ETHNIC-SENSITIVE
SOCIAL WORK PRACTICE

ETHNIC-SENSITIVE SOCIAL WORK PRACTICE

WYNETTA DEVORE, Ed.D.

Syracuse University School of Social Work,
Syracuse, New York

ELFRIEDE G. SCHLESINGER, Ph.D.

Rutgers—The State University of New Jersey,
The School of Social Work,
New Brunswick, New Jersey

Illustrated

Charles E. Merrill Publishing Company
A Bell & Howell Company
Columbus   Toronto   London   Sydney

Copyright © 1981, The C. V. Mosby Company.

Copyright © 1986, Charles E. Merrill Publishing Company.
Columbus, Ohio   43216
A Bell & Howell Company

Library of Congress Catalog Card Number: 80–27538
International Standard Book Number: 0–675–20593–X
Printed in the United States of America
1 2 3 4 5 6 7 8 9 10—91 90 89 88 87 86

Preface

This book is about ethnicity, social class, and social work practice. It was written because for many years we worried about the fact that knowledge about the life-styles and needs of different class and ethnic groups was not sufficiently integrated into principles and methods of social work practice.

There was considerable information about how ethnic and social class membership shapes responses to problems of living. Much rich material is and was available in the sociological and psychological literature. However, social work had made only limited systematic efforts to adapt sociological and psychological insights in a manner congruent with practice needs.

Unlike psychological theories that were used to explain the functioning of individuals and groups—and used as guidelines for intervention—ethnic and class data tended to serve merely as background or identifying information. Few attempts were made to delineate how understanding of class and ethnic factors could contribute to the assessment and intervention process.

We are not suggesting that such efforts were totally lacking. As early as 1917 Mary Richmond cautioned that the caseworker who ignores "national and racial characteristics . . . is liable to surprises."* There are many reasons for the failure to act on Mary

---

*Mary Richmond. 1917. *Social Diagnosis*. New York: Russell Sage Foundation.

Richmond's admonition. Egalitarian motives led many social workers to the conclusion that understanding of basic human needs and the dynamics of human behavior would serve them in their effort to provide equal service to all. Some believed that explicit attention to the relationship between ethnicity, social class, and behavior was somehow incongruent with social work's commitment to equality and the uniqueness of each individual.

The ferment of the sixties forced attention to these matters. The civil rights struggle led to the Black Power movement, which spoke out about the beauty of Blackness. This vitality subsequently generated emerging movements in other ethnic groups. Poverty was rediscovered and some called social work to task for faulting on its commitment to the poor.

The profession of social work did respond to these criticisms. A considerable literature emerged on the behavior and life-style of those groups who found themselves in poverty. This thrust is currently being revised as a body of literature focused on diverse stances or problems and problem resolution is emerging in various professional journals and publications. This new body of literature reflects the fact that the time has arrived when social work can comfortably integrate its commitment to deal with individuals as unique human beings at the same time as it draws on knowledge about ethnic and class related responses to refine and enhance practice.

These responses derive from immersion in various groups and from the way these groups are regarded in the society. They relate not only to issues of inequality and racism but also to dispositions associated with child rearing, appropriate sex role behavior, marriage, dispositions associated with seeking help outside of the immediate family, the discomfort felt when sharing intimate problems, and views about formally organized helping institutions. Much of the available material is scattered through the literature. This book is an attempt to synthesize contemporary perspectives on social work, social class, and ethnicity.

Two basic themes inform this work. The first suggests that ethnicity and social class play a large part in shaping life's problems as well as giving perspectives on problem resolution. The second presumes that social work is a problem-solving endeavor that must pay simultaneous attention to micro and macro problems if it is to respond effectively to the problems within its domain.

Using these perspectives a model of ethnic-sensitive practice is developed. The model incorporates general knowledge of human behavior and specific knowledge about the dispositions and behaviors that are generated at the intersect of ethnicity and social class. We have called these unique dispositions, behaviors, and associated experiences the *ethnic reality.* Also incorporated in the model are what we have termed the *layers of understanding* required for social work practice. Subsumed are (1) a general knowledge of human behaviors, (2) self-awareness—with an emphasis on the need for awareness of one's own ethnic and class background and how these impact on practice, and (3) the impact of the ethnic reality on the life of clients. A series of practice principles that highlight the importance of simultaneous attention to micro and macro tasks is presented. These practice principles emerge out of our review of various approaches to social work practice, including the psychosocial approach, the several problem-solving approaches, and the structural and social provision models.

Major attention is devoted to a review of basic social work skills and how these must be adapted in a manner designed to enhance sensitivity to the needs and dispositions of various groups.

Three chapters focus on work in three problem areas—social work with families, social work with recipients of Aid to Dependent Children, and social work in health care. These chapters are designed to illustrate the model in action.

In developing this book we made an extensive review of diverse literature on ethnicity, on social class, on the life cycle, and on prevailing approaches to social work practice. In synthesizing this material we drew heavily on our own experience as practitioners and social work educators. We also learned a great deal from our colleagues, our students, and others who readily talked with us when they learned what we were about. They told us how they experienced ethnicity and social class and how these characteristics affected their encounters with various helping professions.

This book is designed for social work practitioners, social work educators, and use in both graduate and undergraduate social work programs. It can serve as a primary text in social work practice courses and as a supplementary text in human behavior courses focused on the life cycle, in those intended to illustrate how practitioners can integrate both individual and systemic concerns, and in courses on the family, public welfare, and social work in health care. We believe that our colleagues in related professions such as nursing, medicine, and psychology will find useful material and insights.

This book presents no new approaches to social work practice. Rather, we draw on existing approaches and suggest how these may be enhanced by attention to the ethnic reality. In presenting this model we are acutely aware of the fact that the adaptation of skill, in keeping with the ethnic reality, represents a series of hypotheses about how these adaptations can enhance practice. We make no claim that the proposed procedures have been systematically tested. In this respect we share the weakness of many other models. It is our fervent hope that others will join us in efforts to test these hypotheses in the course of practice.

Neither is this a book about different ethnic and class groups. There are many excellent books devoted to that subject. We draw on available material to suggest how knowledge about various groups can be incorporated into practice. The reader will find that our illustrations deal with some but not all ethnic groups. Our examples focus on American Blacks, Puerto Ricans, Mexican Americans, Asian Americans, and American Indians, as well as a number of Eastern European groups, including Poles and Slavics. Material on Italians and Jews is also included.

We want to make special reference to the fact that no illustrations are given about the group usually referred to as White, Anglo-Saxon Protestants. This group is generally characterized as representing mainstream American values and culture. It is the standards of this group by which many immigrants, migrants, and American Indians are judged. In making this statement we are well aware of the fact that this group has its own important traditions and attitudes. We hope that members of this group are not offended by this omission. Rather we hope they join us in this venture of trying to enhance the relationship between social class, ethnicity, and social work practice. We expect that readers will have certain concerns, anticipating that the effort to incorporate knowledge about ethnicity and social class into guidelines for practice raises the possibility of stereotyping. We are quite aware of this danger. While we have made every effort to avoid such stereotyping, we undoubtedly have not been totally successful. We believe the risk is necessary. No claim is made that all members of the groups discussed will behave or think or feel in the manner suggested by some of the descriptive material. At the same time we saw no other way of highlighting important material. If we have presented incorrect or stereotypical information, we apologize and invite readers' comments about where we erred.

Finally, we want to thank the many people who have helped us in this work. We want to thank our students at Kean College and Rutgers School of Social Work who read and critiqued parts of the manuscript. We owe particular thanks to Susan Abrams, former editor at The C. V. Mosby Company, who encouraged us to embark on this work, and to Diane Bowen, Michelle Turenne, and Peggy Fagen, who patiently struggled with us to its completion. Many contributed examples from their practice and consulted with us in relation to certain ethnic groups. Others were helpful in areas of research; among those persons are Cynthia Alonzo, Geraldine Durden, Karl Esmark, Rosalie De Gillio, Paul Fishkin, Pamela Franey, Peter Garcia, Mildred Gaupp, Beverly R. Guest, Shirley Gurisic, Bertram Jones, Jane Kehoe, Judith Kunz, Catherine E. Marino, Lynn Markowitz, Ina Mitchell, Zaidia L. Mostareo, Stephanie Patti, Debbora Peterson, Dr. Albert Ramirez, Kyle Russ, Marjorie Sklar, Loretta Snook, Tom Sullivan, Micheline Swanson, Mottie Tate, and Janet Tuckman.

David Antebi and Jewlee Bryant were extremely helpful in thinking about and providing the photographs we hope illustrate some of our basic conceptions. Many people—friends, relatives, and students—readily talked with us about their experience as it bears on the issues covered in this book. Those whose names we forgot to mention, thank you and our apologies.

Most importantly, we thank our families—Jewlee and David Bryant and Richard, David, and Adrienne Schlesinger. They were patient when we locked ourselves up in a room to work and listened sympathetically as we moaned and groaned.

We also want to express our appreciation to the secretaries who carefully typed portions of the manuscript—Susan Tiller, Margaret Camisa, and Rose Gonzalez. Particular thanks are due to our colleagues Anne Adams, Marjory Alper, Kenneth Kazmerski, Ida Eiger, Frank Naughton, and Arthur Brown, who read and commented on various portions of the manuscript.

Wynetta Devore
Elfriede G. Schlesinger

Contents

PART

I

CONCEPTUAL FORMULATIONS

In Part I, the conceptual base of ethnic-sensitive practice is developed.

In Chapter 1, material on ethnicity and social class is reviewed with an emphasis on how forces both internal and external to various groups serve to sustain the role of social class and ethnicity as powerful aspects of social life. The mechanisms by which ethnicity, culture, and work impact on dispositions to life's problems are reviewed, and the definition of the ethnic reality is developed.

In Chapter 2, prevailing models of life cycle stages and tasks are reviewed and integrated with information about ethnicity and social class to show how these forces affect transition through the life cycle. Points of stress and coping mechanisms, particularly as these relate to ethnicity and social class, are identified.

Chapter 3 outlines the "layers of understanding" required for social work practice. In Chapter 4, the various approaches to social work practice are reviewed and the extent to which understanding of ethnic and class functions have been incorporated in the basic assumptions and procedures is assessed.

In Chapter 5, a model of ethnic-sensitive practice is presented. The model integrates social work values, the view of social work as a problem-solving endeavor, a perspective which focuses on individual and systemic issues, and the conceptualization on class, ethnicity, and the life cycle.

1

DRAGON E
EXOTIC CHINES
EGG ROLLS
SHRIMP EGG ROLLS
ROAST PORK or VEG. LO
ROAST PORK or VEG. FRIED
HAWAIIAN STEAK
CHINESE BARBECUED CHI
TODAY'S SP
ROAST PORK

David Antebi

CHAPTER

1

The ethnic reality

There are many perspectives on how ethnic group membership, social class, minority group status, and culture affect individual and group life.

In this chapter we examine and assess a number of these perspectives. In so doing, we are guided by one basic objective—to cull those insights that can serve as the basis for the development of practice principles to guide practitioners in their efforts to respond with sensitivity to the values and dispositions that are related to ethnic group membership and position in the social stratification system.

There is a vast body of knowledge that identifies the manner in which ethnicity and membership in various social class groups shape approaches to the problems of living. When these are examined in the context of American society a number of overarching themes emerge. One theme focuses on the sense of cohesion, identity, and solidarity that derives from the association with one's own ethnic group. Another centers on how social class is defined, the consequences of membership in different strata of the society, and inequality.

Central to these considerations is the relationship between ethnic group membership, minority status, social class, and inequality. Those who have been assigned official responsibility "to help" have a particular obligation to be aware of inequality as it derives from ethnicity, minority status, and social class and to demonstrate a special sensitivity to the sources of strength and coping capacity that are often ignored. This book presents some formulations that serve to highlight such understanding.

Major attention is focused on the concept of "ethclass" (Gordon, 1964). This formulation aids in examining the meaning of membership in an ethnic group and in the various social classes.

ETHCLASS AND THE ETHNIC REALITY

In his classic analysis, Gordon suggests that the point at which social class and ethnic group membership intersect be characterized as "ethclass." Gordon uses this concept to explain the role that social class membership plays in defining the basic conditions of life at the same time as it seeks to account for the differences between groups at the same social class level. These differences are in large measure explained by ethnic group membership. We suggest that the intersect of ethnicity and social class, what Gordon has termed ethclass, converge to generate identifiable dispositions and behaviors. We characterize these dispositions and the behaviors which flow from them as the *ethnic reality* or ethclass in action. The concept of the ethnic reality is depicted in Fig. 1.

Dispositions on such matters as appropriate child-rearing practices or proper care for the aged, though in large measure related to social class membership, are often affected by ethnicity.

Ethnic groups

According to Gordon, the ethnic group is a type of group contained within the national boundaries of America defined or set off by race, religion, or national origin. In this view religion is a cultural phenomenon. National origin calls attention to the fact that everyone in the United States, except American Indians, has migrated to this country from elsewhere, often bringing a set of customs, a language, and a unique history. Race is the result of differential concentrations of gene frequencies that are responsible for traits confined to physical manifestations such as skin color or hair form that have no intrinsic connections with cultural patterns and institutions.

Common to the ethnic group is a shared feeling of peoplehood

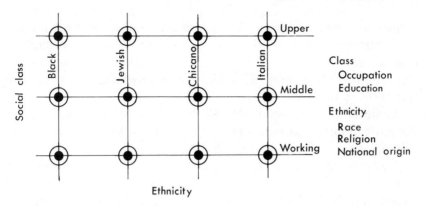

Fig. 1. The ethnic reality: ethclass in action.

The "social space" created by the intersect of social class and ethnicity has been called ethclass. The dispositions and behaviors that flow from this are termed the ethnic reality or ethclass in action.

Ethnicity and the associated sense of "peoplehood" are represented by the vertical axis and stress the fact that ethnicity is a component of social life at all social class levels. Social class is represented by the horizontal axes.

The circles represent the ethnic reality and suggest that as social class intersects with ethnicity a unique configuration is formed.

and a common sense of past and future. This sense of belonging often connotes cohesion, solidarity, and a basis of identity. Ethclass thus serves to clarify differences between groups at the same social class level who in many other ways are quite similar. Intimate relationships are most frequently found between people of the same social class within an ethnic group. These relationships, usually of an emotional nature, reinforce mutual expectations. These expectations and the behaviors that result from them are deeply embedded though often subtle. They may revolve around such issues as appropriate methods for punishing children, anticipated adult-adolescent relationships, public behaviors expected of men and women, the place of the church in family life, or the manner in which aging parents should be regarded.

ETHNICITY

To begin the examination of the ethnic reality we will focus first on the meaning of ethnicity in America today. There are two major factors to consider: (1) the "growth of civilization" has altered and contributed to an increasingly complex basis of self-identification, and (2) varying views of culture and subculture enhance understanding of the role played by ethnic group membership in shaping responses to the joys and problems of living.

In developing the concept of ethclass, Gordon points out that the early hunting societies were characterized by what he terms a "simple model of self-identification."

The rules governing family behavior, and political life and the values guiding them, were intricately and closely intertwined. Group, family, and political life were culturally uniform and took place within a limited and clearly demarcated geographical place. Distinctions between family, social class, ethnic group membership, work, and geography were virtually nonexistent and out of the frame of experience of most people. The development of stable agricultural societies, followed by massive industrialization and urbanization, gave rise to diverse bases of identity. Nation, region of birth, residence, occupation, and social class are but a few of the factors that help to shape our sense of who we are, where we belong, and how to behave.

In diversified and stratified societies each of these bases of group membership suggest varied and at times conflicting bases of identification, guides for behavior, and orientation to the vicissitudes of life. And yet

> . . . the sense of ethnicity has proved to be hardy. As though with a wily cunning of its own, as though there were some essential element in man's nature that demanded it—something that compelled him to merge his lonely individual identity in some ancestral group of fellows smaller by far than the whole human race, smaller often than the nation—the sense of ethnic belonging has survived. It has survived in various forms and with various names, but it has not perished, and twentieth century urban man is closer to his stone-age ancestors than he knows.
> (Gordon, 1964)*

---

*From *Assimilation in American Life: The Role of Race, Religion, and National Origins* by Milton M. Gordon. Copyright © 1964 by Oxford University Press, Inc. Reprinted by permission.

What, then is this compelling force? In order to answer this question the distinctions between ethnicity, culture, and subculture must be understood.

Culture

Culture is a commonly used though not readily defined concept. Dictionary definitions abound with such terms as "explicit and implicit patterns," "artifacts," "symbols," "language," and the like. What do these really convey? Culture refers to the fact that human groups are distinguishable by the manner in which they guide and structure behavior and the meaning ascribed. Cultures differ in their world view, in their perspectives on the rhythms and patterns of life, and in their concept of the essential nature of the human condition. These perspectives are conveyed in a myriad of symbolic and direct ways via language, socialization practices, abstract forms such as art, as well as the mundane artifacts used in daily living.

The ideas and values thus conveyed become part of the routine and habitual dispositions to life that become so thoroughly a part of the self and group life that they require no examination. Forged out of diverse experience in attempting to grapple with natural forces and human interaction, culture guides thinking about these forces. For example, those immersed in a culture that views nature as malleable and controllable by "people" stop to think only about *how* but not *whether* to control nature. If we find ourselves members of a group that views natural forces as evil or controlling they are then to be endured. The basic response patterns, set into the core and substance of group life, involve a variety of injunctions by which every member learns to live. In the view of Kroeber and Kluckhon, culture is the product of action and a major force affecting the nature of subsequent action (Kluckhon 1964). Culture has also been viewed as the "total ways of life" that orient thinking about the universe and the proper nature of human to human and human to God relationship (Valentine, 1968). Margaret Mead describes culture as "a vehicle for the human emotions of human beings to come into some kind of intelligible order" (New York Times, November 19, 1978).

This order derives from the social heritage or way of life of a particular society at a particular time. It is a term appropriately applied when human groupings of "various dimensions share behavioral norms and patterns that differ somewhat from those of other groups" (Gordon, 1964).

Subculture

What is subculture and how does it differ from culture? As societies become more complex, the tenets for appropriate political, religious, and interpersonal behavior are transmitted by varying groups. A subculture or a subsociety is a group that may be distinguishable by ethnic background, or occupation, or religion, or race, or status, or some combination of these characteristics—at the same time as it shares certain features with larger social segments or an overriding culture system. For example, the "Protestant ethic" is often viewed as an overriding American cultural theme and one to which all subgroups in the United States are exposed, regardless of the extent of commitment to this ethic by any particular group. One type of subsociety or subculture is the ethnic group.

Ethnic group

Shibutani and Kwan (1965) suggest that an ethnic group consists of those who conceive of themselves as being alike by virtue of their common ancestry, real or fictitious, and who are so regarded by others. Greeley suggests that there is as yet no conceptual clarity concerning the nature of ethnic groups. The definition of an ethnic group as a collectivity based on presumed common origin is a useful point of departure for discussion (Greeley, 1974). These and other definitions focus on a common past, a common present, and the assumption of a common and shared future.

These definitions all point to the fact that ethnicity or the sense of peoplehood is an integral component of social life—particularly in those respects that involve intimacy and a long-lasting socially based identity.

Minority groups

Before considering how ethnicity is experienced and how its strength and vitality have survived, a discussion of the special characteristics of minority groups is in order. In the context of this book the definition offered by Shibutani and Kwan (1965) is most useful. Minority groups are "the underprivileged in a system of ethnic stratification and people of low standing—people who receive unequal treatment and who therefore come to regard themselves as objects of discrimination."

Adams (1975) suggests that there is a tendency to use the term "ethnic group" when invidious distinctions are not being made and to use the term "minority groups" when invidious distinctions are implied.

Although the term "minority" has been used to describe any number of subgroups who are in some way devalued by the larger society (e.g., women, homosexuals, the aged, the handicapped), it is used here to include those groups that can be characterized as ethnic groups and who are generally viewed as having low status.

Most ethnic groups in the United States have at some point in their history been subjected to varying degrees of discrimination of the type subsumed by the definition. Some continue to be particularly subject to extremely low status.

The sense of ethnicity

All of these definitions convey in a formal sense what is frequently experienced at a "gut" level by people immersed in various ethnic groups.

In assessing the degree to which the sense of ethnicity and peoplehood persist, we examined a variety of materials. These included systematic, quantitative studies as well as novels, plays, and personal documents intended to express more unique emotional experiences. We also talked with a variety of people: the "schooled" (those involved in a cosmopolitan life-style) as well as the less educated. When we asked, sometimes half jokingly, "Do you want to be assimilated?" a number of replies were not unlike those of a well-educated Jewish woman who said: "Do you mean giving up my Jewishness and becoming just like everybody else? If that's what you mean I don't want it. I'm part of this country, and I pay my taxes and I want my children to go to school but I want to remain different in many important ways."*

---

*Conversation with Ellie Jacob.

An older Hungarian woman commented: "You know, when I came to this country I was so happy to be here that I wanted to be a complete American, to do everything the American way. Then I found out that I could not stop being Hungarian, I could not give up the Hungarian ways. I was so economical, so upset about waste that my boss laughed at me. My children are more American but we are still all Hungarian and I like it!"*

Among the sentiments of young Puerto Ricans presented in *Growing Up Puerto Rican* (Cooper, 1972) is that of Rosita, a 16-year-old: "Puerto Ricans are special people because they have special food like rice and beans—Puerto Ricans are very special people and they're different from others. Good different. The way they act and the way they treat each other."

Jenkins (1969) suggests that the phrase "Say it loud, black and proud" has serious psychological purpose in that it attempts to reverse a destructive psychological situation—one in which many Blacks degraded their own physical characteristics and chased "ethereal forms of whiteness."

Mostwin (1972) reports findings of a study of post–World War II Polish immigrants to the United States designed to ascertain the association between migration and changes in the immigrant's ethnic identity. Responses to a structured questionnaire suggested people retain a sense of Polish identity but also come to identify as Americans. The letters that accompanied responses to the structured questionnaires are expressions of the sense of belonging to both groups. "I feel very pro-American in the knowledge that this adopted country has great values and possibilities. I would love to contribute to its greatness, as well as see my children become good citizens—but always aware of their Polish culture and ancestry (Mostwin, 1972)"

Ethnic background as predictor of behavior

In an extensive analysis Greeley (1974) attempted to ascertain the degree to which ethnic background can predict and explain behavior even in the third-generation children of European immigrants. The question is answered in detailed ways in an extensive volume *Ethnicity in the United States*. He states:

---

*Conversation with Margaret Herczag.

We began with a very simple theoretical question. Does a knowledge
of the cultural heritage of an immigrant group help us to understand
its present behavior? On the basis of the evidence presented we
would answer yes. The heritage may not explain everything but it
appears to explain some things.
(Greeley, 1974)

The heritage may well explain the response of some Hispanic
males who believe that their identity as males and human beings is
on the line if their women seek employment to supplement a meager family income. It has been suggested that ethnic identity may
explain the stoic response to pain of some "old Americans," when
compared to the more volatile response and associated fears expressed by some Italians and Jews (Zborowski, 1952).

Ethnicity is experienced and persists because there is a sense of
comfort and ease when a person attends a wedding or funeral that
adheres to familiar rituals and routines; at the same time there is
discomfort when these rituals are carried out in a manner that de-
parts from the tried and true. Ethnicity is expressed in the spontaneous expression of distress by the Jew turned athiest who learns
that some synagogues hire and fire rabbis just as large corporations
deal with various managers in the hierarchy. And it is reinforced by
"kielbase" and "pasta" and "beans and rice" and the joy of eating
these foods in the company of others who appreciate them because
of what they convey.

Ethnicity and language

Ethnicity is experienced and persists through language. It may
be Spanish, Polish, Italian, Hungarian, Yiddish, or a soulful
sound "metered without the intention of the speaker to invoke it"
as in the language of soul (Brown, 1972). A common language provides a psychic bond, a uniqueness that signifies membership in a
particular ethnic group as well as a base for the coordination of
activities both social and political. There are times when it is necessary to cope with the oppression of the mainstream society,
which may forbid the use of the native tongue in the public arena.
Ethnicity may be heard or felt when young Blacks "play the dozens"
or "get their programs togethers." It is the deliberation of the Spanish "a poco a poco," the joy of the Italian "aldia," or the audacity
conveyed by the Yiddish term "chutzpa." Each of these words and

many others retain their ethnic uniqueness in that they are not readily translated into mainstream language, thereby giving the speaker a sense of distinction.

Maintenance of ethnic identity

The interaction of factors both internal and external to the group contribute to the persistence of ethnic identity. One explanation is to be found in the distinction between interaction in primary and secondary groups. The other is the role played by prejudice, racism, discrimination, and certain dominant American cultural themes.

The study of social structure indicates that the groups within which major social relationships take place vary in a number of critical ways. A major distinction—and one of particular importance in relation to the persistence of ethnicity—is the one between primary and secondary groups. Families, play groups, and informal social networks are examples of primary groups, while secondary groups tend to be found in the work place, political and civic organizations, and large bureaucracies.

Primary groups

In primary groups, relationships are most often personal, intimate, and all encompassing. Ideally these are the types of groups where people can "be themselves," where their foibles are understood, and where they are intrinsically loved and wanted.

The major types of activities performed in primary groups highlight their importance in transmitting the ethnic reality. It is these groups that convey values and a sense of belonging, warmth, and cohesion. What is important and striking about the activities so often confined to or mainly carried out within primary groups is that they involve the core of the personality and important emotional relationships (Gordon, 1964).

How do primary groups such as the family and the peer group convey and sustain this "sense of ancestral and future oriented identification" with the group?

It is sustained in subtle reminders conveyed by the way in which children are consoled or admonished, the transmitted clues for appropriate behavior in puberty, and the way in which these are reinforced by the larger society.

The "pull" exerted by family and community and kin as they

seek to keep the young within the fold is well known to most young-sters. The almost universal request made of adolescent girls by their parents that their dates pick them up at home reflects a need to protect and a concern for safety and decorum. Yet, the fact that it also contains the question, albeit implicit—"Is he one of us?"—is not lost. This stage is often preceded by small and subtle actions ranging from looking for the "right" schools, which may really mean looking for neighbors of one's own kind, joining the temple or church "for the children," and sending the children to religious school. It means finding enough money for extras if the extra is a church trip, but lacking sufficient resources to finance the summer at a nonsectarian camp. A three-generational study of Jewish, Ital-ian, and Slavic American women in the Pittsburgh area (Krause, 1978) finds that ethnic group-related differences are transmitted in a number of ways.

An Italian "daughter" describes the tight controls placed on her by her father concerning her social life, thus transmitting in word and nuance the strong need on the part of Italian fathers to protect the chastity of their daughters. "At twenty-five she felt a taste of freedom taking a trip by automobile to Chicago only to find that her father had followed the entire distance to make sure that she was safe"(Krause, 1978). While in college she was permitted to attend social functions only if brought home by her brothers, while they had total freedom to come and go as they wished.

The importance of group identity and "marrying one's own kind" is transmitted and conveyed in extreme responses to "transgression." Where guidelines are clear and parents vehement, there is often pain and turmoil; not infrequently a total rupture in the relationships ensues. Some orthodox Jews may go so far as to "sit shive" for a child who has married out of the group. Sophie suffered the agonies of group identity and societal prejudice when she, a young Italian woman, became pregnant by a Puerto Rican man. When she attempted to introduce her son to his maternal grandmother, this was the mother's reaction:

> They heard the woman from inside the apartment shouting "get out!
> I'll call the police, go away! Go some place with those people who
> kill my daughter. The niggers. Go there. My daughter is dead gone
> finished. No more. I call the police!"
> (Mohr, 1974)

Where parents are permissive and "democratic" in their views concerning cross-ethnic primary relationships, they often voice their concerns in terms of the possible discomfort of the unknown and unfamiliar in a relationship with someone of a different background. The refrain, "Marriage is difficult enough even if you have a lot in common," is well known.

The family, then, usually kind and protective, sometimes destructive, guides the young into the "right" schools, to playing with the "right" kind of children, into marriages with the "right" people, and these more often than not turn out to be "our own kind." "Man's most primal needs and emotions declare themselves first within the family. Man learns his greatest fears, loves, hatreds and hopes within this social unit" (Greeley, 1974).

A myriad of experiences, persons, and things are feared, loved, hated, and wanted. All too often, aspirations, even those of an intense and deeply personal nature, are negatively affected by societal perceptions of what and who we are as this is related to ethnic group membership. And much of what the family transmits—particularly the minority family—has the effect not only of transmitting that which is valued by the group but also clues concerning the manner in which members of the group are likely to be perceived and received. For those who suffer the particular effects of discrimination—those ethnic groups that are also considered minority groups—ethnic identity and its transmission serves as a sense of protection from the larger world. This larger world all too often demeans, frequently by vociferous intent and often out of ignorance. Ethnicity may serve as protection against the message that suggests that if ethnic group identity or related behaviors are abandoned, discrimination will cease. That this message so often proves to be false is exemplified by the fact that Blacks or Hispanics who abandon subtle but characteristic speech patterns and Jews who change their names or have plastic surgery performed to anglicize their features still experience job discrimination.

Ethnicity is protection from the larger world, which stereotypes the Black scholar who possesses no musical or athletic talent and cringes when a thoughtless bystander suggests that he would make a good addition to the local jazz band or baseball team; it provides a retreat for the American Indian who feels hurt and at a loss when told by a harried social worker that stopping to help a friend along the way is irresponsible behavior and no excuse for being late for an important appointment.

These and countless other examples highlight the fact that the "world out there" continues to react to people in terms of ascribed images rather than in individual terms. The ethnic group can give solace and put the "ethnic slur" into perspective. It often does so either via humor or by providing a comfortable setting within which to ventilate anger. Much of that "comfort" is provided by the types of groups characterized as primary.

Acculturation and assimilation

One other aspect of the interaction between ethnic groups and the larger society of which they are a part is important. Gordon's "multidimensional model of the assimilation process" is an articulate and incisive formulation. The "core culture" or "core subsociety" is middle-class and white Protestant.

"Acculturation" and "assimilation" are terms used to describe what happens when groups with different backgrounds and cultures meet. Efforts to describe and understand this process were triggered by the mass migrations of Europeans to the United States, the importation of slaves, and the contact between the original settlers and American Indians. "Acculturation makes one group's culture the point of reference and focuses upon the events and processes by which that group responds to more or less continuous contact by variously accepting, reformulating or rejecting elements of the other culture or cultures" (Keesing, 1964). In Madge's (1964) view, assimilation ". . . denotes the process in which one set of cultural traits is relinquished and a new set acquired, through communication and participation. The change is gradual and may take place in any degree." Gordon (1964) contends that assimilation is a matter of degree and that various types and stages in the assimilation process can be identified.

There is a distinction between "cultural" or "behavioral" assimilation and structural assimilation. In the former some of the major themes or behaviors of the dominant society, particularly its language, have been adopted. When structural assimilation takes place there are extensive primary group relationships between immigrants and members of the core culture, sometimes including intermarriage. Seven types or stages of the assimilation process are

identified: (1) cultural, (2) structural, (3) marital, (4) identifica-
tional, (5) attitude-receptional, (6) behavioral-receptional, and (7)
civic (Gordon, 1964).

When the dominant or mainstream society erects barriers to total particpation by various groups in significant aspects of social
and economic life, only cultural or behavioral assimilation is likely
to take place. Many ethnic groups do not seek total structural assimilation such as that implied by marital assimilation. Indeed,
many groups value their traditions and differences and actively try
to prevent structural assimilation at the same time as they seek social and economic equality.

This view of assimilation has come to replace the earlier belief
in the "melting pot"—it was thought that ethnic groups would lose
their distinct identity and merge into some common framework.
Rather, "the persisting facts of ethnicity demand attention, understanding and accommodation" (Glazer and Moynihan, 1963). The
persistence of ethnic diversity, when accompanied by equal access
to goods, services, and prestige, enriches and enhances the collective life experience.

SOCIAL CLASS

To this point we have focused on the ethnic component of "ethclass" and suggested what ethnicity means, how it is experienced,
and what factors contribute to its persistence. The concept of social
class will now be examined.

Social inequality

No discussion of social class can proceed without consideration
of the meaning of social inequality and stratification. The nature of
inequality has been examined by theorists from Plato to Marx to
Weber to contemporary analysts. All have focused on examining the
conditions that intensify or minimize various forms and types of
inequality.

In contemporary American society inequality is evident in the
fact that some have more income, find themselves in more highly
valued and rewarded occupations, and have more prestige than
others. This in turn affects the extent of individual well-being, specific indicators of health and illness, real and perceived power to
achieve desired ends, the sense of self-respect, and the degree of
dignity conferred by others.

Social class defined

Although there is agreement concerning the existence of inequality, there is an enormous amount of conceptual confusion surrounding the term "social class." Much of the debate revolves around whether there *are* social classes. Some theorists suggest that the term is a useful representation of reality (Hodges, 1964), while others (Wrong, 1959) take the position that social classes are nothing more than convenient fragments of the sociological imagination. Hodges (1964) believes that "social classes are the blended product of shared and analogous occupational orientations, educational backgrounds, economic wherewithal, and life experience."

Gordon suggests that the term "social class" involves the horizontal stratification of a population, related to economic life. It refers to: "differences based on wealth, income, occupation, status, community power, group identification, level of consumption, and family background" (in Duberman, 1976). The experience of social work practitioners and the life experience all of us have shared suggest that the latter positions are accurate reflections of reality.

Measurement of social class

Considerable effort has been made to identify and measure the different strata or classes. A brief review and summary of some of the more commonly used and useful social class measures will be helpful. Much that has been written and said about social class in the United States has used these or analogous classification schemes.

Analysts differ concerning how many classes there are, and on the criteria to be used in assigning people to the various strata. With respect to the former, some, usually of a Marxist orientation, believe that only two classes exist—the rich and the poor. A good many view the society as divided into three categories, the upper, the middle, and the lower classes. The six-part classification scheme developed by Warner (in Duberman, 1976) and the five-class categorization developed by Hollingshead (1958) are commonly used. Warner (1949) views the population as consisting of:

1. The upper-upper class, composed of old wealthy families
2. The lower-upper class, whose wealth is newly acquired
3. The upper-middle class, which consists of successful professional and business people

4. The lower-middle class, generally comprised of white-collar workers

5. The upper-lower class, those whom we tend to think of as blue-collar workers

6. The lower-lower, class, which includes but is not limited to the "derelicts," the "unemployable," or the "dregs of society"

Hollingshead's index of social position is based on the assumption that place of residence, occupation of the head of the household, and number of years of education completed are characteristics of class status. Statistical procedures by which relative weights are assigned to the three factors permit assignment of individuals to one of five strata ranging from Class I, the highest, to Class V, the lowest (Hollingshead, 1958). The index is commonly used as an indicator of social class position.

Several approaches are used in determining how to place individuals in the social class structure. Some are based on subjective perception, while others are related to actual inequalities or differences based on criteria such as those suggested by Hollingshead. In the subjective approach people are asked to place themselves or others on the basis of a number of criteria including perceived power, decision-making authority, and occupation.

Each of these approaches has its limitations and advantages. Centers (1949) suggests that how people rank themselves may be a function of the terminology used. When *Fortune* magazine polled a group of Americans and asked whether they considered themselves upper, middle, or lower class, 80% claimed middle class status. When Centers repeated the study and added a fourth choice—working class—half of the respondents placed themselves in this category. Centers proposed that people did not like the pejorative implications of the term "lower class." It is interesting that the fact that a substantial number of those who would not be designated as working class by "objective" criteria —white-collar workers—identified themselves as working class. Despite some discrepancy between perceived status and position as it is "objectively" defined, studies designed to assess the relationship between objective factors such as education, income, and the prestige assigned to an occupation point to a close relationship. "By obtaining a certain level of education, people qualify for certain occupations and receive a certain income; education is a 'cause' of occupation and income is the 'effect' of that occupation" (Duberman, 1976).

The importance of occupation as a determinant of perceived high status is supported in a study in which respondents were asked to rank ninety occupations in relation to the others. Diverse people across the country consistently ranked such occupations as physician, major governmental officials, and scientists near the top; teachers, bookkeepers, insurance agents, policemen, and farmers somewhere along the middle; and janitors, sharecroppers, and garbage collectors at or near the bottom (in Duberman, 1976).

Social class terminology used here

We share Centers' view that the term "lower class" has pejorative implication, and shall refrain from use of that term except in instances where citing directly from the work of others. The terms "working class" or "under class" will be used to designate members of these groups. For others, the term "middle class" is employed.

Class and rank

Research on the characteristic types of education and occupation that converge to generate different strata of society makes it clear that the highest ranking is assigned to those who perform the tasks most highly valued by American society. Included are those who manage and own major business enterprises, those who play leadership roles in government and education, those who interpret the law, and those who heal the sick. Those who perform menial tasks and take rather than give direction at work are held in low esteem. These rankings are a reflection of basic American tenets. These have been characterized as an emphasis on worldliness, on mastery of nature, and on activism. These basic themes—or ways of structuring and ascribing meaning to behaviors—are translated into standards of adequacy and worthiness and are the basis for gratification and security.

This suggests that much of what is subsumed under the term "social class" is essentially about work and money and the values placed on that work by the larger society. These evaluations are internalized and permeate our lives. The conditions of work, of security, of autonomy and the range and type of experiences to which that work exposes us seep into the very core and substance of our being. It affects the way we feel about work and what we can buy or not with the money we earn.If we earn sufficient money to make meaningful choices about the things we buy, it affects our tastes and preferences in how we furnish our homes, the music we prefer, and the clothes we like to wear. It affects our outlook on the larger world, particularly as this affects our perceptions of life's opportunities and constraints. And, in the view of many, our perception of opportunities and constraints, as these derive from class position, also affect family life, attitudes toward sex, and extent of involvement in the world of politics and voluntary organizations. Importantly, our perceptions affect what we view as problematic in the education our children receive, the marriages and other intimate relationships in which we are involved, and the importance we attach to what is happening in the world beyond our daily existence.

Analysts disagree on the extent to which class-related behaviors are understood and known to those who engage in them. There are those who stress the importance of class consciousness, particularly among the members of the working class, believing that consciousness will generate confrontation of the system that perpetuates inequities.

There are others who still consider the United States to be a "classless society." However, there is little question that social class differences have a discernible effect.

Nature of work in the various social classes

Work may be characterized as monotonous, repetitive, and offering no intellectual challenge or as varied and calling for the utmost in mental efforts. Work varies in regard to the degree of physical exertion required. It differs in the extent of autonomy and the degree of control of the direction, pacing, and timing of work permitted. Often, what is done and when is determined by others, by the speed of the assembly line, or by rigid rules that must be adhered to if the job is to be retained or the work carried out.

What is the nature of work carried out by the members of the different classes?

The working class

At least two segments of the population may be characterized as working class—those in low paid, semi-skilled, or unskilled occupations, and those like the "Blue Collar Aristocrats" (LeMasters, 1975), who are unionized and well paid. Among the latter are construction workers, truck drivers, carpenters, electricians, and others whose work involves considerable decision-making. Also well paid and eligible for substantial fringe benefits are automobile workers; their work is often quite routinized, repetitive, and allows for limited self-direction.

We try to capture the distinctions between the under class and working class by examining the nature of work and by reviewing studies that have attempted to assess how the nature of the work and the relative degree of security or insecurity that attaches to it may generate some differences in perspective. Menial work in our society provides the least financial remuneration and it provides only a low status. Garbage men, domestics, factory workers, attendants, janitors, and street sweepers all provide essential services; yet as they describe their work (Terkel, 1972) a picture of drudgery, physical exertion, routine, and fatigue emerges. The employer pays little attention to safety codes or the environment of the work place. The workers are powerless, having no ability to define their work. There is no dignity, only monotony, heavy labor, and a lack of respect. There is no economic security. Blumberg (1972) points out that these conditions of workaday life inevitably produce cultural responses which reflect an effort to cope with and adapt to the circumstances of failure and adversity. This group of workers lives in a relatively circumscribed world. Work and income limit the opportunities for movement in a variety of social worlds.

Whether the experience is viewed as "narrow" or different from that of the middle class, so often used as a yardstick, becomes a matter of debate. Sennett and Cobb (1972) suggest that for some, particularly urban ethnics, the standards by which they are judged comes from a world "in which human capabilities are measured in terms profoundly alien."

Regardless of the language used, a number of motifs become apparent. Binzen (1970), a journalist who looked at the lives of Black and White inner-city workers, concluded that: "They were unimpressed by abstractions. They wanted meat and potatoes basic education. They wanted homework. They wanted prayers and Bible reading. They wanted physical punishment. They wanted all these things because they had never been exposed to any workable alternatives."

Gans' review (1962) of a number of studies of working-class life points to the tendency of working-class people to be concrete and particularistic, to think anecdotally and to personlize events. There is the general conception that the outside world is not to be trusted. This extends also to a skepticism about caretakers, a reluctance to visit settlement houses, and a fear of doctors and hospitals.

Compare this with the experience of those generally considered to fall in the upper strata of the working class. LeMasters tried to gain some insight into the lives of heavy equipment operators, plumbers, sheet-metal workers, electricians, and other skilled construction workers. As a participant observer he frequented a bar that was a favorite meeting place in one community. Terming these workers "blue collar aristocrats," he points out that they are unionized, earn high pay despite modest education, and appreciate the fact that their work is not monotonous. One worker explains: "I see that the auto workers in Detroit want early retirement. I don't blame the poor bastards. I would want to retire at thirty-five if I had to stand in one place and put fenders on all day." (LeMasters, 1975).

In this group, supervision is loose. For the plumber, a day's work is planned in the morning with the foreman and there is no further contact with him that day unless there is trouble. A good carpenter would view close supervision as a reflection on his competence. "The men like the freedom to move around the job, also the fact that problems of one kind or another develop almost every day—these 'jams' make them think and reassure them that they are not stupid machines" (LeMasters, 1975).

In their attempt to isolate a number of characteristics basic to "those members of the non-agricultural labor force in manual occupations," Miller and Riessman (1972) suggest that this group is subject to internal and external factors that promote instability and insecurity. Related to this is an emphasis on getting by rather than getting ahead. These workers, despite high pay and union protection, are particularly subject to lay-off and to the vagaries of the economic situation. Sick leave and disability provisions in union contracts do not allay the fear of lay-offs or that benefits will be exhausted. This sense of insecurity may account for the reluctance of some steel workers to become foremen, for they fear loss of job seniority should lay-offs occur. This same stress on security appears related to the emphasis noted earlier on the "basics" in education and the reluctance on the part of many to encourage their children to go to college (Miller and Riessman, 1972).

These are broad generalizations, which by their very nature fail to capture the complexity and variation in working-class life and stance. Scanzoni's study of Black working-class families (1971) found that 75% wanted their sons to become physicians, ministers, lawyers, teachers, social workers, or artists. Further, over 80% thought that their children had a chance of attaining these goals.

Regardless of these variations, there are consistencies which emerge. LeMasters (1975) comments:

> In recent years some observers have postulated that social class lines in modern Western society have become so blurred that distinct life-styles can no longer be discerned at different socioeconomic levels. This study tends to support the conclusions of Herbert J. Gans, Bennett M. Berger, Mirra Komarovsky, Gavin MacKenzie, and the Goldthorpe research group in England that the homogenization process, if it exists, is far from complete. Gans is especially emphatic on this point: "the West Enders" he writes "were not frustrated seekers of middle-class values. Their way of life constituted a distinct and independent working-class subculture that bore little resemblance to the middle-class."

The middle class

What is work like for skilled office workers, teachers, dentists, pharmacists, consultants, and factory owners who constitute the broad middle stratum of the population? The description of their work (Terkel, 1972) reveals that in "middle-class" positions they enjoy the work and have a sense of autonomy as they exercise some control over their work. They are positively evaluated by others. Other middle-class occupations are used as guidelines to assess the prestige and value of their work. Money is a concern, and the lower down the middle-class ladder they go the more disappointed they are about the discrepancy between their expectations and what they actually do.

In trying to capture the relationship between the lives of middle-class people, the work they do, and their perceptions of life, a paradox emerges. On the one hand, it is this group that is generally viewed as the "mainstay of America." In the past, middle-class people typified the American virtues—hard work, diligence, thrift, and independence. These characteristics were believed to be essential for those who wanted to climb up the prestige ladder. With the decline of small business and growth of large bureaucratic organizations, "the old middle class ethic is dying out in reality if not in rhetoric" (Blumberg, 1972). These changes in the size and type of organizations have generated an emphasis on conformity and fitting in. Much of this has been highlighted in a number of studies of suburban life—the mecca of the middle class.

These are the people who are eager to get ahead themselves and stress the importance of education for their children. They move readily for jobs, are active in voluntary organizations, and rely heavily on the advice of experts for child-rearing and health practices. They are aware of the importance of having credentials in order to obtain desired jobs and have homes in "good" communities.

According to many analysts, the current nature of middle-class work fosters a need to be well liked. The work itself may call for personality traits that facilitate interaction with a variety of people. Blumberg (1972) suggests that much of the work involves "manipulating persons, not objects." This is true of the farmer who suggests that farming is becoming more management- and less labor-oriented and the copy editor who guides his staff (Terkel, 1974).

The media play on the personal insecurities of the middle class. Television commercials suggest that decaffinated coffee will minimize tensions and antacids will relieve the results of stress. The need to "look right" is emphasized in a thousand ways in the ads for toothpaste and hair spray and deodorant. With few exceptions, it is the life of the middle class that is portrayed in daily soap operas, in the movies, and in mass circulation magazines. The cars, home furnishings, clothing, and jobs portrayed are for the most part those encompassed by the middle-class vision.

The effort to disentangle the impact of social class and ethnic group membership persists. There are those who believe that social class serves as the major definer of basic life experiences. Others view racial and ethnic distinctions—and their convergence with economic position—as the major determinants of life within the various strata. The effort to keep these components separate derives from the conviction that both social class and ethnicity make somewhat distinct and definable contributions to the way people live and feel and think. At the same time, the total consequences of life in any of the social classes cannot be fully assessed without consideration of ethnic group membership.

ETHCLASS IN ACTION—THE ETHNIC REALITY

Thus far discussion has been focused on how ethnicity and social class are experienced and transmitted. It has been suggested that each has a somewhat distinct and separate effect on the lives we lead.

Having examined each separately, we now illustrate how social class and ethnic group membership join to generate ethclass in action or the ethnic reality. The ethnic reality has been defined as involving those dispositions and behavior which flow from this intersect.

Each ethnic group has a unique history with respect to oppression and discrimination, to the relative emphasis and value attached to academic pursuits, to familism, to the respective roles of men and women, and to how religious teachings are translated into dictums for daily living.

In large measure the traditions transmitted by the family, the special inflection of language, and the foods we eat let us know we're among our own, whether "our own" are those in the middle class or in the lower strata.

For the latter the ethnic reality may translate into continuing and persistent discrimination in jobs, housing, and the kind of schooling received, and into the reception received in the work place and by welfare institutions. All too often, those very aspects of heritage that have sustained and are part of a proud tradition do not serve us well in segments of the society that do not value that heritage.

Many of those who have achieved the material goals so highly regarded in this country are frequently reminded of the oppression that still plagues their kindred and of their identification with the group. Some in the lower strata are isolated, whether that isolation is imposed by the larger society or sustained by language barriers. Many of these people do not become "acculturated" in the terms earlier defined. This is often the experience of American Indians when they leave their own communities. The following case situation is illustrative.

When the Anthonys, a Navajo family, moved to the city from the reservation, Mr. Anthony had a job as a fork lift operator. He lost this job when he failed to return at the expected time from a visit to relatives in another state. For the Anthonys, intimate involvement with the family, though separated by distance, is crucial. The importance of "returning on time" is not shared by people of a culture who do not measure time by the western clock.

Since he lost his job, Mr. Anthony has been periodically underemployed or unemployed. When one child was admitted to the hospital with a diagnosis of malnutrition, the possibility of child neglect was raised. Adherence to "American Indian" time is a component of their ethnic reality as is their underclass status. Both serve to intensify their problems with clinics, school, and in the work place.

(Council on Social Work Education, 1965)

Language barriers, strong adherence to culturally based norms, and low-class status often interact to minimize acculturation. Chicano men are usually extremely proud and consider their role as leaders of and providers for their family crucial. Faced with unemployment and a threat to this position, some, like Mr. Ortego, leave.

Mr. Ortego's underemployment and unemployment have continually reminded him of his inferior status in the larger society. He has no power to change his condition. His leadership role, so important to the Chicano head of household, is threatened. All family roles will be affected by his change in status. Mr. Ortego's response to this ethnic reality is to leave. Mrs. Ortego is left alone to seek public welfare. She speaks no English. Her language which has meant comfort and support in an alien place now serves as a barrier to the resources she and her children need so desperately.

(Gonzalez, 1971)

How the ethnic reality affects the behavior of many in the middle strata is illustrated by the following examples. A Black writer describes a social gathering of well-to-do Blacks:

We were the blacks who warmed the hearts of enthusiasts for the American way of life. For each of us had more than one academic degree. And since our median family income was $25,000 or more, we had, as a group, shown the most impressive jump in black earning power. . .

But in spite of our good fortune, it could not be said that we were happy, for something always moved among us that was closer to pain than joy. For we had embraced with a vengeance the values of middle-class America. And yet all of our travails and sweat had simply led us to a place where we were among the most isolated urban people on earth. Most of us worked for middle-class whites, entertained them in our homes, and made tentative stabs at bonhomie with them. But while we sometimes called them "friends," so great was the pervasiveness of American racism that they would never become "family." We were left, then, in a plural society, with only the fellowship and succor of others like ourselves—black men and women who had paid a great price for their comfort. And the proportion of blacks who were pushing their way closer to the economic shelf on which we found ourselves was growing smaller every year. . . But more bothersome was the fact that every year we watched ourselves grow more and more alienated from the brothers and sisters who had not been able to use their energies and education to jump over the obvious barriers when they came down. (Coombs, 1978)*

Brashler (1978) does not share Coombs' view: "Put simply, blacks who've made it, who have it, are saying today that they have more in common than ever before with their white counterparts—and sometimes more in common with them than with their black street brothers." Yet Brashler too casts doubt on his own contention when he recounts the reaction of Rachel, age 22, Black, ad agency receptionist, well dressed and living comfortably. She spots two young Black men on the verge of "pulling a knife" on a man on a train station platform. "Rachel . . . can spot their thing in a second, knows for certain what's in the pockets. Rachel moves, strides quickly for them. She yells, 'Get the hell out! You're just continuing the stereotype.'" She is middle class as defined by the work she does, by her income and purchasing power, and by the life-style that accompanies her job, but she is also Black. And out of that aspect of her identity she prevents a piece of socially destructive behavior; not only because she intrinsically abhors the act, but because that act furthers a negative image of her people. Her efforts to struggle against that image derive not from her class position but

---

*From Coombs, Orde, "Style without the substance of power." *Black Enterprise Magazine*, Vol. IX, No. 5, December 1978, p.32.

from a sense of identity with her Black heritage, a crucial component of her ethnic reality.

Members of different ethnic groups with a history of poverty and discrimination move into certain segments of the middle class at varying rates and paces. When the number who do make this move is relatively small, those people keenly feel the lack of opportunity to interact with others who have shared a similar experience. The number of Italian university professors and writers in the United States is still small (Stone, 1978). Given this, people who haved moved into the middle class have limited opportunity to interact with others who share their occupational aspirations, work experience, and the particular ethnic traditions common to Italian-Americans. A young Italian writer says: "We don't fit in the old neighborhood, but there aren't yet large numbers of us in the 'new' neighborhood. In my present life, I almost never meet Italians, and I notice it." And another Italian writer who wanted to make it into WASP* society describes his experience as it relates to the different food habits of the two groups: "The first adjustment I had to make to WASP middle-class life was leaving the table hungry. The portions are always so tiny and bland, especially to me, coming from a family where they put so much on the table" (Stone, 1978).

An Italian academic reflects the tension between certain ethnic traditions and what he perceives to be class and occupationally related orientations: "These are two things that are totally important to me. . . In ethnic terms, I'm very much an Italian man in terms of my family. But unlike the old notion of the Italian, I'm also a careerist. There's a constant tension between the two" (Stone, 1978). Ethnic reality for these Italian-Americans manifests itself in the struggle to straddle two worlds. The struggle is intensified by the scarcity of colleagues like themselves.

Not all groups experience these same strains. For many Jews, the gap between life in the working class and the move to the middle class was less problematic. "It's very funny. . . If you were Jewish and working class, people said 'Oh, well, Jews are into books.' But if you're Italian and working class then it's 'How did it happen?'" (Stone, 1978). This perception of smooth transition is not

---

*White, Anglo-Saxon, Protestant.

shared by all Jews. The elderly Jewish poor often feel abandoned by young, liberal Jewish intellectuals who put their energies into efforts to raise the status of other minority groups. Some of these same intellectuals feel that their liberal politics are an outgrowth of the Jewish tradition that obliged one to work with the oppressed (Cowan, 1972). Their ethnic reality forces them to confront the fact that some of their own continue to be oppressed.

.   .   .

As we have seen, the sense of ethclass as it has been defined is readily articulated. The nature of the work we do and our ethnic heritage do indeed result in persistent and discernible differences in the life of people of the same social class level who have different ethnic backgrounds. We have suggested that those who do not speak the mainstream language are tied to their own ethnic groups in ways that provide succor at the same time that they confront the system with myriad handicaps. These are often derived from low occupational status, which narrows the range of options and experiences open to them.

Similar barriers are faced by those with strong commitments to powerful and meaningful cultural values that are not understood or appreciated and that indeed are maligned by the larger society. Among these there are many underclass Puerto Ricans, Chicanos, and American Indians.

There are others whose position within the mainstream is much more firmly established. They are "behaviorally assimilated" in that they speak the language, are more firmly ensconced in the work place, and have a greater range of experience with and exposure to the larger society's values and goals. However, their work is assessed as marginal by much of the society and as they struggle with the reality of that work—its hazards and insecurities—they too approach and are approached by various institutions as "lesser beings." The blue-collar workers of varying ethnic backgrounds are in this group, as are those who, though white-collar by designation, are constantly struggling. Among these are the Irish and Italian and Polish and Hungarian workers and many of the Jewish elderly. They have a proud history, an ethnic heritage on which they draw for sustenance as they deal with the work place, their family lives, and the schools.

There are the Black workers who have major ambitions for their children and a persistent experience with negative evaluation by the larger society. They struggle to attain the goods and services and recognition that this society holds out and continues to withhold to some degree at the same time as the barriers are breaking down.

And then there are those who "have made it" when American success goals are used as a yardstick: the Black academicians and business people, the Italian writers, and the Jewish intellectuals. Their "work" entails autonomy and relative economic security and yields prestige.

As each of these groups, as a group, and as individual members of these groups send their children to school, become ill, encounter marital difficulties, and generally live their lives, they bring with them a unique ethnic and class tradition, as well as a personal history within that tradition. As they confront "helpers" or "caretakers" they expect, whether or not they articulate that expectation, that these aspects of their being what we have called ethclass in action will be understood; this despite the fact that many may be unaware that some of their strengths and tensions are related to this aspect of their lives.

Those charged with the responsibility of educating and helping have the obligation to be sensitive to that possibility. Examination of these phenomena must become part and parcel of human service practice.

SUMMARY

Social class and ethnic group membership exert a profound influence on life-style and life chance. The point at which they intersect has been characterized as ethclass. The differences at each intersect are manifested in many ways and include basic dispositions on matters such as child-rearing, sexuality, and the roles of men and women. These dispositions and the behavior which flow from them are defined as the ethnic reality or ethclass in action. Ethnicity and the ethnic reality are transmitted by mechanisms both internal and external to various groups. Values are embedded in individual and group life and, like culture, become part of the routine of daily life.

REFERENCES

Adams, Bert N. 1975. *The family: A sociological interpretation*. Chicago: Rand McNally College Publishing Co.

Binzen, Peter. 1970. *White town U.S.A.* New York: Vintage Books.

Blumberg, Paul. 1972. *The impact of social class*. New York: Thomas Y. Crowell.

Brashler, William. 1978. "The black middle class: making it." *The New York Times Magazine*, December 3.

Brown, Claude. 1972. "The language of soul," in Kochman, Thomas. *Rappin and stylin' out*. Chicago: University of Chicago Press.

Coombs, Orde. 1978. "The black middle class: style without the substance of power." *Black Enterprise*, December.

Cooper, Paulette (Ed.). 1972. *Growing up Puerto Rican*. New York: New American Library.

Council on Social Work Education. 1965. *Casebook on cultural factors in social casework*. New York: The Council.

Cowan, Paul. 1974. "Jews without money: revisited" in Levine, Naomi, and Hochbaum, Marvin (Eds.). *Poor Jews: an American awakening*. New Brunswick, N. J.: Transaction Books.

Duberman, Lucile. 1976. *Social inequality: class and caste in America*. New York: J. B. Lippincott Co.

Faris, Robert E. L. 1964. "Assimilation." In *A dictionary of the social science*. New York: The Macmillan Co.

Gans, Herbert. 1962. *The urban villagers*. New York: The Free Press.

Glazer, Nathan, and Moyhihan, Patrick. 1963. *Beyond the melting pot*. Cambridge: Harvard University Press.

Gonzales, John D. 1976. "El Centro," an NIMH program. Washington, D.C.: U. S. Department of Health, Education, and Welfare.

Gordon, Milton M. 1964. *Assimilation in American life*. New York: Oxford University Press.

Gordon, Milton M. 1973. *Human nature, class and ethnicity*. New York: Oxford University Press.

Greeley, Andrew M. 1974. *Ethnicity in the United States*. New York: John Wiley & Sons, Inc.

Hodges, Harold M., Jr. 1964. *Social stratification*. Cambridge: Schenkman.

Hollingshead, August B., and Redlich, Fredrick C. 1958. *Social class and mental illness: a community study*. New York: John Wiley & Sons, Inc.

Jenkins, Sidney B. 1969. "The impact of black identity crisis on community psychiatry." *Journal of the National Medical Association*, September.

Keesing, Felix M. 1964. "Acculturation." In *A dictionary of the social sciences*. New York: The Macmillan Co.

Kluckhon, Clyde. 1964. "Culture," In *A dictionary of the social sciences.* New York: The Macmillan Co.

Krause, Corrine Azen. 1978. *Grandmothers, mothers and daughters:* an oral history study of ethnicity, mental health and continuity of three generations of Jewish, Italian and Slavic-American women. New York: The Institute on Pluralism and Group Identity of the American Jewish Committee.

LeMasters, E. E. 1975. *Blue collar aristocrats—life styles at a working class tavern.* Madison: University of Wisconsin Press.

Miller, S. M. and Riessman, Frank, 1972. "The working class subculture: a new view." In Blumberg, Paul (Ed.). *The impact of social class.* New York: Thomas Y. Crowell.

Mohr, Nicholasa. 1974. *Nilda.* New York: Bantam Books.

Mostwin, Danuta. 1973. "In search of ethnic identity," *Social Casework,* May.

Scanzoni, John H. 1971. *The black family in modern society.* Boston: Allyn and Bacon.

Sennett, Richard, and Cobb, Jonathan. 1972. *The hidden injuries of class.* New York: Alfred E. Knopf.

Shibutani, Tamotsu, and Kwan, Kian M. 1965. *Ethnic stratification.* New York: The Macmillan Co.

Sotomayor, Marta. 1971. "Mexican-American interaction with social systems," *Social Casework,* May.

Stone, Elizabeth. 1978. "It's still hard to grow up Italian," *The New York Times Magazine,* December 17, 1978.

Terkel, Studs. 1974. *Working people talk about what they do all day and how they feel about what they do.* New York: Pantheon Books.

Valentine, Charles A. 1968. *Culture and poverty: critique and counter proposal.* Chicago: University of Chicago Press.

Warner, W. 1949. *Social class in America.* New York: Harper Books.

Wrong, Dennis. 1959. "The functional theory of stratification: some neglected considerations," *American Sociological Review,* XXIV, December.

CHAPTER
2

Ethnicity and the life cycle

Universal movements and stages of life are governed by major psychophysiological events such as birth, death, adolescence, and sensesence (Gadpaille, 1975). Universal movement suggests universal tasks. The ethnic reality suggests that these tasks are perceived and carried out in a variety of ways by diverse ethnic groups. Thus, the universal task of adolescence is to move toward adult status. Jewish tradition provides the ritual of Bar Mitzvah for boys and Bat Mitzvah for girls to signal movement into adulthood. Italians, having no analogous ritual, by tradition permit male adolescents freedom to explore the world, seeking their manhood.

The movement to each psychophysiological stage may entail varying degrees of stress if the expected tasks cannot be fulfilled in a way that meets the standards of the individual or the ethnic group. Jewish adolescents may resist the Bar Mitzvah or Bat Mitzvah as they struggle to free themselves from parental and group restraint. Grandparents who view the Bar Mitzvah as a ceremony only for boys and men may decry the contemporary trend which includes girls. An Italian male who wants to become an academic may have less time available for the "manly pursuits" so highly valued by many in his groups and risk the taunts of peers or expression of dismay by the family.

VARIOUS CONCEPTIONS ABOUT
THE LIFE CYCLE

The universal movement through life's stages has captured the imagination and attention of many scholars, the most noteworthy being Freud, Erikson, and Piaget.

Though their emphases varied, all sought to identify those aspects of the life cycle that represent crucial points of change, the kind of life experiences during each stage that promote health and well-being, and the social or psychological factors that impede growth and learning. The part played by family and society is touched on by all. Most have pointed out that comfortable progression from one stage to the next takes place when the psychological, physiological, and social tasks or events associated with the preceding stage have been completed in a satisfactory manner.

Anthropologists have called our attention to the diverse rituals and meanings associated with movement from one stage to the next. The extent to which these derive from ingrained beliefs concerning the nature of the universe and person-to-person and person-to-God relationships have often been noted (Van Gennep, 1960). Little attention has been paid to the dynamic interplay between life cycle stages and ethnicity, particularly as it occurs in a multiethnic society.

The work of Erik Erikson will be used in this chapter as a base from which to identify the universal stages of development. The tasks and needs of each stage and the ethnic dispositions which tend to be reflected in the response to the inevitable changes will be examined. Most importantly, emphasis will be placed upon the potential sources of stress or strength as these relate to the juncture of life stage, particular ethnic disposition, and context of the larger American society in which these are played out.

The stages of the life cycle have been identified in a variety of ways. Some, like Erikson, characterize them in relation to the psychosocial tasks entailed (Erikson, 1950). Other theories, particularly those derived from freudian thought, emphasize the progression through various periods of psychosexual development.

The characterization presented here is descriptive of the stages of life which are in large measure determined by physical growth, change, and ultimate decline.

Much activity is guided by and responsive to the physical

changes accompanying childhood, adolescence, adulthood, and old age. For example, it is not possible for children to engage in activities beyond the range of those congruent with physical and cognitive development. It is because of their physically based helplessness that children everywhere require protection and are unable to obtain their own food and such protective shelter and clothing as the elements require. Similarly, menarche and menopause set the boundaries for the childbearing period, and aging inevitably signals some decline in physical faculties. Within these broad limits there is, of course, enormous variability.

In our American society adulthood is a complex stage lasting for several years. The idealized nuclear family, the glorification of youth, and the high value placed on autonomy all serve to give a different stamp to the varying periods of adulthood. The early period of childbearing and rearing may be one of excitement and challenge. As children become adolescents and adults there are shifting role expectations. Activity once cherished—protecting, nurturing— may be seen as interference. For these and other reasons we divide adulthood into several periods. The first of these is emerging adulthood, a time for mate selection and perhaps marriage, as well as for decisions concerning occupation which will ultimately determine one's social class. This is followed by adulthood, the middle stage, which requires skills in relationships with mates, nurturing of children to provide them with a sense of ethnic pride and identity, and, most particularly, skills in developing and maintaining a standard of living satisfactory to one's self and family. At the final stage, later adulthood, one is confronted by the physiological changes that signal aging. Children once requiring nurture begin to claim their freedom. Aging parents require more commitment and, upon their death, there is the struggle to grapple with the loss.

Erikson, Freud, and others postulate that each stage of life involves the mastery of a series of psychosexual, psychological, and social tasks. According to Erikson, if a sense of trust is not developed in infancy the ability to relate positively to those with whom we all must relate subsequently—peers, teachers, and the like—is impaired. The child denied autonomy may in later years lack the sense of adventure that adds much to the fullness of adulthood.

Freud's delineation of psychosexual stages focuses upon stages of development which begin with the gratifications of impulses at the initial oral stage; this gratification continues into the anal stage, when the child becomes able to control the sphincter muscles. The phallic stage provides the pleasure of self-stimulation. At each of these pregenital stages the response of adults in the environment will influence the ability to respond appropriately at the genital stage and beyond.

Our perspective incorporates these theories and others, with an emphasis upon how the tasks are interpreted and defined by various ethnic groups. What message do Slavic children receive from their mothers at the anal stage? Is that message different from the message of an American Indian mother? Focusing then on crucial periods of life as these are bounded by physical growth and change, we identify the following universal stages of the life cycle and accompanying tasks.

I. *Entry*
    TASKS: Survival
           Establishing trust
           Obtaining nurturance, comfort

II. *Childhood*
    TASKS: Developing physical skills
           Acquiring language
           Acquiring cognitive skills
           Acquiring moral judgment
           Acquiring awareness of self
           Acquiring awareness of sex role arrangement
           Moving out of home into peer group, into school

III. *Adolescence*
    TASKS: Coping with physical aspect of puberty
           Coping with psychological aspect of puberty
           Coping with sexual awareness/feelings
           Developing relationships with peers of both sexes
           Seeking to achieve increasing independence from parents
           Developing skills required for independent living

IV. *Emerging adulthood*
    TASKS: Deciding about
               Mate—getting married
               Occupation—career
               Sexual behavior

Developing standards of moral-ethical behavior
Locating and identifying with congenial social group
Developing competence in political-economic area

V. *Adulthood*
TASKS: Relating to
Same sex peers
Heterosexual peers
Mates
Establishing
An occupation or career
A home
Bearing and nurturing children
Developing and maintaining a standard of living
Transmitting sense of peoplehood and the ethnic reality

VI. *Later adulthood*
TASKS: Adapting to
Physiological changes
Emancipation of children
Maintaining relationships with aging parents
Coping with loss of aging parents

VII. *Old age*
TASKS: Combating failing health
Coping with diminishing work role
Passing on wisdom—the ethnic reality

The perception of people and how they move within these stages is subject to enormous variability. Whether children are viewed as small replicas of adults or as emerging human beings, are coddled and pampered or treated matter-of-factly, is often a matter of cultural and class perception. The view of adolescence as the period of preparation for the tasks of adulthood as opposed to one which sees this as the beginning of adulthood is a matter of historical and group perspective.

The discussion that follows develops each stage in greater detail with particular emphasis upon the ethnic reality.

ENTRY

In all societies and at all times the task at birth is to survive the trauma of birth. The neonate is imperfect. Indeed it may be a disappointment to its parents in regard to sex. Its physical appearance reminds one of the aging rather than a new arrival. Hair, skin, eyes, and skull formation give little indication of what the appearance will be as the newborn grows. Preferring its former home, the infant sleeps about 20 hours a day (Lidz, 1976).

Having accomplished birth the infant must rely on those in the surroundings to supply the basic survival needs which are experienced as the discomforts of thirst and hunger. These discomforts are vague, diffused, and relieved by others. The process of becoming "hooked on being human"* has begun, for the centrality of other beings is conveyed by the fact that relief from discomfort can be had in no other way. At the same time, the manner in which infants are touched, fondled, and fed says much to them about the emotions of adults: Are they wanted or merely tolerated? Was their arrival a joy, a disaster, or an event to be neither celebrated nor negated?

The successful experiencing of trust will depend upon the manner in which early needs are met by individuals and the group into which the child has been cast. If adults have insufficient food and lack emotional support needed to cope with the dependent new being, comfort and warmth may be difficult to obtain.

Social class position determines the ability of a parent to supply the concrete needs for nurturance. A prosperous Polish merchant whose shop provides specialty food items in an affluent suburb has ample ability to provide for his infant son. His income is more than sufficient to enable the child to develop in the environment by virtue of the abundance of goods available through his father's middle-class status. The Polish clerk who checks out and bags the groceries in the large supermarket chain is faceless to the many harried shoppers. His job provides a meager income that must be stretched to provide his infant son with the bare necessities. Yet each child has the potential of receiving nurture that comes from the "soothing" sounds of caretakers, the stroking of skin, or the embrace that dispels discomfort (Winch, 1971).

When the media blare out news of the abandonment or killing of a newborn, the inability of the involved individuals to nurture, to welcome, and to guide is highlighted. The fact that such events are

---

*Phrase used by Professor Bredemeier, Rutgers University, "Sociological Theory," circa 1964.

newsworthy points to the fact that most groups and individuals celebrate new life.

At the celebration of baptism the Chicano child becomes a member of the church. At the same time, "campadres" of the parents present themselves as caretakers, assuming responsibility with the parents for continuity in the faith as well as in the group. The giving of gifts celebrates entry and rituals symbolize its importance. Hispanic and European female infants are "marked" by the ceremony of ear piercing. This act identifies them as female, one of us, and in need of protection. The "marking" of a Jewish male infant through circumcision is a "sign of union," a permanent mark that incorporates him into the social group. The gifts given on each of these occasions spell acceptance and ethnic continuity.

The manner of entry and preparation for birth derives in large measure from the ethnic reality. The manner of birth relates to a group's beliefs about the nature of the social order, economic security, and the esteem held for children. Early on, then, the child's life course—the sources of strength, weakness, and struggle—are evident in the nature of the preparation for and management of the event of birth.

The activities of women during pregnancy are often designed to protect the child from real or perceived danger while in the womb, in the belief that adverse behavior may mark the fetus in some way.

In some instances these beliefs and the surrounding rituals are powerful, serve a psychologically reassuring function, and in no way put mother or unborn child at risk.

For example, some Black women avoid eating strawberries while pregnant, fearing that the child may be born with a strawberry shaped birthmark on the stomach. Others are careful about certain aspects of posture, believing that if they fold their arms around their stomach or cross their legs they may cause the cord to wrap around the baby's neck and choke him.

Other ingrained beliefs and fears may lead to actions or failure to act which put mother and baby at risk. There are Navajo women who believe that both mother and child are vulnerable to the influences of witchcraft and therefore keep the news of the pregnancy even from the husband until it is observable (Brownlee, 1978). Wariness of witchcraft may keep the mother from seeking prenatal care, thus risking preventable problems. The Black woman who rubs her stomach with dirty dishwater to ensure an easy delivery or others who insert cobwebs and soot mixed with sugar into the vaginal tract to prevent hemorrhage are placing themselves and their unborn children at risk.

There are those genetic factors linked to ethnic group membership over which parents have little control. Tay-Sachs disease and sickle cell anemia, which plague Jewish and Black families, require identification prior to conception.

For children the major task at entry is to learn to survive in an alien world. The trust that comes from warmth and comfort may be difficult to attain for those who are in ethnic minority groups at lower income levels. Social class and ethnicity in these instances deny parents access to the various resources which would guarantee a joyful entry.

CHILDHOOD

Childhood is the beginning of the life cycle. Each child is a "new recruit" (Koller and Ritchie, 1978) into the ethnic reality, where the universally assigned tasks will be perceived and carried out in specific ways common to each ethnic group. The achievement of these tasks may be termed "socialization," for through this process the child becomes an accepted member of the group, the family, the neighborhood, the larger society. Parents, primarily mothers, are assigned the role of culture bearers and respond to the assignment in various ways that influence the development at this early stage. Fathers, however, are not without influence and with the mother carry responsibility for continuation of the cultural ethos. An American Indian father reflects: "I have been given a child, a life to direct. I will remain in the background and give direction. To yell at them places the child in an embarrassing position. I am not an authority figure."* In such an instance the behavior of children is not polarized into the requirement of submission with the adult holding dominance. Many American Indian tribes reject the ideal of submissive or obedient behavior, placing much stress upon approval and praise (Talbot, 1974).

While this attitude may provide children with an environment

---

*Conversation with Ronald Lewis, DSW.

of contentment and security, there are those mainstream forces which negate the world view out of which these child-rearing modes arise. The permissive child-rearing practices of many American Indians are used as a rationale for the forcible assignment of many American Indian children to boarding schools operated by the Bureau of Indian Affairs. Separated from their families, some may suffer stress to such a degree that it interferes with the physical, mental, and social development (Byler, 1978). The views of many Chinese and Italian fathers are similar to that of the American Indian. Each tends to hold back. The Italian father guides from the sidelines, moving in when circumstances are perceived as diminishing the likelihood that the child will be educated in the "Italian way" (Gambino, 1974). In that case direct parental authority is likely to be invoked. The authority vested in the Chinese father serves to provide an emotional distance between him and his children, leaving child-rearing responsibilities to the mother, who decides what is best for their children. Obedience is expected and received (Kitano, 1974). The imposition of paternal authority and the contrasting practice of noninterference are examples of ethnic dispositions to which children must learn to respond in appropriate ways; however, the adaptations may entail varying levels of stress.

Stress may become evident in the developmental experience of the Slavic child whose parents' emotional involvement vacillates between the closeness of hugs (which tend to bind and incorporate, suggesting that the child has no will of its own) and the abruptness of being pushed away as they seek a separate autonomous existence. The ambivalence is compounded by the need to "be strong for me."

A Slavic mother comments, "You teach children to be strong. . . . Johnnie never had a cold for me. . . . Teach a child to be strong—let life take its course" (Stein, 1976). While this may be viewed as acceptable within the ethnic reality, the child may be at some disadvantage when coming in contact with those outside of the group prepared to respond differently to the needs of children in distress. A visit to the dentist requires strength; no medication for pain is permitted, even though modern dentistry has the ability to reduce pain for all patients. Parents may well prohibit anesthetics as they prepare their children for adult responsibility. For some it may indeed pose a conflict between two worlds; others may internalize this reality and view the stoic approach to pain as valuable in their search for autonomy.

There is the universal expectation that children assume household tasks related to their age and ability. This may be clearly seen in the childhood of Mexican American youngsters who gain status as family members as they carry out errands, care for younger siblings, and share in the family work for the good of all. The reward from parents is an environment of permissiveness, indulgence, perhaps even spoiling but less ambivalent than that for the Slovac child, who is responsible for cleanliness of the household and picking up after play without similar remarks. Work, even for children, is an indication of the capacity for good; laziness suggests work of the devil, gaining no rewards.

Sex-specific experiences and assignment begin early in childhood. The clarity and specificity vary with each ethnic group. Mexican American and Italian males are early taught that they are *men* and that this role entails the obligation of protecting female siblings, even if they are older (Krause, 1978a; Murillo, 1976). Girls in turn derive some sense of their female role expectations by virtue of this assured protection. This is reinforced by learning household and child-rearing skills (Gambino, 1974). They are expected to care for both male and female siblings, clean house, and prepare food while their brothers take on those "outside" chores which are carried out by men in this world. Thus both are prepared for adulthood (Gambino, 1974; Krause, 1978). More specific sex-related experiences take place later as childhood merges into adolescence. Movement out of the home into peer groups and institutional settings provides opportunities to complete several universal tasks. The child in preschool and elementary school settings becomes more aware of language as a tool for communication; this development has begun between the ages of 2 and 4 and, if ethnicity has provided a multilingual environment, he has become easily and unselfconsciously multilingual (Gapaille, 1975). But the bilingual child may find that the school rejects the language that makes him a "real" person. Mexican American children in some cases have been forbidden to speak Spanish in the classroom and on the playground, limiting the institution's ability to test and further the development of cognitive skills. American Indian school children may be similarly lost between their own "real" world and the mainstream, as the boarding school suggests that their culture and their own individuality are undesirable. Such messages give little strength to the positive pull toward trust and autonomy as opposed to mistrust and shame, making childhood a stressful experience.

The conflict around language in the school system is most evident in the experiences of Hispanic groups. However, adult first-generation Jews, Slovacs, and Italians may still recall the slur cast on their native languages during their early years. The persistence of Ukranian, Hungarian, and Greek schools where children are sent by their parents after "regular" school hours attests to the tie to the native language and suggests that the positive aspect of bilingualism as a factor in child development bears serious attention.

Indeed, we would go further and suggest that bilingualism is more likely viewed as problematic when the language of minority groups is involved. The value of learning a second, more "prestigious," language is implicitly acknowledged by the practice of some upper-class families who hire French nannies in order to expose children to a second language early in their lives.

Although the school plays an important part in the experience of childhood, much of life takes place in the home, in the neighborhood, and with extended family. In instances where roles are clearly assigned and economic circumstance not too harsh, child-rearing and tending needs are provided for within the natural ebb and flow of family and community life. In times of change, trauma, or dislocation, tried and true patterns break down and institutional forces come into play.

The ready integration of a Black child into an extended family with a cohesive kinship network provides solace and comfort, material support, and advice on the solution of childhood ills, as well as personnel for babysitting (Brown*; Stack, 1975). Those available may lack the skills needed to provide care in a complex, often threatening urban environment. Youthful cousins and aunts or elderly grandparents may bring love and caring devotion but have limited skills because of inexperience or faltering skills because of the aging process. Yet formal organizations are not readily accepted. Those parents who go outside of the immediate network to protect their young may precipitate family emotional crisis and pay

---

*Conversation with Arthur Brown, MSW.

the price in guilt, as do Slovacs who move outside family boundaries. "Taking care of our own" and "doing things for ourselves" provide for cohesive family systems; at the same time, there is risk when community resources having much to offer are not used. Children have much to do and much to learn.

Socialization is an ongoing process. The positive and negative images developed in childhood, the skills learned, and the attitudes developed are subject to modification based on subsequent life experiences. However, children who have been loved, taught, and given a chance to "test their mettle" without being subjected to extensive familial or societally induced trauma are more likely to be successful and integrated human beings, ready for transition to a crucial and perhaps intrinsically dramatic stage—adolescence.

ADOLESCENCE

The move to adolescence or puberty is both physiologically and socially determined. Although it can never readily be said that childhood has ended, there are events that are indicative of impending manhood and womanhood. The onset of menstrual flow, development of pubic hair, and breast growth in girls are in large measure public and visible, as are the growth of facial hair and the voice change in boys.

The ethnic response to these physiological and anatomical facts is diverse. In some societies these events signal the assumption of the rights and obligations associated with adult life. In others they appear to be treated as unwelcome facts, for they portend the emergence of physiological sexual capability and sexual arousal in a social milieu that seems never quite comfortably prepared to deal with these realities. Whichever the case, adolescence is a time of continued growth and serious preparation for the responsibilities of adult life. Social puberty is of greater concern in our considerations of the ethnic reality, for children move from the asexual world of childhood into a more sexual world in which girls become "ladies" and boys become "men." The "lady" expectation is expressed in this manner: "When I was eleven years old my father came home with a . . . manicure set for me. He told me to keep my nails nice, to sit on the porch, and not to play in the street anymore because it was time for me to be a lady" (Krause, 1978).

Such is the experience of many adolescent females. Although

given the directive to be ladies, much other information necessary for advancing adulthood is withheld, particularly that which pertains to sexual matters.

As the Puerto Rican female child learns the female role through imitation of her mother she receives much affirmation from the entire family. Gradually she takes on more female responsibility in caring for young siblings, the babies; but there is no talk of sex. Knowledge is gained from friends with a similarly meager experience and from overheard conversations of adults.

This practice is not limited to the Puerto Rican experience. Talk of sex is taboo among Irish and Italian people as well (Biddle, 1976; Krause, 1978). Daughters know little of sexual functioning; information that *is* given may move along a continuum from mystery to shame. The designation of particular ethnic groups here serves to keep us in touch with the ethnic reality. We are aware that the education of our children in matters related to sex and sexuality is an issue that transcends the ethnic reality and in many communities becomes a source of much tension.

The course from asexual childhood to sexual adolescence is universally traumatic. But the ethnic reality imposes greater stress for many, and as shown earlier, the message is often unclear. Brown suggests that a Black working-class mother may declare: "You're grown—you can have a baby, but you'd better not—If you do I don't trust you to raise it because you're only a baby yourself."*

Dougherty (1978) reports on the practices in a rural Black Florida community where sexual information is withheld from adolescent females not from lack of knowledge of older women but because they are unable to transmit the information. The adolescent female is allowed one "free baby" because she did not know any better. This baby admits her to adulthood, but if she relinquishes her infant she returns to adolescence with no punishment.

Among Puerto Ricans, male siblings are assigned the protector role, warding off those who would attempt to challenge a girl's virginity or respond in any manner other than friendship (Padillo, 1958). The freedom of the male is encouraged; used wisely, a worldly knowledge is gained which is preparation for the role of husband/father.

---

*Conversation with Arthur Brown, MSW.

In the informal "Palomillas" there is the opportunity to gain knowledge and share experiences in male relationships. Machismo (maleness) is developed and demonstrated, and a reputation is established, based upon skill, knowledge, and experience. This "rite of passage" accomplished, he may move to manhood with prestige in family and community (Murillo, 1976).

The clarity of sex-specific experiences in the ethnic reality is useful to the practitioner. However, absoluteness in defining roles may have adverse effects (Gapaille, 1975) and may lead girls to feel like second-class citizens.

The young Puerto Rican girl may be startled by the onset of menstruation, but within her family and community she is now "senorita" and her activities are more closely observed by the adults (Padillo, 1958). Her brothers, much like their Italian peers, gain greater freedom at this stage of their development, moving into the larger society. Feminine identity as defined by large segments of the culture leave them the well-established, traditional biological function of the maternal role. With sexual boundaries set, boys may suffer greater damage through discrimination, distortions, and curtailment of the potential for more wide-range functioning. To stray from the "pure" masculine image into more esthetic pursuits may cause considerable strain in the father-son relationship.

An Italian artist and college professor, in reminiscing, tells of his father's stress as his interest in art developed. His efforts were not accepted as reasonable work until as a high school student he won a cash prize in an artistic competition. His lost esteem was regained as his father began to speak proudly of his son's accomplishments. The demonstrated power to earn money through the arts restored him to a more favorable masculine role. An adherence to the more rigid sex assignment would have denied him his true identity as artist-teacher.*

Among the tasks of adolescence is movement away from the family of origin into the larger society. This is among the most stressful episodes in the life cycle. While the freedom given to male Italians or Mexican Americans described here is a signal, there is no specific ceremony, no point in time, at which manhood is announced.

For the Jewish adolescent, particularly the male, Bar Mitzvah

---

*Conversation with Leonard Pierro.

is a moment of transition. The ritual reaches through centuries into the past and holds religious and social significance in the present. It is the proclamation of religious maturity at age 13. The expectation is that one becomes Bar Mitzvah, "a man of duty," responsible for his religious activity for the rest of his life. This rite of passage permits the adult privileges of reading the Torah in public and being counted in the "minyan" required for conducting the sabbath service (Birnbaum, 1975). Both transmit the feeling of full-fledged or emerging adulthood.

And yet in the reality of contemporary American society, there is a "lack of fit" between the rituals that signal adulthood and the responsibilities and rights assigned to a 13-year-old boy. The situation of the Jewish female is even more complex. The Bat Mitzvah ritual experienced by some has no long established history of significant standing in Jewish law comparable to the Bar Mitzvah. In some Orthodox congregations females are not accorded religious responsibilities in the same way as are men. However, the "coming of age rite" provides the opportunity for parents and friends to recognize the developing young woman at a gathering of the clan, highlighted by festivities and gift giving—"You are one of us!" (Rosenzweig, 1977). The Bar Mitzvah has significance for all involved—congregation, family, friends, peers. Our focus here is on the 13-year-old given this new status in the Jewish community. The stage of development suggests that its meaning may not "take hold" for some time.

At age 20, a young Jewish man recalled his Bar Mitzvah, stating that he realized that adulthood does not suddenly appear as a result of having taken part in the ritual.* Rather, the event proclaims his potential for development into a "man of duty." A dimension not to be ignored is the conflict of "being Jewish." It is difficult to separate clearly the aspects of adolescence and Jewishness but it is evident that for some a struggle emerges, possibly derived from a societal anti-Semitic attitude. In a hostile world surrounded by hostile persons, religion may become a scapegoat for universal feelings of hostility common among the young. Self-hatred is a phenomenon that cannot be ignored, for it may well continue into later stages of development (Kiel, 1967).

---

*Conversation with Larry Schrager.

The universal tasks of adolescence may be traumatic for some members of all ethnic groups. Clashes between adolescents and those in the older generation may be intensified by cultural conflicts, as the young depart from ethnic and cultural traditions. Some ethnic traditions may intensify adolescent turmoil.

Nevertheless, a review of several studies of adolescent behavior reveals that "turmoil and conflict are not necessarily the hallmark of adolescent development" (King, 1972). Adolescents may not suffer from great identity crises or from poor relationships with parents, siblings, and peers. While many have questions and doubts about themselves, most have the competence to handle stress because of their high level of self-esteem. Where ethnically based guidelines and values are clear-cut, these serve to reinforce competence and minimize trauma.

The sense of peoplehood, ethnicity, has provided Japanese families with the strength to overcome the various onslaughts of their American experience, which included internment at the height of World War II. The emphasis upon ethnic identity has served as a force among others to develop conformity and little social deviance. Rewards for good behavior, as well as punishment for misdeeds, provide elements of social control reinforced by a sense of dependency, duty, and responsibility, with some messages of shame or guilt giving clear directions for ethnic behavior (Kitano, 1976).

The point midway between childhood and adulthood may be variously defined or for some groups omitted; yet experience has shown that something happens to children that changes their bodies, and their voices and their perspectives—which suggests that childhood is waning and a new, more responsible person is developing.

EMERGING ADULTHOOD

Adolescence with or without trauma centers about the search for self within the context of family and community, both having intimate connections to the ethnic reality. As adolescents emerge into adulthood, energy is directed into wider areas. There is increasing potential for intimacy, emotional commitment, and giving to others. It is the time during which wives and husbands are wooed and won, past relationships deepen or vanish, and emancipation from parents continues (Valliant, 1972). It is a time of decision-making.

Perhaps the question, "Who am I?" arises. Decisions center about mate selection and marriage, employment or career opportunities, ethical behavior at this more advanced stage of development, identifying with congenial peers, and participation in the larger political arena.

Mate selection

While we may hold to the American ideal of freedom to select one's own marriage partner, we recall earlier examples cited of parental decisions to locate in certain neighborhoods and to provide recreation for the purpose of having children associate with other families "like us." The result of these decisions may bear fruit at this stage of the individual's life cycle. The Italian parents may withhold permission for a daughter to go out until they know "who he is" and "who his family is"—an Italian male is more acceptable and more likely to continue the ethnic tradition (Krause, 1978).

Although there is continual mention of the freedom of Italian males, there is an expectation of behavior that is respectful and moral in relation to women. In reviewing his experiences within the family as a young man, an Italian adult recalls the disappointment felt by his father who suspected that he was keeping his intended wife—an Italian young woman—out too late, realizing that his son was returning home much after midnight. The concern was with caring for, respecting, the young woman. He was much more comfortable when he learned that the young woman had been home at a respectable hour and that the son had then met and socialized with a group of men until the late hour. The father's regard for women included not only those in his family but those who would bcome members.* The mate selection process, for these reasons, is often fraught with conflict. Nevertheless, there is increasing intermarriage.

We suggest that a majority of young people are urged by their families to seek partners from within their own ethnic group.

Ethnic dispositions relating to the role of woman as caretaker are questioned as young women reevaluate that role. This activity, however, places them at risk of diluting and losing many of the characteristics that made them "female" and initially attractive to

---

*Conversation with Frank Becallo, MSW.

their ethnic male counterparts. Murillo cites the example of a Chicano male graduate student in conflict about his decision to marry a particular young woman. He wishes her to maintain the old ways, which require her to be devoted to her husband and children, serve his needs, support his actions and decisions, and take care of the home. She opposes this and is in conflict with her fiance (Murillo, 1976). As emerging adults both are in the process of preparing for a career; but for the woman, a Chicana, this is a relatively new adventure, the more familiar career being that of wife/mother.

For young Jewish women there is less of a problem. The plan to work continues a tradition established long ago by grandmothers and mothers whose diverse occupations were important to the survival of the family. Jewish tradition more easily accepts employment of women, which brings money into the home. In the present, however, the emerging Jewish woman has a choice. The Jewish value of education is traditional, but in the past was more reserved for men. Women now attend college in equal numbers with men and may experience conflict as they make the choice. "As a young Jewish woman I am achievement oriented, committed to individual achievement, accomplishment and career—but, I am equally committed to marriage. What then of my children? If I am to be a responsible mother then I must remain at home with my young children." Such is the ethnic dilmma shared by Italian and Slavic young women (Krause, 1978b).

Asians, both Chinese and Japanese, anticipate that their children will acquire as much education as possible—high school, college, graduate school. In order to accomplish this families will make great sacrifices, thus endowing the family with pride. Success is a means to the upward mobility anxiously sought after (Kitano, 1976).

But entry into the work force is often difficult for ethnic minorities. Of particular note are those American Indians who have attended Bureau of Indian Affairs (BIA) boarding schools. Led to believe that they have the competence that comes with a high school diploma, young adults discover that in fact the level of achievement is at the seventh or eighth grade. This limitation denies the opportunities needed for self-esteem and movement to the adult level. The reality is more likely a job of lesser status. Attempts to perform the occupational tasks result in disappointment, feeling of failure, and negative identity. Acceptance of such an image related to work is reflected in the comment of a young Plains Indian: "My brother is a heavy machine operator, that's a pretty good job for an Indian" (Allen, 1977). A possible response to the devastation is a high rate of suicide among young Indian males, who appear to have poorer mental health than the average American population. Although Havighurst denies the influence of attendance at BIA schools, citing the low rate of suicide *in* boarding school, we suggest that consideration be given to this experience as one among many during the life cycle that perpetuate mistrust. Byler describes the social characteristics of an Indian most inclined toward suicide: "He has lived with a number of ineffective or inappropriate parental substitutes because of family disruption. . . . He has spent time in boarding schools and moved from one to another" (Byler, 1978). Efforts to make Indian children "white" may destroy them before they have a chance at adult status.

More recently Howze (1979) has observed the emerging Black male in a poor urban setting and discovered a high suicide rate to be "a primary means of coping with problems." Among those problems is the inability to achieve an important position in their value system—a good job. Jobs bring status, place an individual and his family in a particular social class. The better the job, the higher the status. Young adults with no job or hopes for a job which will supply the wherewithal to assume adult responsibility seek what appear to us to be irrational solutions.

Emancipation through self-support and/or marriage, a reasonable expectation for the emerging adult, may be elusive for those who are members of extended families where their incomes are essential to the survival of the group. This is vividly expressed: "Me and Otis could be married, but they ruined all that. . . . Magnolia knows that it be money getting away from her. I couldn't spend time with her and the kids and be giving her the money I do now. I'd have my husband to look after" (Stack, 1975). Ruby, the narrator, describes the pressures exerted to keep her within the group; this young Black woman is entrapped by the kinship network which has so much potential for ethnic cohesion. She is anxious to move on to full adulthood but constrained by her ethnic reality.

Sexuality

Seldom do ethnic groups prepare their young for adult sexual encounters. Sexuality, a primary aspect of adulthood, remains hidden from male and female children. Information about menstruation, sexual intercourse, conception, and childbirth is often withheld or is related in vague terms by adults. Lack of preparation for menarche leaves many young women startled. Krause reports that a significant number of women, in her study of Jewish, Italian, and Slavic women, were totally unprepared for menstruation and so were frightened, distressed, surprised, or believed themselves to be injured. Most unprepared were Italian women (Krause, 1978), who are beset by strong taboos against discussion or exchange of information about anatomy and physiology. Although we expect menarche to occur during adolescence, it is significant here; lack of earlier information influences behavior or responses in early adulthood. Preparation for parenthood and marriage is lacking in most ethnic groups. There are few guidelines provided for parents, who are inexperienced amateurs throughout most of their incumbency (Hill, 1974); and so, like their parents, young adults stumble onto adulthood "ready or not."

In the Puerto Rican life cycle it is clear that, "ready or not," a child moves directly into adulthood by virtue of physically mothering or fathering a child. This circumstance confers adult status, and one is expected to assume adult roles and behavior, which may mean dropping out of school to take on employment (Hidalgo, 1974).

In order to have the competency to move to adulthood we have suggested several universal tasks to be accomplished by all young persons. There are those ethnic characteristics that give assistance and support in mate selection, career choice, developing ethical behavior, and finding congenial friends. At the same time there are those ethnic forces that deter movement, as well as mainstream forces which deny the accomplishment of political competence; thus many, particularly those of minority status, are accused of noninvolvement. And so the Mexican American is seen as a nonjoiner of voluntary associations and as having a fatalistic view of the world, feeling no control over government or schools. In their ethnic minority status the young as well as adults have seen the situation as hopeless. Earlier experiences have been fruitless. Continual failure and hardship give little reason for hope. There have been in recent times those emerging adults who have called the mainstream into question through organizations such as the Young Lords, La Raza, and Operation PUSH. They intend to move confidently into adulthood ready for the tasks of generativity.

ADULTHOOD

Generativity, an aspect of adulthood suggested by Erikson, is primarily concerned with establishing and guiding the next generation; it is a time of productivity and creativity (Erikson, 1950). It is the longest stage in the life cycle, during which individuals assume responsibility for the care of others, primarily through the role of parent, but also in varying career, job, and political experiences.

Children move from entry to adolescence and emerge into adulthood under the supervision of adults. They are the bearers of ethnicity, a task that is accomplished for the most part unconsciously. But in this process adults give children a sense of belonging to a special group that has special food, a language of its own, exciting holidays, and celebrations with family and friends; usually there is devotion to a particular religion. Recollections of an ethnic childhood may include a father aware of discrimination against Polish-Americans who remained proud of their Polish American identity and openly contemptuous of the "cowardice" of Poles who anglicized their last names. As an adult Thomas Napierkowski has the Polish heritage thus transmitted by his father. As an adult he feels a conscious need to help his children to grow up to be Polish Americans. This means that he is their protector when their names are garbled; when they are called "Polack" or are victims of the insensitive Polish joke, an experience that brings a tightness to his chest (Napierkowski, 1976). To be the bearer of ethnicity is not always a pleasant task. The Polish experience is paralleled by Italians, who recoil from the term "dago" or "wop"; Puerto Ricans from "spick"; or Asians from "chink" or "jap"; Blacks from the viciousness of "nigger." As one assumes the role of adult protector and feels increasing pride in this achievement, the realization occurs that the ethnic heritage held so dearly may be viewed by others as a joke.

Other adult Polish Americans speak of a childhood in which aspects of Polish heritage were set aside in order to become American—the Polish language was unspoken and English was used daily. To speak Polish would be to call attention to the fact of Polish descent, which may serve as a barrier to upward mobility (Wrobel, 1973). The purpose of this conscious denial of ethnicity is to protect children from the experiences of discrimination. Adults, each in their own way, function as protectors of their young from the hidden injuries of ethnicity.

Color, the banner of ethnicity for Blacks, identifies them immediately. The parent again becomes the protector as well as the bearer of ethnicity. In moving their children toward an ethnic awareness they enable them to understand that their black skin is not just wrapping paper around them but a part of them (Harrison-Ross, 1973); that their hair, though kinky, is not "bad"; and that they are Yourba's Children. An extreme example of parental failure may be seen in Pecola Breedlove, a central figure in Toni Morrison's novel, *The Bluest Eye* (1972). Pecola wishes for "blue eyes, prettier than the sky, prettier than Alice-and-Jerry storybook eyes." Such a wish cannot be fulfilled. Unprotected by her parents, she becomes unable to cope with life. Most parents understand and do protect their young, knowing that they will not acquire "blue eyes." They also know that with them they would not suffer from the effects of racism that calls their skin color, hair texture, and lack of blue eyes into question. Such racism is manifested in harassment from the mainstream society.

There is in addition the task of nurture of the young through the provision of basic needs of food, clothing, and shelter. These are provided through the income received from activity in the work place. The job and the level of income it produces will determine the social class of the family.

Middle-aged, middle-class Blacks have spent time in adolescence and emerging adulthood investing in an education that has moved them to this level. Both men and women have made this investment despite institutional racism. As adults they marry and together gain a social status that provides them with the ability to provide their children with opportunities *they* missed in childhood. These may include music lessons, recreational activities, and perhaps private schools.

Work for many ethnic adults is an absorbing experience. Middle-class Blacks manifest the Puritan orientation toward work and success more than any other group in our population (Willie, 1974).

This leaves them little time for recreation and other community experiences. The regard for work is shared by Slavic Americans, who live to work and who believe that, if one cannot work, one is useless. "Work is the capacity for good, not to work lets in bad. Work is God's work, laziness is the devil's work" (Stein, 1976). And so this group has labored at almost any employment to be found, but primarily in blue-collar occupations. When both husband and wife work, this yields a comfortable existence. Efforts to move into the professional ranks may be viewed as more problematical and deflecting from the tasks of generativity.

It is important to note that ethnicity may discourage certain types of employment; although employment is not ruled out, the Italian American woman rarely works as a domestic. Such employment in the home of others is seen as a usurpation of the family loyalty. And so such employment has been left to Irish, German, Black, Hispanic, English, Scandinavian, and French women (Gambino, 1974). The primary responsibility for Italian women is to maintain the home, nurture the children, keep a home that is immaculately clean (a symbol of a sound family), and attend to the needs of her husband. The response to this adult female expectation was noted in one of our Italian undergraduate students. An exceptional student in her thirties, she was proud of her Italian heritage and during her senior year was deeply involved in preparations for her teenage daughter's wedding. However, 1 year after graduation she appeared at a college function 15 pounds lighter, with a new hair style and a special radiance. In that year she had found employment and separated from her husband. She explained that part of the difficulty had been the energy that it took for her to be the good Italian wife/mother. She added the role of student quite successfully but lost favor in the community. Her children, like many others, disapprove of her new life-style and her rejection of their father. But it is her feeling that part of their discomfort is her rejection of the Italian way of life she had taught them as bearer of the ethnicity. As culture-bearer she played the woman's role of nurturer, supportive wife, and mother. The Italian woman as center of her home is successful if she is responsible for the care and well-being of husband and children (Krause, 1978). Her conclusions show considerable insight into aspects of ethnic disposition and move her well along into an understanding of herself.

This Italian woman chose to be a single parent; it has its risks.

But for many Black women the choice was not as conscious. Many Black women assume this head of family status by virtue of being widowed, separated, divorced, single, or separated from their husbands involuntarily—often by jail. Emasculation of the Black male by institutional racism has made him less available instrumentally and expressively to his family. The low-income Black woman, unlike the middle-class Black woman described earlier, is aware that the woman, wife, may become the primary support for her children, a role she does not cherish; she wishes for a more viable family unit (Painter, 1977). Generativity, caring for the next generation, is acted out alone, but not without difficulty. Greater energy is needed to accomplish the universal tasks.

Admittedly there is a lack of preparation for marriage and parenthood. We have indicated such in the discussion of emerging adulthood. Individuals take on these roles without adequate credentials although subtle ethnic messages as to how to behave are conveyed. The Puerto Rican male pushed into adulthood by circumstance of fatherhood knows the meaning of *machismo*, a desirable combination of virtues of courage and fearlessness. As *macho* he is the head of his family, responsible for their protection and well-being, defender of their honor. His word is his contract (Abad, Ramos, and Boyce, 1974). His wife knows that she will be protected and carries out her motherliness, being particular about teaching her children *respecto*, an esteem for individuals based upon personal attributes rather than class.

Consider another Hispanic group, Mexican Americans, whose adult responsibility continually includes the bearing of children. Denied this potential for fulfillment, there is the risk of personal disaster for Mexican American women. Such is the experience of a group of low-income women who, apparently without consent, have been sterilized, denying them the opportunity to continue to bear children. Their feminine identity is denied and their social identity jeopardized. They become cut off from social networks of godparents, friends, and relatives. They suffer insomnia, depression, and social isolation. Adulthood for them is incomplete; they have not been protected by machismo, which found itself powerless against the mainstream force (Ainsworth, 1979).

Jewish men, like Hispanic men, are expected to protect their women. Adults are expected to marry. Marriage is "mitzvah" (duty);

besides procreation it provides companionship and fulfillment. The Biblical directive, "Be fruitful and multiply, it is not good for man to be alone; I will make him a helpmate," legitimizes the expectation, but the vow of the groom makes public his intention: "Be my wife in accordance with the law of Moses and Israel. I will work for you, I will honor you, support and maintain you as it becomes Jewish husbands who work for their wives, honoring and supporting them faithfully" (Birnbaum, 1975).

Biblical directive again provides clues for appropriate behavior for the Jewish housewife. She is trusted by her husband, obeyed by her servants, admired by the community, kind to the poor and needy; she cares well for her household and is not idle. "And in return her children rise up and call her blessed and her husband praises her" (Proverbs 31:10-31). This passage also gives affirmation to the Jewish tradition of work for adult women; indeed, the work allows for creativity, a characteristic of this adult phase. It includes selecting a field and planting a vineyard, making linen garments and selling them to a merchant, taking produce to the market for sale, as well as making her own clothes. And so Judaism provides guidelines for adults that are similar to those that are implicit in other groups. It also provides some direction for child-rearing. A coordination of the efforts of both the father and the mother places them at the same level of authority in regard to the children.

The influence of the mother in rearing of the children gives her greater potential as culture-bearer. Each group, however, benefits if there is a tradition to give support to present behavior. Ancient Asian tradition of filial piety provides a framework for parent-child relations among Chinese and Japanese. In action the directive is for reciprocal obligations from parent to child and child to parent in the day-to-day family interactions as well as in major family decisions (Kitano, 1976).

In the Jewish and Asian families men are assured of their position as protector, head of household. On many occasions Black men seeking the role of protector are denied the role and their manhood. More often the media and literature present him in relation to the things he cannot do in the position of husband-father; they say little about what Black men may be really like, alluding only to toughness and ignoring tenderness (Hannerz, 1969).

The term "boy," too often applied to all Black males regardless of age, suggests a childlike, helpless state of dependency. Examples of the result of such treatment may be found in the work of Liebow (1967), Hannerz (1969), and Billingsley (1968). Ethnicity again is denied affirmation; so, when the Black male attempts to take his place as head of the household, he is rebuffed. The public school teacher talks to his wife. If he is a single parent teachers do not expect him to show interest in the education of his children. The assumption is of incompetence by virtue of heritage.

Child-rearing

The intricate day-to-day tasks of child care require much concentration, for the outcome will influence the future. Given the privilege of motherhood, the Slovac American mother's ethnic behavior may deny her children early autonomy by binding them to her, letting them know that they have no mind of their own, no will of their own, no separate existence apart from her. They are expected to be strong, resist adversity and fight worry, and begin to understand the importance of work by picking up after their play (Stein, 1976).

A contrasting practice permits the American Indian child more freedom. An Indian child may have available innumerable adult family members who assume responsibility for his care. Parents do not see themselves as figures of authority but as guides or role models. This style, however, has placed Native American children in jeopardy, for the mainstream interpretation has been that these children are running wild without the care of their parents. Permissiveness, allowing for individual development, is a different but effective way of discipline accepted by the American Indian community. And so they are continually amazed when parents who were regarded as excellent caregivers are considered to be unfit, thereby losing custody of their children, who are placed in foster care or BIA schools. Slavic American and Native American children then may suffer in different ways from the ethnic behaviors of their parents who follow ethnic tradition. Unfortunately the American Indian children are in greater jeopardy for, once removed from their families, their experiences prevent the learning of skills necessary in later stages of development. They have no parental or community models. Their social growth and development are hampered (Byler, 1978).

Friends

For the adult there are dimensions of living that move beyond spouse and children to peer friendships. These round out one's existence and provide confidantes and associates for recreation. The initial source for these friendships is the extended family and then members of the same ethnic group, which often means the same religious affiliation.

The hierarchy of friendship for the Italian begins with those who are "sangu du me sangu" (blood of my blood), adds "compari" and "comare" (godparents), who are intimate friends in addition. Beyond these there are those who demand respect but not intimacy and those with whom one may associate by reason of work (Gambino, 1974).

"Compadrazo" and "compadres" are terms that identify those Mexican American adults who hold the same status as compari or comare. They are godparents and most cherished friends. They are reliable in times of stress imposed by various insensitive institutions. In times of joy they are available for the celebration, for they are family.

While the Mexican American adult male has freedom of movement in the larger society, the woman is expected to remain close to the home and so her friendship group contains her daughters, even after they have gained maturity, and other female relatives, such as cousins and nieces. There is comfort here and the women often become confidantes (Murillo, 1976).

When friends are outside of the immediate family they may be found in the neighborhood but they are not as close as family (Wrobel, 1973).

As ethnic adults attempted to find the friendship of others like them, they formed ethnic communities, ethnic islands; sometimes these are labeled "ghetto" or "barrio" in the negative sense of the word. These may be communities of rejected people who, despite the barrenness of their existence, find a sense of belonging and cohesion that is characteristic of ethnic commmunities where adults attempt to maintain their homes. It is here that they find friends and a church. Howell (1973) suggests that in such a Polish neighborhood a homeowner may work in a local factory; his wife remains home to care for the children. On Wednesday evenings he bowls in an all-male league but on most evenings he stops by the local tavern to drink with the boys (LeMasters, 1975). On Tuesday his wife occasionally plays bingo and on Sunday she goes to church (he goes only on special occasions). Their neighbors are their best friends but they maintain relatively close relationships with their parents, siblings, and extended family and are wary of outsiders (Howell, 1973). This pattern is found again and again within the ethnic groups we are concerned with. Blacks have long maintained kinship networks that have provided emotional as well as financial resources. Stack, in her study of kinship networks, has established their presence for low-income families, while Willie and McAdoo have done the same for middle-income families (McAdoo, 1978, 1979; Willie, 1976).

An analysis of Krause's data indicated that Italian and Slavic families in Pittsburgh often lived within a reasonable proximity—some at the same address, others in the same neighborhood, and still others in different neighborhoods with similar zip codes. Jewish women tended to live in more distant cities. Those Slavic and Italian women remaining in Pittsburgh visited as frequently as daily, while Jewish women were more likely to visit weekly. In each instance there is evidence of adults who provide each other through the generations support, a sense of family, and ethnic continuity.

Outside the family circle the adult task of relating to peers is achieved in the ethnic neighborhood where the sense of peoplehood pervades the environment and the ethnic reality is surely in action. The daily or weekly contact among the grandmothers, mothers, and daughters studied by Krause gives evidence of a major adult task, that of maintaining generational ties. The adult stands between the young and the aged, sometimes pushed by both forces. Again the response to the older generation may be guided by ethnic tradition. This tradition is broad, covering all ethnic groups.

LATER ADULTHOOD

To recognize that one is in later adulthood is to realize that time is in constant motion and with this movement there are physiological and emotional changes. The climacteric tells women very clearly that their child-bearing years are ending. What then will be the life for women whose ethnic assignment was to bear children and care for them? Time has moved them into adulthood and independence, but in many instances the ethnic dispositions permit and encourage a closeness which may be observed by determining the geographical distance. It is not unlikely that Italian, Polish, or Black emancipated children and their families remain in the neighborhood. Those who move perhaps from the city to the suburbs are seen as far away (Gans, 1962).

The telephone is a resource that provides the possibility, daily or weekly, for communication. This does not appear to be limited to a particular ethnic group when both generations are in the same community.

The expectation for care of aging parents manifests itself in various ways. There are those who visit daily or telephone several times a day, as well as those who visit infrequently; the latter were in the minority (Krause, 1978).

It is difficult to measure the depth of relationships, but McAdoo (1979) attempts to determine the sense of pressure felt by adults as they shared their resources with their parents and other family members. Stating generally that they felt no sense of obligation because "this is what is done in families," 45% feel pressure to share ranging from "a little" (16%), to "a great deal" (8%), to "some" (21%). The sense of generation and ethnicity both remain strong. Most ethnic older Americans expect some measure of regard from the younger generation. Time, technology, and life-style have all contributed to the need for older family members to adapt to a world which, although it holds them in regard, does not respond in the old ways.

OLD AGE

Many elderly persons in our society arrived here early in their youth from societies that were primarily agrarian. The Chicano and the Chinese, though different in so many ways, shared this agrarian experience and similar patterns of family life. The extended family had need of each family member. In the Chicano family mature men and women were the workers; the aged provided knowledge, based on their experience, and cared for the very young. They were useful members of the family (Maldando, 1975). Similarly, Chinese families were self-contained units in which the elderly had no fear of unemployment. Even before physical decline, they retired, living on the fruits of their children's labor. Their advice was sought on important matters. The young held them in high regard and infants grew up in their grandparents' arms.

Aging is a proud station in life. This has been the pattern of life for generations, but change has come to cause tensions not anticipated. Technology has caused families to move to urban centers where employment provides greater opportunities for the young. The extended family changes in form as an urban life-style evolves. The result for the aging Chicanos and Chinese is a world unknown to their grandparents.

Settled in Chinatowns or barrios, the elderly watch the young move into more heterogeneous communities in the city or the suburbs. The respect and regard remain but the extended family under one roof is less common than in Mexico or China or even in earlier periods in America. In the city, their children do not need their knowledge, skills, and experience.

Cheng, in a 1978 study of the elder Chinese in San Diego County, California, presents "Chinese-ness" characteristics among older Chinese that enable them to maintain their sense of peoplehood in a changing society. Among these characteristics are:

Expectation of children supporting and helping them in their old age.

"Clanishness"—living in neighborhoods with Chinese neighbors and belonging to Chinese associations.

Celebration of family happenings with family and friends—birthdays especially.

Identification of themselves as Chinese or Chinese in America, regardless of the dialect they speak.

These ethnic dispositions and others provide the framework around which daily life may be constructed with some assurance of success and comfort. The activities of youth and early adulthood which included various areas of work are less available. This has sustained many throughout their lives.

In Chapter 1 the importance of work in relation to ethnicity and social class was discussed. As old age approaches, work performed with ease in earlier years becomes a burden. Limitations are obvious. There are those who, recognizing this, would not accept employment if it were appropriate and available. The lack of work may be humiliating for others. Earlier we have noted the Slavic American drive for work which is perceived as good. When aging requires retirement for the Slavic male, a change in behavior of many may be noticed. Rather than admit to the threat of aging, which implies incapacity, inactivity, weakness, and dependency, attempts may be made to work even more vigorously. This invariably fails. Having used this option, retirement follows and with it, for many, depression, apathy, despair, over assumed uselessness. Time used in the past at labor is used in wandering aimlessly around the home and neighborhood. Once a respected figure, he now becomes dependent, aimless, perpetually in slow motion; his wife and children respond by becoming bossy (Stein, 1976).

Stein poses the possibility that in some instances long-hidden conflicts surface in regard to loss of authority, power, and respect even though there is evidence of the apparent universal respect and deference for the aging.

The last vestiges of power and authority which came with work diminish and the fruits of that labor become the center of power struggles. Land, houses, property—the last symbols of power, authority, and prestige—represent independence; at the same time, declining age suggests that some authority or power should be assigned to the young. But the Slavic disposition in the elderly suggests caution; to be taken care of is dependence. Good intentions are not worthy of trust and so rather than retiring peacefully like some American Indians the Slavic elderly have great potential for tension and stress (Stein, 1976).

The authority that wanes for the Slavic elderly maintains itself in the life of the Native American. An Iroquois woman describes the position of older women in her tribe:

> The clan is the basic structure of the Iroquois family and of most other Native American families. The Clan mother is the oldest woman in that family group. Her authority reigns over every aspect of that family's daily life even to the nominations of the chiefs. The men voted, the women give the symbols of office to the new chief. (Haile, 1976).

With a definite role to perform there is no time for retirement. As Curely describes his grandmother, a Navajo, a picture similar to the early life of the Chicano and Chinese evolves, but with different results. Mr. Curely's grandmother never "worked" outside of the home. Her education was received from her grandmother, who taught her to behold and revere the land. She learned of the balance and order in creation; of the relationship between mountains, rivers, trees, and the wind. Her work at home was to open the gate for the sheep and goats to forage for food. It is now her turn as grandmother to teach these things to her grandchildren. The world is somehow different, the gate is opened by the grandchildren while she continues to pray at dawn. This will be taught to her grandchildren, along with knowledge of the morning as the time in which good things exist—good health, increased wealth, and wisdom. This is not a job from which one retires; it is what must be done. The new role is teaching her grandchildren the lessons of her grandmother. Like her Iroquois sister she is in the position of wielding wisdom and knowledge, sought after when the order and balance of the world seem to be undone. Retirement, rather than excluding her from the family clan, incorporates her more completely into the role of teacher, a process that is inevitable and definite (Curely, 1978).

The role of the grandmother is clear in these American Indian families. Seldom do we hear mention of loneliness, yet in other groups this is an important issue. Much of the stress could be removed by relationships with grandchildren in the manner of the American Indian. This is illustrated in Krause's sample of Italian grandmothers.

Grandchildren provide the opportunity to tell the family history; such exchanges seem to be initiated by grandchild or grandparent. Seldom do parents appear to encourage the telling of the story. Studies indicate that it is often the third generation that attempts to revive family history (Robertson, 1977).

But grandparenting provides other opportunities and resources. These range from child care and financial support to serving as role models to playing a modulating influence in family strife (Robertson, 1977). But grandchildren cannot be expected to assume major responsibility for giving life vitality; other sources must be explored.

Kinship ties among all generations would seem to be a resource, particularly if all are in the same household. Such is not always the case. Given the reality of the oppressive results of institutional racism, many elderly Blacks reside with children, grandchildren, and great-grandchildren without receiving emotional support. The arrangement is necessary, but economic difficulties minimize the likelihood that support will be forthcoming. Nevertheless, there are many Black older people living alone. Findings of a study in San Diego County have also been noted in other works (Faulkner, Heisel, and Simms, 1975; Jackson, 1978). Along with other ethnic groups, Blacks prefer to live in the vicinity of family members. Contact with them may be limited in certain urban areas due to their fear of the environment. The threat of violence is a reality in many urban centers. This may reinforce loneliness and isolation from family and friends even when there is a need and a desire and physical health permits (Faulkner, Heisel, and Simms, 1975). In areas of less danger, recreational activities that are enjoyed include church activities, family picnics, card playing, and getting together to talk.

Religion plays an important part in the life of many. Church attendance has provided spiritual involvement for some and a basis of social life for others (Stanford, 1978). Others have found positions of status that are self-affirming and provide for respect and honor in the community. The Black church is among the very few Black institutions in our society that is independent of control by the mainstream society. It is entirely controlled and supported by the Black community, with elder Blacks often holding important administrative positions.

We have continually stressed the importance of kinship and neighborhood ties as positive aspects of this stage of the life cycle. However, it is important that we consider the possible negative aspects of this disposition. In 1978 Cohler and Lieberman reported on a study of the assumption that close ties with family and friends fostered personal adjustment and reduced the impact of otherwise stressful events. The study included Irish, Italians, and Polish Americans who were middle-aged and older. The presence of an extensive network was stressful for Italian and Polish women. Socialized to be caretakers in earlier life stages, they cared for their children and various other kin. As children grew and became more independent of parents, women seemed to show an increasing involvement in themselves, moving away from the caretaker roles. This was particularly evident in the Italian and Polish women, less evident in the Irish women. The presence and demands of an extensive social network appeared to have an adverse impact on mental health.

As role expectations and personalities change over the years, distress may be evoked by the demands for caring for others. The ethnic community is not a positive environment for all aging persons, particularly those women who seek release from earlier caretaking roles which are demanded by their ethnic reality.

Ethnicity indeed has its strengths and weaknesses. It has power to hold a people together, yet there is the potential for stress when the demands are excessive. Most aged people have the universal task of combating failing health and diminishing capacity and confronting the ultimate reality of death. Health problems that become critical often generate unacceptable "solutions." The nursing home has become a viable alternative for many. For others it is not a reasonable solution. Many Slavic families find nursing care homes repulsive (Stein, 1976). This is also true for many Chicanos (Sotomayor, 1977).

"Continuity is a fundamental necessity for human life, collectively and individually" (Myerhoff, 1978). Our elderly people offer us continuity in the social, cultural, historical, and spiritual aspects of our lives (Meyerhoff, 1978). Their death places the responsibility for that continuity upon those at earlier stages of life. We know little of ethnic dispositions in relation to death. Black, Japanese, and Mexican American residents of Los Angeles were studied by Kalish and Reynolds (1976), casting some light upon how these ethnic groups feel about death, dying, and grieving. A study of funeral customs of Black Americans (Devore, 1979), which examined similarities in African and American rituals and Negro spirituals such as "Soon I will be done with the trouble of dis world" or "Swing low sweet chariot, coming for to carry me home," gives a Black perspective in which death for many is a release from the oppression of the mainstream.

Native Americans view death as part of life and are able to visualize themselves as performers in the "Dance of Death." No matter what the tribal burial custom may be, in sleeping, sitting, or fetal positions, life is to be lived to the fullest and death accepted as a natural conclusion (Dial, 1978).

Death does not wait for the last stage of the life cycle, but if one is able to survive the pervasive reality is that death will be at the end of this stage. It may be faced with integrity or despair, with an acceptance of decline that recognizes the affirmation of the past, or with submission to the forces which seem designed to make life unbearable.

SUMMARY

The stages of the life cycle are acted out in as many variations as there are groups. The stage of development will not only give us clues as to the universal tasks needed to be achieved but an indication of the ethnic dispositions that are imposed upon those tasks. Life cycle stage, universal task, and ethnic disposition are all items of data, along with social class, which are essential for our practice.

REFERENCES

Abad, Vincente, Ramos, Juan, and Boyce, Elizabeth. 1974. "A model for delivery of mental health services to Spanish-speaking minorities." *American Journal of Orthopsychiatry, 44*(4), July.

Ainsworth, Diane. 1979. "Cultural cross fires." *Human Behavior*, March.

Biddle, Ellen Horgan. 1976. "The American Catholic family." In Mindel, Charles H., and Habenstein, Robert W. (Eds.). *Ethnic families in America: patterns and variations.* New York: Elsevier Scientific Publishing Co.

Billingsley, Andrew. 1968. *Black families in white America.* Englewood Cliffs, N. J.: Prentice-Hall, Inc.

Birnbaum, Phillip. 1975. *A book of Jewish concepts* (rev. ed.). New York: Hebrew Publishing Co.

Brownlee, Ann Templeton. 1978. *Community, culture and care: a cross-cultural guide for health workers.* St. Louis: The C. V. Mosby Co.

Byler, William. 1978. "The destruction of American Indian families." In Unger, Steven (Ed.). *The destruction of American Indian families.* New York: Association on American Indian Affairs.

Cheng, Eva. 1978. *The elder Chinese.* San Diego: Center on Aging, San Diego State University.

Cohler, Bertram J., and Lieberman, Morton A. 1978. "Social relations and mental health among three European ethnic groups." Chicago: University of Chicago.

Curley, Larry, 1978. "Retirement—an Indian perspective." In Stanford, E. Percil (Ed.). *Retirement: concepts and realities.* San Diego: Center on Aging, San Diego State University.

Devore Wynetta. 1979. "The funeral practices of Black Americans." Union, N.J.: Kean College of New Jersey.

Dial, Adolph L. 1978. "Death and life of Native Americans." *The Indian Historian, 11*(3), Summer.

Dougherty, Molly C. 1978. *Becoming a woman in rural Black culture.* New York: Holt, Rinehart and Winston.

Erikson, Erik. 1950. *Childhood and society* (2nd ed.). New York: W. W. Norton & Co.

Faulkner, Audrey Olsen, Heisel, Marsel A., and Simms, Peacolia. 1975. "Life strength and life stresses—explorations in the measurement of the mental health of the Black aged." *American Journal of Orthopsychiatry,* *45*(1), January.

Gadpaille, Warrin J. 1975. *The cycles of sex* (edited by Lucy Freeman). New York: Charles Scribner's Sons.

Gambino, Richard. 1974. *Blood of my blood—the dilemma of the Italian Americans.* Garden City, N.Y.: Anchor Books—Anchor Press/Doubleday.

Gans, Herbert. 1962. *The urban villagers: group and class in the life of Italian-Americans.* New York: The Free Press.

Haile, Elizabeth. 1976. "The Native American untold story." In *Untold stories.* New York: United Presbyterian Church, Third World Women Liaison.

Hannerz, Ulf. 1969. *Soulside–inquiries into ghetto culture and community.* New York: Columbia University Press.

Harang, Lucy J. 1976. "The Chinese American family." In Mindel, Charles H., and Habenstein, Robert W. (Eds.). *Ethnic families in America: patterns and variations.* New York: Elsevier Scientific Publishing Co.

Harrison, Phyllis, Ross, M. D., and Wyden, Barbara. 1973. *The Black child—a parents guide.* New York: Peter W. Wyden, Inc. Publisher.

Hidalgo, Hilda. 1974. "The Puerto Rican." In *Ethnic differences influencing the delivery of rehabilitation services.* Washington, D.C.: National Rehabilitation Association.

Hill, Reuben. 1974. "Modern systems theory and the family." In Sussman, Marvin B. (Ed.). *Sourcebook in marriage and the family* (4th ed.). Boston: Houghton-Mifflin Co.

Howell, Joseph T. 1973. *Hard living on Clay Street—portraits of blue collar families.* Garden City, N.Y.: Anchor Books.

Howze, Beverly. 1979. "Black suicides—final acts of alienation." *Human Behavior,* February.

Jackson, Jacquelyn, and Walls, Bertram E. 1978. "Myths and realities about aged Blacks." In Brown, Mollie (Ed.). *Readings in gerontology* (2nd ed.). St. Louis: The C. V. Mosby Co.

Kalish, Richard A., and Reynolds, David. 1976. *Death and ethnicity.* Los Angeles: University of Southern California Press.

King, Stanley H. 1972. "Coping and growth in adolescence." *Seminars in Psychiatry,* *4*(4), November.

Kitano, Harry H. L. 1974. *Race relations.* Englewood Cliffs, N.J.: Prentice-Hall, Inc.

Kitano, Harry H. L. 1976. *Japanese Americans* (ed. 2). Englewood Cliffs, N.J.: Prentice-Hall, Inc.

Koller, Marvin R., and Ritchie, Oscar W. 1978. *Socialization of childhood* (2nd ed.). Englewood Cliffs, N.J.: Prentice-Hall, Inc.

Krause, Corinne Azen. 1978. *Grandmothers, mothers and daughters: an oral history study of ethnicity, mental health and continuity of three generations of Jewish, Italian and Slavic-American women.* New York: The Institute of Pluralism and Group Identity of the American Jewish Committee.

Krause, Corinne Azen. "Grandmothers, mothers and daughters: especially those who are Jewish." Paper presented at the Meeting on the Role of Women American Jewish Committee, June 1978.

LeMasters, E. E. 1975. *Blue collar aristocrats.* Madison: University of Wisconsin Press.

Lidz, Theodore. 1976. *The person* (rev. ed.). New York: Basic Books, Inc.

Maldonado, David, Jr. 1975. "The Chinese aged." *Social Work, 20*(3), May.

McAdoo, Harriet Pipes. 1978. "Factors related to stability in upwardly mobile Black families." *Journal of Marriage and the Family, 40*(6), November.

McAdoo, Harriet Pipes. 1979. "Black kinship." *Psychology Today, 12*(12), May.

Merian, Lewis. 1956. "The effects of boarding schools on Indian family life." In Unger, Steven (Ed.). *The destruction of American Indian families.* New York: Association of American Indian Affairs.

Morrison, Toni. 1972. *The bluest eye.* New York: Pocket Books, Holt, Rinehart & Winston, Inc.

Murillo, Nathan. 1978. "The Mexican American family." In Martinez, Richard Aguigo (Ed.). *Hispanic culture and health care—fact, fiction, folklore.* St. Louis: The C. V. Mosby Co.

Myerhoff, Barbara J. 1978. "A symbol perfected in death: continuity and ritual and the life and death of an elderly Jew." In Myerhoff, Barbara J. and Simić, Andrei (Eds.). *Life's career—aging: cultural variations on growing old.* Bevery Hills: Sage Publications.

Napierkowski, Thomas. 1976. "Stepchild of America: growing up Polish." In Novac, Michael (Ed.). *Growing up Slavic in America.* Bayville, N.Y.: EMPAC.

Padillo, Elena. 1958. *Up from Puerto Rico.* New York: Columbia University Press.

Painter, Diann Holland. 1977. "Black women and the family." In Chapman, Jane Roberts, and Gates, Margaret (Eds.). *Women into wives—the legal and economic impact of marriage.* Beverly Hills: Sage Press.

Robertson, Joan F. 1977. "Grandmotherhood—a study of role conceptions." *Journal of Marriage and the Family, 39*(1), February.

Rosenzweig, Efraim M. 1977. *We Jews: invitation to a dialogue.* New York: Hawthorn Books, Inc.

Sotomayor, Marta. 1977. "Language, culture, and ethnicity in developing self-concept." *Social Work, 58*(4) April.

Stack, Carol B. 1975. *All our kin—strategies for survival in a Black community.* New York: Harper Colophon Books, Harper & Row.

Stanford, E. Percil. 1978. *The elder Black.* San Diego: Center on Aging, San Diego State University.

Stein, Howard F. 1976. "A dialectical model of health and illness—attitudes and behavior among Slovac-Americans." *International Journal of Mental Health,* 5(2).

Talbot, Toby (Ed.). 1974. *The world of the child—clinical and cultural studies from birth to adolescence.* New York: Jason Aronson.

Valliant, George E., and McArthur, Charles C. 1972. "Natural history of male psychologic health: the adult life cycle from 18-50." *American Journal of Psychiatry,* November, 26.

Van Gennep, Arnold. 1960. *The rites of passage.* London: Routledge and Kegan Paul.

Willie, Charles V. 1974. "The Black family and social class." *American Journal of Orthopsychiatry,* 44(1), January, 35, 45.

Winch, Robert F. 1971. *The modern family* (3rd ed.). New York: Holt, Rinehart and Winston.

Wrobel, Paul. 1973. "Becoming a Polish American: a personal point of view." In Ryan, Joseph A. (Ed.). *White ethnics: their life in working class America.* Englewood Cliffs, N.J.: Prentice-Hall, Inc.

David Antebi

CHAPTER

3

The layers of understanding

A mother's struggle

The past 6 years have been a lonely, unrelieved ordeal for Mrs. Verna Davis. At age 35 she has four children—Lillian, 17; Harold, 13; Richard, 10; and Jimmy, 6. Soon after Jimmy was born her husband Charles deserted the family. In the emergency Mrs. Davis' younger sister Louise moved into the home and for the next 2 years looked after the children while Mrs. Davis went to work as a domestic. Louise married and moved into a home of her own, causing Mrs. Davis to quit her job and apply for public assistance. In another year, however, Lillian was able to take on some responsibility for her younger brothers. This enabled Mrs. Davis to work nights as a cleaning woman in an office building.

One night last summer while preparing dinner before leaving for her job, Mrs. Davis suffered third-degree burns on her hands and arms when grease in a skillet burst into flames. Since then the family has been managing on public assistance, for Mrs. Davis cannot yet use her right hand. It was her concern for Lillian that brought Mrs. Davis to the Family Service Center. Lillian, formerly a good student, began to cut classes last spring and lost interest in her studies.

When Mrs. Davis meets with the social worker at the Family Service Center she brings not only the problem of Lillian's truancy, but her particular perspective on that problem and the many others that have plagued her for the past 6 years. Her view of these is influenced by her personality, life cycle stage, family of origin, views about work and education, and response to illness as well as to economic stress. Previous experiences with social service agencies, primarily public welfare agencies, have shaped her expectations of the client role. The social worker brings a professional perspective which recognizes Mrs. Davis' hope for insights into Lillian's difficulties and the availability of resources to help the family attain a greater sense of well-being. The professional perspective consists of four components which we term the "layers of understanding."

These layers are comprised of knowledge, attitudes, and skills that are important for all approaches to practice. These are:

1. A basic knowledge of human behavior
2. A self-awareness, including insights into one's own ethnicity and an understanding of how that may influence professional practice
3. The impact of the ethnic reality upon the daily life of clients
4. The adaptation and modification of skills and techniques in response to the ethnic reality

Most of these have and continue to be considered basic ingredients of professional practice. Indeed, they are incorporated into the "Working Definition of Social Work Practice."* They are reviewed here in order to highlight their basic thrust and to suggest additional dimensions required for ethnic sensitive practice. The situation of Mrs. Davis and her family illustrates how and why these "layers" must be incorporated into ethnic-sensitive practice.

LAYER 1: BASIC KNOWLEDGE OF HUMAN BEHAVIOR

The working definition suggests that the following knowledge areas are needed to guide social work practice: human development and behavior characterized by emphasis on the wholeness of the individual and the reciprocal influences of man and his total environment—human, social, economic, and cultural.

Human development and the life cycle

With this in mind the possibility of success is enhanced if the worker has basic knowledge of human development from entry to

---

*Social Work, 3(2), April 1958.

old age. Attention is then focused on the fact that Mrs. Davis is approaching middle age with the apprehensions that accompany movement to that stage of life. Her four children range from childhood to adolescence; each is attempting to complete the associated developmental tasks. At the moment Lillian appears to have the greatest problem. Knowledge of family interaction suggests that her brothers may be affected by her behavior in ways yet to be expressed. Because she has had total responsibility for the rearing of four children, Mrs. Davis has used a variety of coping mechanisms which have included seeking help from her family, obtaining tedious employment, and resorting to public assistance.

Charles Davis abandoned his wife and children soon after the birth of Jimmy. His actions may have elicited a variety of responses from his wife, ranging from anger to relief. Attuned to all of these possibilities, a worker will consider the possibility that his departure may have engendered a variety of responses by the children, related to their stages in the life cycle. This includes Jimmy, who, from the time of his birth, has related to only one parent. His experience is unlike that of his siblings, who had known the presence of both mother and father in the early years.

Without warning, grease and fire combine to cause serious injury to Mrs. Davis and deprive her of the ability to support herself and her children. She is able, however, to continue to assume other adult responsibilities assigned to her. But out of concern for teenaged Lillian, who appears to be floundering, she contacts the social service agency. The pressures upon Lillian seem to be denying her the joys of carefree adolescence.

Social role

Knowledge of the concept of "social role" adds even greater vitality to our understanding of the Davis family (Strean, 1974). In all families each member is assigned a role related to age, usually to sex, and to other positions in the family. Particular behaviors have been assigned to each role and, when the expected complementarity does not occur, problems may be anticipated. Individuals are often expected to fulfill roles for which they have few skills or are assigned more roles than they desire or can manage. This appears to be the case in this family. Although the social worker enters at the time of Lillian's difficulty, the data collection process will no doubt reveal problems in role performance by others which relate to Charles Davis' leaving. When he abdicated the father-husband role he left them for his wife to perform in addition to her own mother-nurturer role, which may have already been taxed at that point by the care of her newborn child. Accepting these roles, Mrs. Davis entered the work force. She assigned some of the mother role to her sister. After Louise's marriage Mrs. Davis was forced to look to other resources. In a short time young Lillian was required to assume a mother-nurturer role. Her past life experience may not have provided her with sufficient skills for this role, which she may prefer not to hold, wishing rather to concentrate on her roles of daughter, sibling, and teenage confidante. The burden of numerous roles may be the inadvertent cause of the accident. In any event it thrusts Mrs. Davis into the sick role. In this adverse position she is unable to carry out any of her roles effectively and adds another role, welfare client. The sick role must be played in a particular way in our society (Parsons, 1958). Even though no blame is placed upon Mrs. Davis, the welfare system and her family will expect her to "get well soon," by using the appropriate health care providers, and return to her regularly assigned tasks as soon as possible. Unfortunately, if her progress is slower than seems necessary she may become suspect. Extended dependency in the sick and client roles threatens the family system, which up to this time had maintained a satisfactory equilibrium.

Systems theory

The incorporation of general systems theory into social work practice has provided a means by which we may gain a clearer perspective of the reciprocal influences between the individual and the total environment as decreed in the working definition. From this evolves the concept of the family as a social system (Hill, 1974). This knowledge gives greater insights into the Davis family. The members are seen as interdependent, with the behavior of each affecting the behavior of others. Lillian's truancy causes discomfort not only for her mother but for her brothers, who may have new roles to perform or who may suffer ridicule because Lillian is in trouble.

As a boundary maintaining unit the family has struggled to support itself financially; the boundary has been partially open to allow for transactions with the welfare, health, and educational systems.

The family has shown itself to be successful at equilibrium seeking and adaptation. Each stressful event has required new behaviors which have been acquired and used successfully up to this point. Desertion, illness, truancy all impose stress with the potential for crisis. This has not been the case so far. Mrs. Davis, as head of the family, has performed the traditional tasks of providing food, clothing, shelter, and socialization and maintaining order and family morale.

Understanding of personality

Her success or failure is in large measure dependent upon the uniqueness of her personality and the characteristics which she has developed to enable her to adjust to her life situation. The social worker who meets Mrs. Davis finds a warm, good-humored woman who is less confident about her ability to cope than she was before the trouble with Lillian began. In order to help her cope with the problem she brings, the worker must know something of her past reactions to trauma and loss. Her history suggests a high degree of emotional stability, the ability to assume responsibility, and a capacity for trust and friendliness. Though distressed by the turn of events, there seems no evident pathological depression or withdrawal. She wants help so that all will be well with her eldest child. It is her hope that this agency is organized in such a way that the social worker will be able to help her to return her family to a more comfortable state.

Knowledge of agency structure, goals, and functions

Mrs. Davis' meeting with the worker has been preceded by her request for services, which was handled by the receptionist who gave her a date for an appointment. It was at this meeting that "intake" occurred and decisions made about the ability of the agency to assist Mrs. Davis. The function of this Family Service Center is to provide services for those who are concerned primarily with interpersonal relationships. It is a people-changing agency. Had Mrs. Davis been seeking vocational rehabilitation or supplementary monetary assistance she would have been referred to other agencies that have defined such services as their function. Having determined that services can be provided, Mrs. Davis is assigned another worker so that the services may begin. The organizational aspects of the agency have immediately begun to influence Mrs. Davis' experience. The worker too is influenced by structure, goals, and functions. Recognizing this, a worker must become aware of the ways in which the organization may constrain as well as facilitate effective practice. An understanding of the agency contraints which will inhibit work with Mrs. Davis is essential. The worker may deem a visit to Mrs. Davis' home essential, while agency policy discourages visits into the projects where Mrs. Davis lives. In order to provide the services needed, the worker must recognize and use those organizational resources which facilitate practice. This may include funds for transportation which enable Mrs. Davis and Lillian to visit the agency without using their meager public assistance income.

The agency provides a supervisor who will assist in decision-making regarding services to Mrs. Davis. Perhaps a consultant may be available to assist in areas where social worker and supervisor need greater insights and supports. The structure demands a director and a lay board since this is a voluntary agency.

Unwittingly Mrs. Davis has entered into a bureaucracy, for the social agency as described by Wilensky and Lebeaux (1958) is a bureaucracy, a form of organization typical of our complex industrial society. This agency specializes in direct service, with a casework emphasis serving families within a particular geographical location.

Although Mrs. Davis may be unaware of the structure and its influence the worker must be aware of the structure as well as the organization's interdependence with other agencies. Mrs. Davis' relationship with the public welfare agency comes immediately to mind, but during the course of the relationship contact with the public school would seem to be a reasonable expectation as well as those with other agencies which might supply various outlets for Richard, Harold, and Jimmy. At some point vocational rehabilitation service may be considered for Mrs. Davis as her hand heals.

This knowledge of the setting in which the worker carries out the professional responsibility may be used in ways that enhance Mrs. Davis' chance to return equilibrium to her family.

LAYER 2: SELF-AWARENESS, INCLUDING INSIGHTS INTO ONE'S OWN ETHNICITY AND AN UNDERSTANDING OF HOW THAT MAY INFLUENCE PROFESSIONAL PRACTICE

The working definition proposes that workers have knowledge of themselves "which enables them to be aware of and to take responsibility for their own emotions and attitudes as they affect professional function."*

Self-awareness is an essential area of knowledge, because the disciplined and aware self remains one of the profession's major tools that must be developed into a fine instrument. The beginning of the honing process is the heightening of self-awareness—the ability to look at and recognize *Me*, not always nice, sometimes judgmental, prejudiced, and noncaring. It is the ability to recognize when the judgmental noncaring self interferes with the ability to reach out, to explore, to help others mobilize their coping capacity. Self-awareness involves the capacity to recognize that the foibles and strengths of those we aim to serve may trigger our tendencies for great empathy or destructiveness. And it refers to the ability to make use of this type of understanding to attempt holding in check those narcissistic or destructive impulses which impede service delivery.

Although considered essential for practice, educators acknowledge difficulty in "teaching" self-awareness. Hamilton (1954) identified self-awareness in social work practice as attendant learning; when pursued as an object in itself it becomes more elusive. It must be "caught." Then how does one catch it? A beginning point is self-acceptance.

In "Getting at the 'Who' of Me," Schulman (1978) poses three questions:

1. Who am I?
2. Who do others think I am?
3. Who would I like to be?

The answers begin to tap the ability to recognize with some accuracy our perceptions of ourselves, the perceptions of others about us, and our dreams of what we might be.

Short exercises have been designed to enable practitioners to begin to answer these questions. The actual process involves a lifetime and the answers change continually during a professional career.

The initial question, "Who am I?" must move from a superficial one, which would identify the various roles assumed, to a level at which it is expanded to "Who am I in relation to my feelings about myself and others?" This subjective question has the ability to bring to the surface material thought to be carefully hidden. Answering these questions is part of "catching" self-awareness. It grows from

---

Social Work, 3(2), April 1958.

within and has been described as a process midway between know-ing and feeling. One may be aware of something without being able to describe it (Grossbard, 1954).

Crucial to this process is social workers' awareness of their own ethnicity and the ability to recognize how it affects their practice. "Who am I in the ethnic sense?" may be added to the original ques-tion. This may be followed by: "What does that mean to me?" and "How does it shape my perceptions of persons who are my clients?"

The childhood experience of a social worker in an ethnic setting points out how such experiences will influence practitioners who have begun to answer the "Who am I?" questions.

I am the youngest of two daughters born to middle class first gener-ation Jewish parents. I was born and raised in an apartment house in Brooklyn, New York, where I remained until I was married at 20 years of age. The neighborhood in which I lived consisted predomi-nantly of Jewish and Italian families where traditions were followed and young children growing up fulfilled their parents' expectations. This was a very protected environment in one sense in that until high school I did not have any contact with people other than those of Jewish or Italian ancestry. However, Brooklyn was then a rela-tively safe place to live, and at an early age I traveled by bus or train to pursue different interests.

Reflecting back, I think of both my parents as dominant figures in my growing up. My father, a laborer, believing in the old work ethic, working long hours each day. However, when he came home life centered around him. My mother and father raised my sister and me on love, understanding, and consideration for others allowing flexibility to discover my own self.

My parents were simple people. Religious ritual played a mini-mal part in their life. They did not even go to synagogue on the High Holy Days, though my mother fasted on Yom Kippur, the Day of Atonement, and fussed because my sister, father, friends, and I in-sisted on eating.

But the family was most concerned about their fellow Jews in Europe, and the fate of Israel was eagerly followed on radio and tele-vision.

There was no question that I identified as a Jew. When I dated non-Jewish boys, my mother could not help but show her concern on her face.

Thinking back on this I realize that without much verbalization my parents conveyed a strong sense of family, derived strength—

and some pain—from their identity as Jews. I realize now that when I see Jewish clients who are in marital distress, or where parents treat children with lack of consideration my "gut reaction" is negative and judgmental.

Without ever having been told so in so many words I realize that I grew up with the sense that that's not how Jews are supposed to be. And somehow, in realizing that "my own people" don't always shape up to ideals, I also begin to realize who I am in relation to other kinds of people. For I recognize that just as I approached "my own" from a dim, somewhat unarticulated perception of what "they were supposed to be," I was viewing others in the same vein.

"Textbook learning" about Blacks, or Chicanos, or Orientals was not sufficient to overcome the effects of media or other experiences. I began to both "think and feel through" my reactions.

When workers begin to "think and feel through" the impact of their own ethnicity on their perception of themselves and others, there is more involved than the particular ethnic identity. What emerges is a total perception of "appropriate" family life, fact and fantasy about economic wherewithal and roles, and the like.

The Jewish practitioner from a lower middle class, intact Jewish family where children "fulfilled their parents' expectations" must be aware of a possible tendency to be judgmental toward Lillian—the daughter in the family described earlier—who is truant and begins to bring pain and tumoil to the family. "Who am I in the ethnic sense?" becomes more complex in an era when more and more people intermarry.

Dual ethnic background

Intermarriage is becoming more common in our society. Persons who share the same religious backgrounds but different ethnic histories as well as those with totally different religious heritage are marrying and establishing families. The social worker who has a partner of another ethnic background or is the child of such a marriage has more influences to consider. The answer to "Who am I in the ethnic sense?" then becomes less simple. The following account by a social worker is illustrative:

My father is Irish Catholic and my mother German-Lutheran. I identified with the Irish ethos to some degree because, first, my father was the dominant member of the family; secondly, my religion was

Catholic—our parish church staffed by Irish clergy. There was little contact with my mother's family because disapproval of her marriage kept them at a distance. External social pressures tended to force identification with paternal ethnicity, as my name was Irish. I don't remember, though of course I realized I shared an Irish heritage, ever having a feeling of a shared future with the Irish as a group.

I in turn married a man whose background was overwhelmingly Italian, in spite of a French great-grandmother. My children have no ethnic identification that I can perceive. St. Patrick's Day is just another day; Columbus Day is a school holiday.

When workers of dual heritage begin to "think and feel through" the impact of ethnicity on their perceptions of themselves they may return to an earlier question: "Who am I?" The pervasive influence of an Irish Catholic heritage did not in this particular instance carry with it the sense of peoplehood with shared future. In the background there is the lost German-Lutheran heritage imposed by the rejection of a daughter who would not marry within the ethnic group.

Given the generalized perspective that women are expected to care for children, and not go to work outside of the home, this worker must be wary that this same expectation is not imposed upon Mrs. Davis, who has few other alternatives. Her own experience of being rejected by her mother's family may make her more sensitive to Mrs. Davis' rejection by Mr. Davis several years ago. Of utmost importance for the worker who has little sense of ethnic identification must be the realization that for many others ethnicity is a force that shapes movement through the life cycle, and determines appropriate marriage partners, language, certain dietary selections, and the various subtleties of daily life.

A heightened self-awareness and a greater awareness of ethnicity as it influences the practitioners' personal and professional life form the second layer of understanding.

LAYER 3: THE IMPACT OF THE ETHNIC REALITY UPON THE DAILY LIFE OF THE CLIENT

At the beginning of this chapter Verna Davis and her family were introduced. They were presented in relation to the first layer of understanding, a basic knowledge of human behavior. We did not identify their ethnic group membership, although their social class was evident from their present circumstances. If this family is now identified as Black we may measure the impact of the ethnic reality upon them and move closer to a consideration of ethnic-sensitive practice.

It must always be recognized that ethnicity is but one of the many pieces of identifying information necessary for assessment in any approach to practice. We know Mrs. Davis' age, sex, marital status, employment status, and names and ages of her children; we know that Lillian, the eldest, presents the immediate problem. This additional ethnic data enables the worker to establish the Davis' ethclass and the dispositions that may surround that juncture.

"Working-class Black" suggests a historical perspective that has placed this family along with other Blacks in a minority, powerless position. Potential barriers to successful family life are compounded by the position in which poor Black men often find themselves. Frustrated in their attempt to fulfill the universal task of adulthood, they decide it may be better to be absent. Experience with the mainstream society has shown that Black women are more acceptable as family representatives. The welfare department and schools seem to address their attention to women rather than men. Jobs, when they are available, often require physical strength and basic skills lacking in men who have had few opportunities for physical development (Liebow, 1967). Available laboring jobs offer few opportunities for exposure to the subtleties of the larger society (Hannerz, 1969; Liebow, 1967). At the birth of another child Charles Davis, probably sensing increasing difficulty in his ability to protect his wife and children, abandoned them.

Responding to the emergency, Mrs. Davis' sister moved into the household and remained there for the next 2 years. Such a response to the stress of kin may be considered to be an ethnic disposition. It is expected that a family member will respond and so an attenuated extended family is formed consisting of Verna Davis, now a single parent, her sister Louise, and four children. Billingsley (1968) suggests that this is but one of the many variations in Black family structures which place emphasis upon the responsibility of kin, particularly as the family strives for economic independence. Stack's study of kinship ties in the Flats of Jackson Harbor highlights the sense of responsibility for kin even beyond the expected blood ties

(Stack, 1975). This is not to say that such supports are not available in other ethnic groups but that they may be more prominent as an ethnic reality for working-class or underclass Black families (McAdoo, 1978). Louise is not "taking from" Verna; she is giving her services, allowing for her sister to move into roles not carried out before.

The husband's departure puts Mrs. Davis in a position of leading the family. Though some would then characterize her as a matriarch, this is a deceptive and inaccurate description. Matriarchy implies power and control. She has limited power and limited resources. Her position may be defined more precisely as matrifocal. This leadership role has been thrust upon her, not acquired through lineage. It is a de facto status (Hannerz, 1969), the result of her ethclass position.

Her powerlessness is reflected in her inability to provide an atmosphere in which Lillian may have a carefree adolescence, a respite before adulthood. Neither is she able to protect her sons Harold, Richard, and Jimmy from the various insults of racism. All of her children are oppressed, and it is her task to provide them with as many viable coping techniques as possible to help them develop a maturity and creativity that strengthen them, enabling them to work their way through environmental situations with dexterity (Ladner, 1972).

In this ethclass environment children are more responsible for their own protection. Black children at the middle- and upper-class level may expect and receive greater protection from their parents. This is not the case with Mrs. Davis. Her strengths are used up in the daily drudgery, which supplies the basic needs for her family. The social worker must assess the institutional resources in relation to their responses to the Davis children and their peers and must also be aware that the children's response to their ethnic reality involves the development of sophisticated coping mechanisms.

Lillian is unable to cope with the many roles given her: supervisor of siblings, student, perhaps even mother confidante. She would rather be an adolescent struggling with the tasks that, when accomplished, will give her adult status. She has this responsibility too soon. Her truancy may be a response to this interruption in her life cycle development. She is not necessarily a rebellious, acting-out, phobic child determined to defy the school and her parent. Rather, an ethnic-sensitive worker recognizes the impact of working- or underclass status and ethnicity which work together to produce for Lillian a situation of sufficient discomfort that she avoids school, where she has had earlier success.

The impact of the ethnic reality upon the daily life of clients is evident at all phases of the life cycle and in any environment in which they may find themselves. The following family experience focuses upon individuals in the adult years of their lives.

Poor health has caused a parent to be placed in a nursing home. This often generates trauma, although protection and care are available. Difficulties are compounded by and related to the ethnic reality and life cycle stages.

> Bella Meyer spent her adult life working with her husband David in their small variety store and caring for their two children, Rose and Mark. The children grew and left home to establish their own households and families. David, her husband, died when they were both age 60. Soon after David's untimely death Bella's health failed and she became a resident of Ashbrook Manor, a nonsectarian nursing home. Mrs. Meyer is Jewish. After a year in the home she is unhappy. A hearing impairment causes her great despair and so she is unpleasant to the other residents and prefers to be alone. The nurses on her unit have almost turned against her because of her attitude.
>
> Her daughter, Rose Niemann, is employed as a clerk-typist in a local insurance company. She visits her mother regularly but stays only a few minutes because she is on her lunch hour. Mark, a shoe salesman, seldom visits. Both of the children make contributions to their mother's care.
>
> Rose's and Mark's children visit their grandmother only on holidays.

The impact of the ethnic reality upon Mrs. Meyer's life may be overlooked in a nonsectarian setting that has no commitment to her Jewishness. The primary purpose of the nursing home is to provide care for aging persons with failing health. In this setting she is denied the traditional aspects of Jewish family life.

The food, although healthful, lacks what Mrs. Meyer calls "tahm" (character). Food has been an important part of her life. She had previously been able to express love and sociability not only to her family but to her friends as well by preparing and serving food. Here, like all patients, she is cut off from daily family life and the tasks of a caregiver—for a Jewish woman this may well be devastating.

Reverence for the Jewish aging may be seen in an extensive network of charities and provisions in the development of residential settings. This adheres to historical concepts which expect a caring regard and respect for the elderly, and for parents by their children (Linden, 1967). And Mrs. Meyer's children do care. They have not totally abandoned her. But they are involved in small, nuclear family units. And these do not readily lend themselves to incorporation of a frail, disgruntled elderly person. She feels alienated and rejected; the nonsectarian nursing home, devoid of "Yiddishkeit," intensifies her already profound sense of isolation and alienation.

The ancient belief that as a Jew she is one of the "chosen people" has at times given her a sense of comfort, of having been favored by God. But God and tradition have failed her. When she draws on this heritage in her communication with others, they don't understand and may interpret her behavior as snobbery or superiority, thus yielding rejection by the nursing staff who are unaware of the tradition or its significance in Mrs. Meyer's life (Linden, 1967).

Aging and poor health engulf Mrs. Meyer in the despair of old age. The productivity of her earlier years in which she carried out a historical tradition of laboring women is no longer possible. Her daughter Rose is able to carry out tradition through her employment and uses some of her resources to aid in the support of her mother. At middle age she is torn between her regard for her aging mother and the needs of her own family. This is the struggle of many women, but for Rose there is the ethnic disposition which places particular emphasis upon both relationships. She is constant in her attention to her mother, although she limits visits to "looking in" during her lunch hour. The visits are regular. On the other hand, her brother Mark is less attentive. He may well be considered to be neglectful except for his regular financial contribution. This behavior can be considered from the perspective of the intense mother-son interactions found in some Jewish families. There are indications that overprotective and affectionate mothers may withhold love for the purpose of discipline. The resultant stress felt by sons may, as the mother grows older, be observed in behavior similar to Mark's. He contributes regularly to her support but refuses close contact (Linden, 1967). Add this to Mrs. Meyer's despair. Her son carries out his filial duty by contributing to her support, but to her his behavior involves rejection. She does not enjoy the rest and peace that should come from a reverent son; neither do her grand-children bring her joy.

The social worker who observes Bella Meyer finds an ailing old woman who complains of poor hearing to the extent that the staff avoids contact with her. The worker who has grasp of the layers of understanding is able to expand upon this initial observation and sees more of Mrs. Meyer, who is now an older Jewish woman in failing health. She has been removed from the Jewish community, which has given her support and a sense of well-being, and placed in a nursing home, which does not respond to her ethnic needs in any way. Her age denies her the satisfaction of work, and her children do not give to her in ways that she feels are appropriate in Jewish families. This information, added to knowledge about the ad-ministrative structure of the nursing home, enables the social worker to seek alternatives in health care which would respond more to Mrs. Meyer's ethnic needs as well as those of other Jewish residents.

As the social worker seeks alternatives that will enhance Mrs. Meyer's life at Ashbrook Manor, there must be an awareness that his or her own ethnicity may influence the perspectives on the life of others. The Meyer family cannot respond in ways that are com-pletely familiar to the Irish, Italian, or Black social worker and must not be viewed from that perspective.

Verna Davis and Bella Meyer both have problems which may well be alleviated through social work intervention. When their so-cial worker and others have gained a professional perspective, which includes the layers of understanding presented here, they may be expected to become more effective in the practice, more aware of themselves and others.

SUMMARY

This chapter has identified the layers of understanding for social work practice. These are:

1. A basic knowledge of human behavior
2. An insight into one's own ethnicity and how that may influence one's perspective
3. The impact of the ethnic reality upon daily life of clients

These are the first three of four layers which lead to ethnic-sensitive practice. The fourth layer is comprised of those skills already available to the profession. They must be reviewed, reconsidered, adapted, and modified in relation to the ethnic reality. Chapter 6 addresses this fourth layer of understanding:

4. The adaptation and modification of skills (and techniques) in response to the ethnic reality

REFERENCES

Billingsley, Andrew. 1968. *Black families in white America.* Englewood Cliffs, N.J.: Prentice-Hall, Inc.

Grossbard, Hyman. 1954. "Methodology for developing self-awareness." *Social Casework,* 35(9), November.

Hamilton, Gordon. 1954. "Self-awareness in professional education." *Social Casework,* 35(9), November.

Hannerz, Ulf. 1969. *Soulside—inquiries in ghetto culture and community.* New York: Columbia University Press.

Hill, Reuben. 1974. "Modern systems theory and the family." In *Sourcebook in marriage and family.* Boston: Houghton-Mifflin Co.

Ladner, Joyce A. 1972. *Tomorrow's tomorrow—the Black woman.* New York: Anchor Books, Doubleday & Co.

Liebow, Elliot. 1967. *Tally's corner: a study of Negro street-corner men.* Boston: Little, Brown and Co.

Linden, Maurice E. 1967. "Emotional problems in aging." In *The psychodynamics of American Jewish life: an anthology.* New York: Twayne Publishers Inc.

McAdoo, Harriet. 1978. "The impact of upward mobility on kin-help patterns and the reciprocal obligations in Black families." *Journal of Marriage and the Family, 40,* November.

Parson, Talcott. 1958. "Definitions of health and illness in the light of American values and social structure." In Jaco, E. Gartly (Ed.). *Patients, physicians and illness: a sourcebook in behavioral science and health* (2nd ed.). New York: The Free Press.

Schulman, Eveline D. 1978. *Intervention in human services* (2nd ed.). St. Louis: The C. V. Mosby Co.

Stack, Carol. 1975. *All our kin—strategies for survival in a Black community.* New York: Harper & Row, Harper Publishers, Colophon Books.

Strean, Herbert. 1974. "Role theory." In Turner, Francis J. *Social work treatment: interlocking theoretical approaches.* New York: The Free Press.

Wilensky, Harold L., and Lebeaux, Charles. 1958. *Industrial society and social welfare.* New York: Russell Sage Foundation.

David Antebi

CHAPTER

4

Approaches to social work practice and the ethnic reality

In the preceding chapters we elaborated our perspective on ethnicity, social class, and the life cycle and presented conceptual formulations intended to develop an image of how these affect perception of problems in living. These are important dimensions of human functioning which have received insufficient attention in the social work practice literature.

In this chapter major focus is on reviewing a number of prevailing approaches to social work practice and assessing the extent to which attention has been paid to the ethnic reality. In making this assessment we are sensitive to the fact that there are divergent points of view regarding the theoretical formulations about how human beings are shaped and the relationship of these theories to the problem-solving activities which social work undertakes.

A strong social reform stance has long been taken by many in the profession. For some adherents to this perspective the major sources of individual and social dysfunction are to be found in social structural inequity. Those committed to this view of the human condition explain behavior in sociological and structural terms; they advocate interventive strategies designed to effect social and environmental change.

For some, major understanding of human functioning is to be found in psychologically based explanations of human behavior.

These in turn have influenced the selection of helping strategies.

A large group has sought to understand how the interplay between social and psychological forces impinge on and shape the individual; both bodies of thought are drawn upon in the effort to heighten understanding and generate appropriate helping strategies.

For some these varying perspectives have come to "dictate the purpose of the social worker's practice" (Pincus and Minahan, 1973) and deflect attention from work designed to develop a "social work frame of reference derived from a clear notion of the function and purpose of the profession" (Pincus and Minahan, 1973). This kind of thinking has generated a number of efforts to distinguish between social work practice principles and strategies on the one hand, and the diverse theoretical orientations which aid in understanding the specific problems with which social workers deal (Fischer, 1978; Pincus and Minahan, 1973).

These divergent points of view have bearing on our assessment of prevailing approaches, as do the varying definitions of theory, assumptions, models, practice theory, and the like.

We begin by reviewing the common usage of these terms; following this we summarize a number of the major points of view concerning the role of theory, concepts, and knowledge about human behavior in the practice of social work. We then turn our attention to a number of practice models and examine them in light of our perspective on the ethnic reality.

We conclude by presenting the point of view on the relationship between theory and practice which guides our work.

ASSUMPTIONS, THEORIES, AND MODELS
Assumptions and theories

These terms are often used interchangeably. In some respects such usage is justified. At least one dictionary defines an assumption as "something taken for granted" and indicates that it is a term synonymous with theory and hypothesis. In this same dictionary we learn that a "theory is a coherent group of general propositions used as principles of explanations for a class of phenomena" or a "proposed explanation whose status is still conjectural in contrast to well established propositions that are regarded as reporting matters of actual fact" (American College Dictionary, 1970). Turner (1974) defines a theory as a "logical explanation of the interrelatedness of a set of facts that have been empirically verified or are capable of being verified." A proposition is "anything stated or affirmed for discussion or illustration" (American College Dictionary, 1970).

These abstract definitions and distinctions assume importance because they all focus on systematic delineation of concepts used in behavioral and social science inquiry and the relationship between them. Essentially, these definitions suggest that when we speak of a relationship between social class and ethnic group membership and the way people feel about marriage, child rearing, or work, we have some evidence—based on systematic inquiry—that these relationships exist. Similarly, when it is proposed that there is a connection between childhood experiences with loving or hostile relationships and adult personality patterns, persistent, systematic observation supports the existence of this relationship.

A crucial component of the definition of theory presented is the term "conjectural." This highlights the fact that the assertions made are ever open to revision and calls our attention to the need for continuing and persistent study.

Also important is the term "proposition" and the way it is used here— "something affirmed." This indicates that the relationships under scrutiny have been sufficiently well investigated and supported by scientific inquiry so that little doubt remains concerning the truth or validity of assertions made.

Few of the theories used in the social and behavioral sciences have been put to this kind of rigorous test, or in Turner's term "empirically verified." This is true whether we speak about psychological or sociological theories.

This by no means negates the major importance of such bodies of theory as psychoanalytic theory, or behaviorist theory, or theories about social class, ethnicity, and the life cycle; these form the foundation of much of our work and thinking. That they are not to be viewed as immutable fact alerts practitioners to the ever-present need to look for new relationships and to approach problems with a fresh and open stance.

Models

In contrast to a theory which looks at a class of interrelated facts and seeks to explain the logical relationship between them, a model is a visual or metaphoric image of an area of interest. Often likened to a model of a ship or plane, it describes or presents an image of the phenomena of interest, while a theory explains the relationships between them. This can be illustrated by reference to the material presented in Chapter 1. A number of prevailing definitions of social class and ethnic group were reviewed and the intersect between the two defined as "ethclass." In our view this is essentially a description of how these two sets of concepts interact and can be translated into an image of how people function at this intersect.

Like most models, this kind of description begins to explain the relationship between social class and ethnic group membership, by suggesting that the two are inextricably linked in a manner which generates ethclass. No claim has been made that persistent scientific investigation shows that these relationships are in the nature of undisputable fact.

Much of the knowledge with which social work deals can legitimately be characterized as deriving from varying models of human behavior. The perspective on ethnicity, social class, and the life cycle presented here can be characterized as a model which describes important components about our clients and their world. Like all models, it has potential for moving beyond description to explaining major areas of thought, feeling, and experience.

PREVAILING VIEWS ON THE RELATIONSHIP BETWEEN UNDERSTANDING OF HUMAN BEHAVIOR AND INTERVENTIVE PROCEDURES

Attention is now focused on the relationship between theories, models, and the helping activities which social work undertakes.

Ideally, the various theories of personality and social systems are translated into principles of helping practice (Siporin, 1975). For example, the life cycle model identifies points of transition and suggests potential points and types of stress for members of different ethnic groups. This aids the social worker in identifying behaviors indicative of stress or smooth transition. Stress may be revealed in parent-child conflict triggered by disagreement over adherence to ethclass versus mainstream standards. For example, an Italian adolescent girl may refuse to adhere to the strict supervision of dating which her family seeks to impose. Identification of the trouble and its source can generate social worker activity designed to aid both parent and child in understanding and coping with the difficulty. Joint interviewing of parents and child by a worker familiar with the culture might be directed toward identifying possible points of compromise. A "good theory" would aid in predicting whether this approach would reduce the stress.

The logical flow from explanation and description of our clients and their world—to identification of problematic behavior—to guidelines for helping—is the ideal process. Some hold firm to this ideal, believing that ultimately all practice must be generated by causal knowledge about human behavior (Turner, 1974). Others suggest that causal knowledge may not provide an adequate base for practice, and that the psychological and social theories on which we have so long relied to date provide limited direction for intervention (Fischer, 1978; Reid,1978).

Fisher makes a distinction between causal/developmental knowledge and intervention knowledge. The former answers the question "Why" and aids in understanding and "diagnosing"; the latter answers the question "What" and deals with theories, principles, and procedures of induced change (Fischer, 1978). Considerable doubt is cast on the assumption that understanding the cause of or history of problems provides clues about what is sustaining the problem, or guidelines for intervention. This view is not shared by all. Middleman and Goldberg (1974) contend that understanding of the cause of a problem goes a long way toward defining it and projecting solutions.

Practice theory

Fischer (1978) views practice theory as consisting of two elements: (1) systematic interpretation of those principles which help to understand the phenomena of interest, and (2) clear delineation of principles of inducing change. Siporin defines practice theory as composed of two levels. The first focuses on how social work affects personality and social systems change. Included here is "assessment theory" which is focused on how judgments are made about what the problem is, how it is defined, and the type of change objectives selected. Intervention theory is focused on how changes are to be effected—that is, on interventive procedures. The second level of practice theory identified by Siporin centers on the various theoretical orientations to helping. These tend to adhere to a body of foundation knowledge, in the form of personality and social theories. Each has a distinctive set of assessment and intervention theories as well as practice principles, strategies, and procedures. In this second level of practice theory it is clearly demonstrated how the view of the human condition assumed by the theory guides and informs problem definition and intervention (Siporin, 1975).

Both Fischer and Siporin advocate an eclectic stance. Fischer emphasizes an approach to selection based on (1) practice principles and procedures which have been tested and found effective, and (2) which are congruent with basic social work values. He explicitly rejects the search for integration based on the divergent theories or causal knowledge (Fischer, 1978). Siporin (1975) proposes a fluid, eclectic stance suggesting integration from diverse schools of thought and doctrines.

PREVAILING APPROACHES TO SOCIAL WORK PRACTICE

Considerable work remains to be done in clarifying the relationship between what is known and believed about human behavior and about the cause of problems, and how social work uses that knowledge.

A number of distinct, though inevitably overlapping, approaches to social work practice can be identified. For the most part these approaches are based on a body of assumptions about and descriptions of the human condition; the related practice procedures represent an attempt to translate the understanding of how people function into principles for problem resolution.

There are any number of ways to categorize and characterize the various social work practice models. Four major approaches are identified here: (1) the psychosocial approach, (2) the problem solving approaches, (3) the social provision and structural approaches, and (4) the systems approach. There are of course other approaches, including the existential and the interactionist. We do not mean to slight these, or to suggest that these are not important approaches to practice. Rather, emphasis is on those which, in our view, have been the most frequently used by social workers in a wide arena of practice. Major components of these other approaches are subsumed by those models reviewed here.

In reviewing and assessing the basic approaches, we summarize the assumptions on which they are based and the related interventive procedures. Particular attention is paid to matters concerning the ethnic reality.

We pose a series of questions designed to determine whether attention has been paid to matters pertaining to the special needs and life-styles of various ethnic and minority groups.

1. Does the approach give recognition to the part played by membership in varying groups in shaping people's lives?
2. Is the approach based on narrow "culture-bound" perspectives on human behavior or is it sufficiently fluid and broad based so as to generate interpretations of behavior that are consonant with world views and outlooks which differ from those most prevalent in mainstream America?
3. Have interventive procedures been proposed which guide practitioners in their use of knowledge concerning the different world view of various groups?

THE PSYCHOSOCIAL APPROACH

In some respects, it is inappropriate to speak of a distinct psychosocial approach to social work practice. In many ways, the term "psychosocial" and the view inherent in the term that people are both psychological and sociological beings is synonymous with social work's perspective. Indeed, Turner (1974) suggests that it is a term fully the "prerogative of our profession." And yet "psychosocial therapy" has come to be associated with a particular view of the human condition and approaches to practice, the full ramifications of which are not uniformly shared. As a result of this, the configuration of ideas and treatment approaches termed psychosocial practice can be viewed as separate and apart from the more general view, shared by most social workers, that many of the issues with which they deal can in large measure be understood in psychosocial terms.

Nevertheless, psychosocial therapy has come to be associated with a relatively distinct view of the human condition and has generated interventive objectives and approaches which are not uniformly shared by all social workers. For these reasons the psychosocial approach is treated as a distinct perspective on practice.

The psychosocial approach has a long and honorable history; much attention has and continues to be focused on efforts to refine, reformulate, and specify the basic assumptions, interventive strate-gies, and techniques which continue to evolve.

Assumptions

Part and parcel of the view that people are psychosocial beings is the assumption that we are in large measure governed by unique past histories and the internal dynamic generated by those histories. This view of human beings translates into a perspective on practice which emphasizes the need to maintain dual focus on "psychologi-cal and sociological man, that is on intrapersonal man, interper-sonal man and intersystemic man" (Turner, 1974).

Richmond (1917) emphasized this dual perspective in her defi-nition of social casework as "those processes which develop a per-sonality through adjustments consciously effected, individual by in-dividual, between men and their social environment."

A number of pervasive themes emerge. These include a belief that all people have both the responsibility and capacity to partici-pate in shaping their own destiny. People are social beings who reach their potential in the course of relationships with family, friends, small groups, and the community. Belief in the capacity to choose and to make decisions from among alternatives is related to the belief that each of us is unique and unpredictable; thus all have the capacity to "rise up above and beyond . . . history" (Turner, 1978). This does not negate the fact that genetic endowment, per-sonal history, and the environment are most important in shaping actions.

The view that the past has major bearing on behavior in the present is stressed. Considerable importance is attached to noncon-scious phenomena, which influence but do not determine behavior. Psychoanalytic insights into human behavior are vital. These in-clude that aspect of Freudian thought which assumes that all indi-viduals throughout life are characterized by libidinal and aggressive drives which make a "continuing and unique demand upon the en-vironment" (Hollis, 1972). At the same time the personality includes a set of adaptive qualities termed "the ego."

The psychosocial approach is also heavily influenced by sociolog-ical conceptions. The family, the social group, and the community affect social functioning in major ways. Increasingly the influence of socioeconomic status, ethnicity, and the family are stressed (Turner, 1978).

Hollis (1972) proposes that breakdown in social adjustment can be traced to three interacting sources: (1) infantile needs and drives left over from childhood that cause the individual to make inappropriate demands on the adult world, (2) a current life situation that exerts excessive pressures, and (3) faulty ego and superego functioning.

Problems which stem from persisting infantile needs and drives generate a variety of pathologies and disturbance in the capacity to assume adult responsibilities. Or, they may be generated by environmental pressures, such as economic deprivation, racial and ethnic discrimination, inadequate education, and inadequate housing. Family conflict and loss occasioned by illness, death, or separation are also viewed as environmental or current life pressures. Faulty ego functioning is manifested in distorted perceptions of factors operating both external and internal to the individual. Breakdown is often triggered by disturbance in more than one of these areas, as they tend to interact and affect functioning.

Turner (1978) suggests that the goal of psychosocial therapy is "the achievement of optimal psychosocial functioning within the client's potential and in a manner that recognizes and respects their value system." These goals may be accomplished through the development of human relationships, available material and service resources, as well as human resources in the environment. Involvement with a psychosocial therapist may effect change in cognitive, emotive, behavioral, or material areas so that there is relief from suffering.

In summary, the psychosocial approach stresses the interplay of individual and environment, the effect of past and present, the effect of nonconscious factors on the personality, and the impact of present environmental as well as psychologically induced sources of stress and coping capacity. There is major attention to psychoanalytic conceptions of human behavior, and how these explain the presenting difficulties.

Assumptions and the ethnic reality. The definition of the ethnic reality calls attention to those aspects of the ethnic experience which provide sources of pride, a comfortable sense of belonging, various networks of family and community, and a range of approaches to coping which have withstood the test of time. At the same time it highlights the persistent negation of valued traditions and the turmoils experienced by ethnic groups as they encounter the majority culture. Particular attention is paid to the effects of discrimination in such spheres as jobs, housing, schooling, and the like.

Review of the major tenets of psychosocial theory indicates that the roles of ethnicity and social class are incorporated in this perspective. Hollis, Turner, Strean, and others all emphasize the destructive effects of discrimination, poor housing, and poverty. The effect of destructive stereotyping is mentioned by many.

And yet, two major gaps are apparent. First, there is no clear or detailed indication as to how race, ethnicity, and class converge to shape individuals and contribute to the problems for which they seek help. This gap is noted by many social work analysts (Fischer, 1978; Reid, 1978; Turner, 1974).

A second omission, or perhaps distortion, is the tendency to stress the negative and dysfunctional aspects of the ethnic reality. Attention is commonly and explicitly called to the disabling effects of discrimination or low socioeconomic status. However, the unique and often beneficial effect of membership in various groups is often ignored (Mirelowitz, 1979; President's Commission on Mental Health, 1978).

Good psychosocial practice should be ever-mindful of those sources of identity which derive from a sense of peoplehood and those sources of difficulty which stem from systemic inequity. The consideration of past history in relation to present functioning should present positive and negative aspects of the ethnic reality. The classic statements of the approach do not help us here. There have been efforts to make these kinds of connections (Grier and Cobbs, 1968).

The American Indians' perspective on time and the priority some give to kin over work relations is frequently cited (Good Tracks, 1973). Related behaviors as these clash with the values of the larger society can indeed cause trouble. When work schedules are not met, jobs can be lost and result in much pain and turmoil.

Similarly, Italian fathers who, by mainstream standards, hover over their daughters (Krause, 1978) may well inhibit the thrust toward independence of late adolescence and early adulthood. But there is another aspect to these types of experiences. In a hostile world, or a world which devalues certain subcultural dispositions, concerned kin and a powerful belief system go a long way toward providing emotional sustenance. The loss of job may seem negligible compared to the sense of satisfaction obtained from doing what is expected by family. Overprotection may be experienced as "smothering" at the same time that it provides a sense of being loved, comforted, and cared for in well-known ways.

Our reading of the best that has been written about the psychosocial approach suggests that insufficient attention has been paid to these matters, despite the fact that Hollis and others take great care to point out that practitioners must be attuned to these differences.

Interventive procedures

The methods of intervention embodied in the term "psychosocial" have been characterized in a number of ways. Here particular attention is given to the typology developed and tested by Hollis (1972); in her classic work she proposes that casework intervention essentially involves the following procedures: (1) sustainment, direct influence, and ventilation; (2) reflective discussion of the person-situation configuration; and (3) reflective consideration of dynamic and developmental factors. These are focused on "forms of communication" between client and workers. Also of importance is "milieu" or "environmental work." This typology of casework "treatment communications" or the "casework process" has been tested. Client-worker interactions were systematically examined to determine if they fit the categories described. The work appeared to indicate that much of worker-client communication does proceed as outlined. Milieu and environmental work were not included in the research procedures.

Sustainment, direct influence, and ventilation. Hollis' presentation of the major components of sustainment, direct influence, and ventilation culls out much that is essential both in casework and other forms of social work practice. She calls attention to the inherent discomfort and anxiety related to needing help, to the fears engendered by self-revelation, and to doubts concerning the outcome. Sympathetic listening and noncritical acceptance are stressed. The importance of providing reassurance, while not losing sight of those realities which may make reassurance inappropriate, is pointed out. The need to render a variety of concrete services, vital in their own right and symbolic of the worker's interest in the client, is highlighted.

Reflective discussion of the person-situation configuration. This procedure places emphasis upon the need to draw clients into discussion focused on their functioning in the major areas of their lives. The practitioner must be alert to distorted perceptions whereby individuals are able to see only one side of persons or situations which have impact upon their present life circumstance. A father, afraid that his son might be "stupid" like his own brother, may not notice his son's positive accomplishments. Or, parents trying to cope with their adolescent in turmoil see only the "negative" behavior and deliberately or inadvertently cut off communication (Hollis, 1972).

When using this procedure practitioners may need to consider the possibility that if the client and worker are members of different racial groups this may interfere with the reflective-discussion process. A difference in race between practitioner and client may produce hostility which will need to be identified and clarified (Hollis, 1972).

When focus is on decision making, consequences, and alternatives, workers try to help clients think about the effects of their actions on others or themselves. These may be of a practical nature, concerning possible changes to be made in residence or employment. They may involve more intimate, emotional issues including decisions concerning marriage, divorce, or adoption. Always, every effort should be made not to explain, but to enable clients to come to "see," on their own, typical behavioral patterns as they affect themselves and others. Helping people to become aware of hidden feelings or to express feared feelings is viewed as helpful.

Reflective consideration of dynamic and developmental factors. In this type of client-worker interaction it is assumed that intrapsychic forces of which people are unaware may strongly influence behavior. Emphasis then is on pursuing "some of the intrapsychic reasons for feeling, attitudes and ways of acting." The historical basis of factors in the person's past history which may help to explain the reason for certain feelings is explored.

Environmental work. Environmental work is essentially focused on intervention in those problematic systems of which the client is a part. All the procedures previously outlined may be employed in various combinations. Diverse resources, including those people with whom the client has emotional relationships, are used.

Varying worker roles are identified—provider, locator or creator of resources, interpreter, mediator, and aggressive intervener. The importance of advocacy is stressed.

Turner (1978) expands on these important distinctions by pointing to "significant environments as components of treatment." The network of relationships in which people are involved should be viewed as a component of treatment, not merely as sources of information. Turner also points to the importance of paying attention to the settings within which service is rendered. Such factors as sponsorship and congruence with client values may be crucial. While not all clients are concerned with "ethnic sponsorship," for some this may be most important. Some Black clients may look for the agency endorsed by the Urban League, while a Hungarian client may feel most comfortable in a program sponsored by the Hungarian Reformed Church.

We have summarized a number of the procedures that serve as the basis for psychosocial practice. Hollis (1972) proposes that workers who become involved in dynamic or developmental matters and pay major attention to these in intervention must have a thorough familiarity with both conscious and unconscious aspects of personality functioning. She also suggests that workers who are not adept in applying casework skills to environmental work will be less able to help clients with intra- or interpersonal problems.

Interventive procedures and the ethnic reality

The review of basic psychosocial procedures as outlined by Hollis suggests that we must answer our question "Does the model guide practitioners in their use of the ethnic reality?" in the negative. In other work Hollis (1965) does propose practice modifications presumed to be more consonant with working-class orientations. She suggests that the differences are in emphasis and cautions against stereotyping.

In our perusal of many case examples in the major work there is virtually no mention made of class or ethnic group membership. Although "persons-in-situations" are presented, their situations are marital conflict, problematic parent-child interaction, and the life-threatening or fearsome situations related to illness. These are the "gut" and "heart" of the kinds of problems with which social workers try to help people. But people in marital conflict are also Black,

Italian, Jewish, Chicano, or Puerto Rican. They may at the same time be threatened with job loss, not merely making a decision about vocational change, or contemplating the advantages of a promotion that means moving to another part of the country, removing them from kin.

Turner (1970) has demonstrated that clients and workers from different ethnic groups do have different value orientations. These differences affect the outcome of treatment when various aspects of psychosocial functioning are assessed. Despite this awareness limited if any attention is paid to the possible usefulness of these findings in identifying the components of treatment.

For instance, "reflective consideration of the situation" and self-disclosure are alien to many Mexican-Americans and American Indians. For some, to tell a stranger about weakness or family turmoil runs counter to the core and substance of their being. Some American Indians reject discussion on intimate matters unless there is mutual sharing. Some Indian women, experiencing marital difficulties, will in the course of discussing these with a female social worker believe that she too has had similar experiences. Their expectations are that these are to be mutually shared, that perhaps the two can help each other. Certainly there is little in social work education which prepares the social worker for such reciprocal interaction. Quite to the contrary, it is expected that social workers will not bring their problems into the encounter with the client. Adaptations of this kind involve more than the kinds of transference relationships which are commonly thought to effect client-worker interaction. Experiencing of transference phenomena on the part of the worker is not ruled out. But what is at issue here is a major difference in perspective on the circumstances under which it is appropriate to discuss problems, and how the worker is viewed. An issue to which we shall pay some attention is whether the view of the "relationship" can be modified to incorporate these kinds of perspectives.

What emerges from our examination of some classic work on the psychosocial approach is that the approach is congruent with the kind of attention to the ethnic reality with which we are concerned. However, when we review the case examples, and other suggestions for practice, we find that there is a dearth of material which aids in operationalizing this approach.

THE PROBLEM-SOLVING APPROACHES

Rather than pursue the psychosocial approach concentrating on psychoanalytic insights, a significant number of practitioners look to the problem-solving approaches as the framework to be used for the helping process. Prominent among these are Helen Harris Perlman (1957), and William Reid and Laura Epstein (Reid, 1978; Reid and Epstein, 1972). Perlman may be considered the originator of the "problem-solving framework," presented in her classic work (Perlman, 1957). Recently Reid and Epstein have introduced a more structured model termed "task-centered casework" (Reid, 1978; Reid and Epstein, 1972). These two approaches are reviewed here, realizing that there are other theories within this group.

Common to these approaches is reliance on a wide range of theoretical stances. Few reject freudian conceptions; they are, however, not as committed to them as are those who proceed from the assumptions as outlined in the psychosocial approach. Ego psychology, learning theory, role theory, and communication theory are among the theoretical foundations drawn upon by the proponents of the problem-solving approaches.

The basic problem-solving approach as developed by Perlman and the task-centered system of Reid and Epstein are treated separately. We begin with the basic assumptions put forth by Perlman.

PROBLEM-SOLVING FRAMEWORK
Assumptions

Intrinsic is the view that all of human life is a problem-solving process; difficulties in coping with problems are based on lack of opportunity, ability, or motivation.

In the course of human growth, individuals develop problem-solving capacities which become basic features of the personalities. To deal effectively with diverse problems, including recurrent life cycle tasks, requisite resources and opportunities must be available. Excessive stress, crisis, or inadequate resources impair coping capacity. Interpersonal conflict, insufficient resources, deficient or dissatisfying role performance, and difficulties in moving through the stages of the life cycle as anticipated are all viewed as problems.

There is less emphasis than in the psychosocial approach on the importance of personal pathology in the etiology of problems. Equilibrium may be restored and optimal functioning regained when "competence is restored or strengthened and when needed social and welfare services are provided" (Siporin, 1975). Past experiences, present perceptions and reactions to the problem, as well as future aspirations join together to form the person with a problem. Of primary importance is today's reality. Knowledge of current living situations by which persons are "being molded and battered" provide the facts necessary for the problem-solving process to be activated (Perlman, 1957).

The person's response to the process is influenced by the structure and functioning of the personality which has been molded by inherited and constitutional equipment as well as interactions with the physical and social environment. There are, however, blocks which may impede the process. These may include a lack of material provisions available to the client; ignorance or misapprehension about the facts of the problem and the way of dealing with it; or a lack of physical and emotional energy to invest in problem-solving.

Culture and its influence on individual development is discussed. In describing the person, Perlman presents the individual operating as a physical, psychological, social entity—a product of constitutional makeup, physical and social environment, past experience, present perceptions and reactions, as well as future aspirations. She adds that "the time schedules that we keep, the way we eat, dress, talk to other persons and respect we show for property and the rights of others and our personal expectations for success are an indication of our incorporation of societal standards and ideas" (Perlman, 1957).

The goal in problem-solving is to provide necessary resources, restore equilibrium and optimal functioning through a process that places emphasis upon contemporary reality, and present problem-ridden situations. These resources are of both a concrete and an interpersonal nature.

Assumptions and the ethnic reality. There are no contradictions between this model and the concept of the ethnic reality. There is considerable congruence between the notion that effective coping is contingent on the availability of adequate resources and opportunities and our view that, for the most part, the ethnic reality often simultaneously serves as a source of stress and strength. While the dysfunctional effect of personality pathology is not neglected, greater emphasis is placed on restoration of competence and provision of resources in delineated problem areas. This is consonant with our stress on the systemic source of problems often faced by ethnic and minority groups.

Interventive procedures

Perlman suggests that the problem-solving event has five components: (1) the person, (2) the problem, (3) the place, (4) a professional person, and (5) a process. It is through the process that problem-solving operations take place within a meaningful relationship. This process includes three essential procedures which are intended to move people from a state of discomfort to one in which they are able to cope with problems using their own skills (Perlman, 1957).

Ascertaining and clarification of facts. This initial step requires that the caseworker establish the facts of the individual's situation—that is, the "why" and "what" factors as they are perceived. These facts include the feelings and behaviors manifested by people as they struggle with the problem and respond to the "objective reality" in "subjective" ways. While this is identified as the initial step, it must be recognized that ascertaining and clarification are a continuing responsibility throughout the problem-solving event.

Thinking through the facts. While the problem-solving process places emphasis upon collaboration between social worker and client, the professional has a major responsibility in "thinking through the facts." This thorough consideration requires that the "facts" are "turned over, probed into, reorganized, and examined in relation to one another while their significance is viewed in relation to various pieces of knowledge gathered from other experiences and disciplines." Enabling clients to speak about the problem with its facts and emotional impact allows for their "entry" into the thinking-through process, thus establishing the two-pronged problem solving approach.

Making some choice or decision. Once the facts are presented and thought through by both parties, decisions must be made. They may take the form of overt action or changes in behavior related to the problem. The question at this phase is "What will happen if _____?" Often, in order to accomplish this phase, material means or accessible opportunities must be made available to the person, as they are essential to problem resolution.

Perlman contends that, in order to be effective, these modes of action must involve a systematically organized process that is a conscious, focused, goal-directed activity involving client and case-worker.

Interventive procedures and the ethnic reality

The problem-solving approach as delineated by Perlman does call attention to the part played by membership in varying subgroups in influencing behavior. However, little if any explicit attention is paid to the influence of social class. Case examples provide the facts of age, sex, and family composition. Occasional reference is made to social class membership or income.

The practitioner who uses this model as a base for practice must add fact-ascertaining questions which deal with ethnicity if these are viewed as a crucial characteristic of the client, as a social fact of their environment. Attention must be paid to the values which derive from ethnic identity and social class position (Mostwin, 1972).

The process of "thinking through" of the facts associated with the ethnic reality would add critical information as the decision-making phase is approached.

The procedures proposed provide few guides for the practitioner in use of knowledge concerning varying world views of the many ethnic groups seeking help with the myriad problems that occur in daily life.

TASK-CENTERED CASEWORK

The task-centered approach was first formulated by Reid and Epstein in 1972. When initially developed it resembled other structured, time-limited approaches, geared to alleviation of specific problems (Reid, 1978). It drew on components of structured forms of brief casework (Reid and Shyne, 1969), aspects of Perlman's problem-solving approach (Perlman, 1957), the perspective on the client task put forth by Studt (1968), and the specification of casework methods presented by Hollis (Hollis, 1964; Reid, 1967).

Since its inception, extensive work has been carried out to test and refine the model (Reid, 1977, 1978).

Assumptions

The theoretical system stresses the importance of attention to problems in the terms identified and defined by clients. In keeping with the view presented by Perlman, the human capacity for autonomous problem-solving and the ability to begin to carry out action to obtain desired ends are stressed. This perspective was developed by incorporation of assumptions concerning the role of human action in alleviating psychosocial problems. Problems are viewed as unsatisfied wants, usually involving conditions a person wants to change.

Dissatisfaction may be with oneself, with others, or with an all-encompassing life situation. In sharp contrast to psychosocial theory, problem-oriented theory as defined by Reid and Epstein does not focus on remote or historical origins of a problem but looks primarily to contemporary causal factors. Attention is centered on those problems which the client and practitioner can act to change. "Wants," "beliefs," and "affects" are crucial determinants of action (Reid, 1978).

The possible role of the unconscious in influencing human action is not ruled out. However, given the emphasis on the present, it is assumed that problems as defined by clients can be managed without efforts to gain insight into unconscious dynamics (Reid, 1978).

In their view, theories designed to explain personality dynamics and disorders, the function of social systems, and other factors aid in problem assessment. However, these theories provide no clues concerning how people perceive problems, nor do they explain the relationship between personal and environmental factors. Furthermore, there are competing theories to explain similar problems. The worker is left with limited guides for action.

While not rejecting the possibility that such theories are potentially capable of being tested and providing guidelines for action, this is not the case at present. Focus is on development of theory which centers on problems of individuals and families, how their problems came to be, and how they can be resolved (Reid, 1978).

The approach to personality theory is "pragmatic" and "eclectic." Practitioners are free to draw on any theory or combination of theories if they seem to add to understanding of the situation (Epstein, 1977).

Another major set of assumptions discussed by Epstein is important here. These revolve around the view of poverty, the characteristics of poor clients, and how these contrast with other perspectives on the poor. As a case in point Epstein reviews prevailing views on the "multiproblem family." It is frequently suggested that these families are poor, members of minority groups, and often headed by women. In her view they are often described as having dirty children and dirty homes and as uneducated. Their "obdurate tendency to avoid or discontinue contact" (Epstein, 1977) and their overriding interest in obtaining concrete services is frequently stressed in the literature. These traits are often seen as the result of faulty personality development. Epstein contends that these descriptions, and the prescriptions which follow from them, derive from "pseudo explanations" which do not lend themselves to the development of treatment technologies capable of effecting desired changes. She suggests that given the persistent and severe inequities endemic in modern society which minimize the access to resources for so many, "no treatment technology of any kind has the capability of addressing itself to managing or controlling influences so vast" (Epstein, 1977). Substitution of the term "families with special hardships" for the term "multiproblem family" is proposed. Fundamental resolutions to the problems experienced by these families "rest upon development of social policies to mitigate the oppressive restraints of racial, ethnic and sex discrimination; poverty; unavailability of quality education; day care; and the like" (Epstein, 1977).

Assumptions and the ethnic reality. Reid and Epstein point out that much of the impetus for development and refinement of the model was based on an interest in providing more effective service to the poor. The critique of certain prevailing views of the poor has been noted, as has the emphasis on the delivery of concrete services. The insistence on working with problems only in the terms identified by the client is stressed. These thrusts are a major step in the direction of ethnic-sensitive practice as we have defined it. When clients truly have the freedom to reject problem definitions which do not concur with their own views, the risk of attributing personality pathology to systemically induced behaviors and events is minimized.

For example, many American Indians feel that responsibility to family takes precedence over responsibility to the work place. Knowing this, the social worker is unlikely to characterize as lazy an American Indian who explains his failure to work on a given day because of family obligations. If the ethnic reality of an American

Indian man is understood it is unlikely that he will be characterized as lazy or unmotivated.

The extent to which adherence to such subcultural perspectives leads to frequent job loss may become the issue of concern if he chooses to make it so. He is free to define the "problem" and to deal with it on his terms. Once viewed this way, consideration of various options is possible without recourse to the pathological label. For example, can his need to work regularly be reconciled with the responsibilities to family and friends as these are defined by his own group? In some instances a new "client" or group of clients can emerge. These may be fellow employees or a supervisor who understand the kinds of commitments he has and are able and willing to make adaptations in required work routines.

Interventive procedures

It is a basic premise of the system that clients' expressed requests are most important. This is stressed throughout the work. The importance of helping clients to obtain what they ask for, within ethical limits, is emphasized. This is true regardless of the practitioner's reservation about the "worthiness" of the request or the suspicion that what is "really wanted" is different from what is stated. Indeed, if intervention proceeds from the basic values inherent in this assumption, action taken on the behalf of clients in relation to problems not acknowledged by them constitutes a violation of the basic value.

Individuals may be said to be clients only when they have accepted the social worker's offer to help or acknowledge a problem. Considerable thought is given to the "involuntary client," those people referred to social agencies for a variety of situations which have brought them into conflict with the law—parents thought to be abusing their children are an example. Epstein suggests that, where intervention is necessary, such as removal of children from their parents' care against their wishes, it should not be termed "treatment"; rather it should be seen for what it is: "authoritative, socially approved coercion to safeguard a child's life" (Epstein, 1977).

Reid and Epstein are among a number of theorists who point to the importance of a structure, a framework, and a clearly specified objective of intervention (Fischer, 1978; Reid, 1978; Reid and Epstein, 1972). There is evidence that short-term intervention with time limits set in advance and jointly determined by client and worker is at least as, if not more, effective than work carried out on a more open-ended basis.

In the task-centered model, distinction is made between activities engaged in jointly by client and worker or by the worker on the client's behalf, and techniques used by workers.

The major task-centered activities have been delineated in a number of ways (Reid, 1977, 1978). Basically they center on the following: (1) problem specification, (2) establishing the presence of acknowledged problems, (3) determining desired changes, (4) developing working explanations, (5) eliciting prior problem-solving efforts, (6) obtaining contextual data, (7) forming the contract, (8) task planning and implementation, and (9) establishing incentives and rationale.

Problem specification and establishing the presence of acknowledged problems. When clients come for help on their own, this step is clearcut and focused on making sure that the agency is in a position to help. Discussion with the referred and the involuntary client must center on determining whether the person acknowledges a problem and wants to work on it with agency personnel and such resources as are available. In such situations a number of possibilities emerge: (1) no "acknowledged problem" is agreed upon; (2) there is agreement between those who referred the person and the client about the nature of the problem; (3) the problem may be different in scope than as defined by the referring persons. Emphasis is always on "what is troubling the client" (Reid, 1977). However, the worker does try to help the person to think about alternative ways in which the problem may be viewed. The example cited by Reid is a case in point. The child referred for "fighting" thinks he/she is "picked on" and therefore fights. While this may not be an accurate description of the state of affairs, it is a starting point for action intended to help the youngster understand that it is the fighting which may cause him/her to lose friends, be picked on, and the like.

Specifying conditions to be changed and determining desired changes. Problems are viewed as conditions that clients want to change. Specification and clarification of the circumstances under which the problem surfaces is crucial. For example, in working with a young man who wants help in reducing outbursts of temper in his interaction with his girlfriend, it is important to know what aspects of their interaction and respective behaviors trigger the outbursts. Determining desired changes would then involve clarification of what is desired: does he want to change his behavior, her behavior, both?

Developing working explanations, eliciting prior problem-solving efforts, obtaining contextual data. This type of activity involves the worker and the client in collaborative effort to clarify how problems arose and how this or similar problems have been managed in the past. Important in this connection are attempts to understand their belief system, their cognitive ability, and social and physical function, and how the overall social and physical environment is affecting them. Material bearing on socioeconomic and ethnic identification, and the dispositions which may be related to these, are involved here.

Forming the contract. Contracts establish explicit agreements between client and worker on what is to be done and how. Although the contract may be reformulated, a crucial aspect of the task-centered approach is the "principle that the purposes and nature of the worker client relationship will be controlled by explicit agreements rather than by the practitioner's hidden agenda" (Reid, 1977).

Task planning and implementation. This phase is viewed as the core of the approach (Reid, 1977). Tasks are designated and obstacles to their completion assessed. Much "in-session" work is focused on rehearsing and planning for activities to be carried on outside the sessions. Crucial is the client's expressed willingness to carry out the tasks taken on. Client commitment as measured on a five-point scale is the best predictor of progress (Reid, 1977). There is great stress on having people begin to work on the task before the next contact with the social worker. For example, one makes some effort to look for a job during that time period. The worker makes sure that the plan for action involves things which the client is capable of doing.

Establishing incentives and rationale. Here stress is on assuring that the involved individuals will view the potential results as being of sufficient benefit so as to make difficult action worthwhile. Both positive and negative consequences for the client and for others are reviewed. This may involve, as in their example, anticipating the pros and cons of asking for a raise, or the negative consequences of not seeking attention for a hazardous illness. An important incentive may be helping the client to anticipate a sense of mastery from task accomplishment, praise, or other kinds of approval (Reid, 1977).

Interventive procedures and the ethnic reality

As we have noted earlier, there is little doubt that Reid and Epstein are keenly aware of the debilitating effects of poverty and discrimination. Furthermore, they emphasize the importance of awareness of values and self perceptions as these arise from ethnic and social class membership. They stress the fact that problems occur in contexts which relate to socioeconomic and ethnic identifications and point out that "unfortunately no effective system has been developed for mapping the context of psychosocial problems" (Reid, 1977).

They too tend to emphasize the problems associated with discrimination but do not point to particular coping strategies which various cultural and racial groups have developed.

In some respects the focus on structure and time limits may run counter to the perspectives on time held by different groups. Adherence to different time schedules and the discomfort with self-disclosure of American Indians and some Hispanic groups are examples. Time-limited, structured approaches are responsive to the high level of motivation to reduce distress which is generated by a breakdown in coping capacity. While this may well be true for many groups, we wonder whether the pride which so many people have in "managing on their own" should not be given greater attention than we discern. Marital problems of long standing, child neglect which has not reached disastrous proportions, and school problems which involve many people are all examples of situations in which extensive time may be needed to build trust. It is possible that the "failures" in this and other approaches are in some measure related to the fact that insufficient time has been allotted to recognizing particular dispositions to problem identification and resolution that relate to the ethnic reality. The approach requires a high degree of rationality, which may be incongruent with the world view of some cultural groups.* The emphasis on structure and time limits may muffle sen-

---

*Conversation with Professor Daniel Katz, Graduate School of Social Work, Rutgers University.

sitivity to the "dual perspective" (Norton, 1978) which increases awareness of the possible and actual points of conflict between the minority client's perspective and that of the dominant society. Clashes generated by the dual perspective may well be encountered by worker and client struggling to specify an acknowledged problem.

This may well be the case in the situation described by Jones, in which American Indians are frequently referred to the local child welfare agency because of presumed child neglect. To the outsider it appears that children are left untended while their parents go to the "native drinking center" (Jones, 1976). Discussion with the distraught parents may reveal that appearances notwithstanding, the children are not left unattended, for in their housing complex, parents arrange to check on each others' children; attendance at the "drinking center" is part of the ritualized and accepted behavior within the group. The distinction between attributed and acknowledged problems is a crucial one in this kind of situation. However, only thorough knowledge of the beliefs and behavior of the group, and what the consequences are for the children, will enable the worker to make a sensitive judgment as to whether child neglect is involved or not.

Similarly, knowledge of Jewish tradition becomes most important in working with the young Jewish woman who comes to a counseling center, distraught because her parents have threatened to "sit shive" for her should she go through with her plans to marry a non-Jewish man. This threat to consider dead those young people who marry out of group may be very real, and represents a basic point of conflict between people caught in different worlds.

We doubt whether situations such as these are amenable to the highly structured, time-limited actions projected. We agree that "pinning down the elements of the problem to be changed" may need to proceed quickly. The agency must make a decision as to whether children are in real danger. The young woman needs some quick help in identifying whether her major loyalties are to her parents or her boyfriend, for she may lose a valued relationship if she wavers too much. But beyond this, we contend that support, and examination of the ethnically derived aspect of response, takes time and continued exploration.

As is true with other approaches, we find no explicit effort to adapt the guidelines for task-centered intervention for work with people who may approach their problems from varying value perspectives.

THE SOCIAL PROVISION AND STRUCTURAL APPROACHES

Approaches which highlight social structural inequity as a major source of difficulty have long been an integral part of the social work practice literature. The work of Addams (1910) and Wald (1951) exemplified this perspective. They were followed by Reynolds (1938), Titmus (1968), Younghusband (1964), and Kahn (1965).*

Recent efforts to explicate the relationship between the social context and social work practice principles (Meyer, 1976) are exemplified by Germain's (1979) and Germain's and Gitterman's (1980) ecological approach and Meyer's (1976) ecosystems perspective. Germain proposes that: "Practice is directed toward improving the transactions between people and environments in order to enhance adaptive capacities and improve environments for all who function within them." Out of this perspective a number of "action principles" are derived. These relate to: "efforts at adaptation and organism environmental transactions . . . those transactions between people and environments are sought that will nourish both parts of the interdependent system" (Germain, 1979).

A similar theme is presented by Meyer, who suggests that the "interface between person and environment is fluid." Furthermore, it is not possible to make clear distinctions between internal or external cause and effect (Meyer, 1976). Meyer identifies a policy-oriented practitioner whose focus is developmental services and who is guided by an ecosystem perspective, a "life model" of practice, and a clear sense of social accountability (Meyer, 1976). She pays considerable attention to the "way people live" and identifies life cycle stages, tasks, the potential crises and problems associated with these, as well as institutional resources available and needed.

Common to these approaches is the view that social institutional sources of stress play a major part in generating problems at the same time as interventive actions must be geared to "individualized understanding of people in terms of their institutional membership" (Siporin, 1975).

---

*We acknowledge the work of Siporin (1975) in helping us to arrive at this formulation.

THE STRUCTURAL APPROACH*

A detailed model which identifies social institutional sources of stress and specifies social work actions generated by such a perspective is presented by Middleman and Goldberg (1974). They identify theirs as a structural approach, examined here in some detail because both assumptions and related practice principles are explicitly delineated.

Assumptions

This approach is derived from two basic assumptions: (1) individual problems are perceived as a function of social disorganization and not as individual pathology; and (2) all social workers, regardless of where they work, have an obligation to pursue social change efforts as an integral part of their ongoing assignment.

In their view it is destructive and dysfunctional to define social problems in psychological terms. Many of those served by social work—minority groups, the aged, the poor—are "neither the cause of, nor the appropriate locus for change efforts aimed at lessening the problems they confront."

Much of social work efforts are expended in working with and on behalf of people who do not adequately deal with the situations in which they find themselves. "Inadequacy" is a relative term, which essentially refers to the disparity between skills or resources and situational requirements. If it is expected that people ought to be skillful and resourceful in response to the requirements of varied situations, then those lacking the necessary coping skills are perceived as inadequate. On the other hand, when situational demands are inappropriate and not sufficiently responsive to individual or collective need, then the situation is perceived as inadequate. "Thus to say that a given man is inadequate is at one and the same time both a description of disparity between that man and a particular situation, and a value judgment attributing blame for that disparity." Middleman and Goldberg put major responsibility for that disparity on inadequate social provision, racial discrimination, and organizational arrangements.

Based on this perspective, they conceptualize social work roles in terms of two bipolar dimensions—"locus of concern" and "per-

---

*All citations from Middleman and Goldberg (1974).

sons engaged." Locus of concern identifies the reason for social work intervention. The concern may focus on (1) the problems of a particular individual such as members of a minority group who confront discrimination in employment and cannot find a job, or (2) the larger category of individuals who suffer from the same problem—"a general category of persons identified as sufferers by definition of a social problem."

"Persons engaged" calls attention to those people with whom the social worker interacts in response to the problem. Those engaged may be the "sufferer" and/or others. This may involve a process by which the social worker facilitates action by clients and family and community networks to help themselves and each other; or attention may be focused on more explicit social change activity. This can range from effort to effect legislative change, to organizing for specific community services, to marshalling informal community supports in time of crisis.

The major targets of intervention are always the conditions which inhibit functioning and increase suffering. "The social worker intervenes to improve the quality of the relationship between people and their social environment by bringing to bear, changing, or creating social structures."

Assumptions and the ethnic reality. The congruence between many of the assumptions of the structural approach and our perspective on the ethnic reality is in many respects self-evident. We have established that a sense of class and ethnicity is strongly experienced in everyday life, and that many ethnic groups and all minority groups are held in low esteem by various segments of the society. We have also suggested that it is not uncommon to find that certain culturally derived behaviors are viewed as deviant.

Such interpretations, which often arise out of mainstream expectations, define culturally derived behaviors as inadequate, and pay insufficient attention to the situations out of which they emerge.

Clearly, the basic assumptions of the structural approach are consonant with our view concerning the part played by the ethnic reality in generating many of the problems at issue.

However, like the proponents of other approaches, Middleman and Goldberg leave the implicit impression that matters of race and ethnicity are primarily problematic. They do not call explicit attention to the particular sources of strength or coping capacity which such group identification often generates. While they hint at this when they point to the social worker's role in facilitating mutual aid activities, they do not make it explicit.

Interventive procedures

Middleman and Goldberg identify four basic principles of the approach, major social work roles, and skills.

In this section we summarize and discuss these principles. The "Principle of Accountability" to the client is based on the assumption that people are capable of defining their own need, and that the social worker's major task is reduction of pressures as viewed by the client. The primary tool for putting this principle into action is the contract established between the practitioner and client. Through this agreement a practitioner together with the client may identify a point of stress, determine how it ought to be relieved, and take on the tasks that will accomplish the goal. Stress may emanate from problematic interpersonal relationships, illness, social structural flaws, or the very nature of tasks to be accomplished such as learning in school. The plan for action may fail. The contract may then be revised or activity halted.

The "Principle of Following the Demands of the Client Task" is based on the view that client need and not worker skill or disposition determines worker activity. In their operational definition of this principle, Middleman and Goldberg begin to delineate the practice implications which flow from a perspective that views the environment as the primary target of change at the same time as individual problems are approached with sensitive awareness to uniqueness. By suggesting that workers "look beyond each client to see if there are others facing the same task," they highlight the fact that problems are often of a collective and structurally induced nature. Their contention that workers must take different roles at different times points to the need to and the importance of being guided by client need rather than worker need or agency or other institutional constraints. Focus on the roles of broker, mediator, and advocate suggests that inadequate service structures often mitigate against adequate problem resolution. The various activities designed to carry out the terms of the contract called for by this principle require work with the clients (1) on their behalf, (2) in behalf of themselves and others; and (3) with others in behalf of the clients.

At times this may necessitate activity in all areas. For example, a child who feels hurt because of racist slurs in school needs help in talking about this to a teacher. At the same time, efforts to involve school personnel in creating a less racist atmosphere may be indicated. Confrontation or social action may be necessary if there are other children having similar experiences. Inherent in this conception is role flexibility.

"The Principle of Maximizing Potential Supports in the Client's Environment" points to the need to modify or create new structures. Viewed as the essential thrust of the structural approach, this principle points to a number of needed activities. For example, on finding that a group of adolescents in a school have not learned to read, it is incumbent on the worker to try to get a special reading program started. Or, when agency intake procedures delay service delivery, action aimed at altering and speeding up the intake process is called for. Workers, though central at key points of stress, should continually be aware of and help to maximize the use and development of diverse support systems in the community.

The "Principle of Least Contest" directs the worker to exert the least pressure necessary to accomplish the client task. Specifically it is proposed that, when an environmental source of difficulty is identified, effort is made to change the environment before engaging in more vigorous protest activities.

In summary, the structural approach views systemic inequity as the major source of client stress, and effort to modify or create less dysfunctional structures as the social worker's major obligation.

Interventive procedures and the ethnic reality

A review of the basic principles of the approach highlights the keen sensitivity to matters of concern to members of minority groups. Many of the examples center on people suffering the effects of deprivation or racism and target interventions geared to minimize their negative consequences. More than any approach we have reviewed, it would appear that the principles, if consistently followed, would of necessity generate ethnic-sensitive practice. It seems unlikely that workers who truly adhere to these principles would negate the needs for protection from intimate disclosure of many American Indians, the various pain responses of certain ethnic groups, "Black pride," or stoicism in the face of adversity which is the hallmark of Slavic groups. However, we do not find any specific suggestions as to whether or how these principles might be modified or adapted to deal with varied ethnically based response.

THE SYSTEMS APPROACH

Most of the models we have reviewed in the preceding section are to varying degrees based on substantive theoretical orientations, which in turn shape and give focus to interventive procedures.

In the introduction to this chapter, the reader's attention was called to the fact that some social work theoreticians have sought to identify approaches to social work practice which are independent of various substantive theories derived from other domains of interest; instead, they seek to identify a "social work frame of reference," related to the basic values, function, and purposes of the profession.

Pincus and Minahan (1973) present such a model. They define social work practice as a "goal-oriented planned change process." The model uses a general systems approach as an organizing framework. It is intended for application in a wide range of settings. Effort is made to avoid the often noted dichotomies between person/environment, clinical practice/social action, and microsystem/macrosystem change. In their view, "the strength of the profession lies in recognizing and working with the connections between these elements" (Pincus and Minahan, 1973).

Assumptions

Two basic concepts form this approach—"resources" and "interaction" between people and the social environment (Pincus and Minahan, 1973). A resource is defined as "anything that is used to achieve goals, solve problems, alleviate distress, accomplish life tasks or realize aspirations and values." Resources are usually used in interaction with others. Thus, there is interdependence between resources, people, and varying informal and formal systems. The former include family, friends, and neighbors; the latter, the societal, governmental, and voluntary health, educational, and social welfare services.

This perspective helps to identify five areas of concern to social work: (1) the absence of needed resources, (2) the absence of linkages between people and resource systems or between resource systems, (3) problematic interaction between people within the same resource system, (4) problematic interaction between resource systems, and (5) problematic individual internal problem-solving or coping resources.

Assumptions and the ethnic reality. This approach derives its basic thrust from the values and purposes of social work. By definition this focuses attention on the many gaps in institutional life which prevent people from reaching their full potential. There is no question that the gaps related to discrimination, cultural differences, and the like have always been recognized by our profession. The emphasis on resources and environment implicitly calls attention to those problems and strengths related to the ethnic reality. However, Pincus and Minahan do not explicitly devote themselves to these issues, although their examples do point to problems experienced by minority people as they confront mainstream institutions.

The assumptions, on which this systems or generalist approach are based, are, like all the others we have reviewed, congruent with a view which takes account of the ethnic reality. However, no explicit attention is paid to these matters.

Interventive procedures

Pincus and Minahan refer to the social work "mode of action" and discuss several components. These are reviewed in the following paragraphs.

Helping people enhance and more effectively utilize their own coping capacities. This is quickly identified as a unifying aspect of the systems approach which is committed to joint effort with clients to change those aspects of their lives which are causing discomfort.

Establishing initial linkage between people and resources. A primary responsibility is the location of those individuals or institutions with ability to assist the worker and client in their planned change effort. Once located, they are enlisted to join in the effort. Needless to say, this effort is not always successful but the investment is an essential procedure.

Facilitating interaction within resource systems. In this process the social worker looks within the resource system to ensure that resources are being used in a manner congruent with client need. Concretely this involves effort to minimize bureaucratic red tape and generally to examine policies to assure that they maximize rather than minimize client functioning.

Influencing social policy. It is here that Pincus and Minahan verbalize an aspect of micro-practice which is often not clearly articulated. Since practice is carried out in agencies where services span the life cycle from early childhood to programs for the aging, there is knowledge about and access to data on social problems, environmental conditions, and the response of social service delivery systems to those who require supports. This access places social work in a position to influence public policy.

Dispensing material resources. Again we may refer to models described earlier. Concrete services are the backbone of practice in many areas. Food, clothing, employment, and shelter may be all that an individual or family needs to enable it to cope with life. Lacks in these areas may be *the* major problems with which people need help. Given the assurance of regular meals and sufficient snacks, acting-out school children may become the vivacious, motivated, above-average students they were meant to be.

Serving as agents of social control. Despite desires to the contrary, there are those persons who are labeled as deviant. They have had experiences in prison, mental hospitals, and a variety of other psychiatric treatment centers. Society often requires that their activities be supervised and/or monitored. Children who live in situations where they are threatened with abuse and/or neglect have need of protection. Adequate care must be provided.

Interventive procedures and the ethnic reality

There can be no quarrel with the validity of the "mode of action" as an approach to practice. However, much like the other approaches reviewed here, it gives little recognition to the impact of ethnicity upon the life of clients.

In an elaboration of data collection skills there is a suggestion that much may be learned by a walk through a community in the process of change. Such a walk does provide beginning information. Food stores and newspapers on newsstands give clues to ethnicity, as do converted religious structures (Pincus and Minahan, 1973). Methods for interpretation of such data and its significance in the daily life of individuals and the community at large are lacking. To view the "ethnic street" without considering its residents' response to their ethnicity and social class omits important variables in the data collection process.

A concise systems approach to practice is presented. Procedures which would make use of the various areas of knowledge a practitioner may need to acquire related to ethnicity, social class, and the wide variations of lifestyles that emerge from the impact of the ethnic reality are not presented.

SUMMARY OF APPROACHES TO PRACTICE

This review of the major approaches to social work practice indicates that, with few exceptions, the assumptions on which practice is based are not in contradiction with prevailing understandings of cultural, class, and ethnic diversity. Our summary of interventive procedures highlights the point we have made repeatedly, that is, limited attention has been paid to modifying or generating procedures which heighten the practitioner's skill in working sensitively with people of various ethnic and class backgrounds.

All of the models reviewed share adherence to basic social work values. The dignity of the individual, the right to self-determination, the need for an adequate standard of living, and satisfying, growth-enhancing relaionships are uniformly noted. Differences emerge about what social workers need to know and do in order to achieve these lofty objectives.

It is quite apparent that those social workers who believe that past personal experience and nonconscious factors have a major bearing on how people feel in the present structure their practice differently from those who emphasize the importance of institutional barriers, both past and present. Both groups draw on a wide range of psychological and sociological knowledge. However, their theoretical differences influence the manner by which these are incorporated in practice.

These differences are reflected in how problems are defined, what kinds of needs are stressed, the stucture of the worker-client relationship, and the type of activity undertaken (Germain, 1979).

Our view of the theory-practice relationship

Based on our review and experience, we have little question that knowledge, theory, and values guide problem definition and affect the kinds of assessments that are made. For example, accurate understanding of ethnically derived responses to illness, or aging, or education will affect assessment when problems surface. These assessments in turn have bearing on interventive principles and strategies selected. The Slavic mother who appears to neglect childhood illnesses may not be neglectful but simply adhering to an ethnic dictum in which apparently minor illnesses are to be endured. Given this knowledge, one is less likely to define her as a neglecting parent. Whether intervention is focused on her feelings about being a mother, education to help her to recognize "dangerous symptoms," or support to help her live comfortably in a culture which permits indulgence of "minor symptoms" is, in our view, a function of the theory of human behavior to which one subscribes. At the same time all social workers would share the goal of maximizing the mother's and the child's physical and emotional well-being.

Much of what follows represents our effort to delineate the relationship between knowledge and theory about the ethnic reality, other knowledge about human behavior, social work values, and interventive approaches.

REFERENCES

Addams, Jane. 1910. *Twenty years at Hull House.* New York: The Macmillan Co.

Epstein, Laura. 1977. *How to provide social services with task-centered methods: report of the Task-Centered Service Project, Volume I.* Chicago: The School of Social Service Administration, University of Chicago.

Fischer, Joel. 1978. *Effective casework practice: an eclectic approach.* New York: McGraw-Hill Book Co.

Germain, Carol B. (Ed.). 1979. *Social work practice: people and environments.* New York: Columbia University Press.

Germain, Carol B., and Gitterman, Alex. 1980. *The life model of social work practice.* New York: Columbia University Press.

Good Tracks, Jimm. C. 1973. "Native American non interference." *Social Work, 18*(6), November.

Greir, William H., and Cobbs, G. 1969. *Black rage.* New York: Bantam Books.

Hollis, Florence. 1965. "Casework and social class." *Social Casework, 46,* October.

Hollis, Florence. 1972. *Casework: a psychosocial therapy* (2nd ed.). New York: Random House.

Jones, Dorothy M. 1976. "The mystique of expertise in social services: an Alaska example." *Journal of Sociology and Social Welfare, 3*(3), January.

Kahn, Alfred J. 1965. "New policies and service models: the next phase." *American Journal of Orthopsychiatry, 35.*

Krause, Corinne Azen. 1978. *Grandmothers, mothers and daughters: an oral history study of ethnicity, mental health and continuity of three generations of Jewish, Italian and Slavic American women.* New York: The American Jewish Committee.

Meyer, Carol H. 1976. *Social work practice* (2nd ed.). New York: The Free Press.

Middleman, Ruth, and Goldberg, Gale. 1974. *Social service delivery: a structural approach to practice.* New York: Columbia University Press.

Mirelowitz, Seymour. 1979. "Implications of racism for social work practice." *Journal of Sociology and Social Welfare, 6*(3), May.

Mostwin, Danuta. 1972. "In search of ethnic identity." *Social Casework, 53,* May.

Norton, Dolores G. 1978. *The dual perspective.* New York: Council on Social Work Education.

Perlman, Helen H. 1957. *Social casework.* Chicago: University of Chicago Press.

Pincus, Allen, and Minahan, Anne. 1973. *Social work practice: model and method.* Itasca, Il.: F. E. Peacock Publishers, Inc.

President's Commission on Mental Health. 1978. *Task Panel Reports,* Volume III, Appendix.

Reid, William J. 1977. *A study of the characteristics and effectiveness of task-centered methods.* Chicago: The School of Social Service Administration.

Reid, William J. 1978. *The task-centered system.* New York: Columbia University Press.

Reid, William J., and Epstein, Laura. 1972. *Task-centered casework.* New York: Columbia University Press.

Reynolds. Bertha C. 1938. "Treatment processes as developed by social work." *Proceedings, National Conference of Social Work.* New York: Columbia University Press.

Siporin, Max. 1975. *Introduction to social work practice.* New York: The Macmillan Co.

Strean, Herbert S. 1974. "Role theory." In Turner, Francis J. (Ed.). *Social work treatment.* New York: The Free Press

Studt, Elliot. 1968. "Social work theory and implication for the practice of methods." *Social Work Education Reporter, 16*(2).

Titmuss, Richard. 1968. *Commitment to welfare.* New York: Pantheon Books.

Turner, Francis J. 1970. "Ethnic difference and client performance." *Social Service Review, 44,* March.

Turner, Francis J. 1974. "Some considerations on the place of theory in current social work practice." In Turner, Francis J. (Ed.). *Social work treatment*. New York: The Free Press.

Turner, Francis J. 1978. *Psychosocial therapy*. New York: The Free Press.

Wald, Lillian. 1951. *The house on Henry Street*. New York: Holt, Rinehart and Winston.

Younghusband, Eileen. 1964. *Social work and social change*. London: George Allen and Uwin.

CHAPTER
5

A model for ethnic-sensitive practice

In this chapter, a model for ethnic-sensitive practice is developed. The model builds on (1) social work values, (2) the conception of the ethnic reality and its relationship to the life cycle, (3) the layers of understanding, and (4) the view of social work as a problem-solving endeavor. From these are derived the assumptions and practice principles on which this model is based.

A synthesis of the perspectives presented in the preceding chapters suggests that:

> Social work practice needs to be grounded in understanding of the diverse group memberships people hold. Particular attention must be paid to ethnicity and social class, and how these contribute to individual and group identity, disposition to basic life tasks, coping styles and the constellation of problems likely to be encountered. These, together with individual history, and genetic and physiological disposition, contribute to the development of personality structure and group life.

In the first section of this chapter the major assumptions of the model are identified. The basic practice principles follow. The basic assumptions are:

1. Individual and collective history have bearing on problem generation and solution

2. The present is most important
3. Nonconscious phenomena affect individual functioning
4. Ethnicity is a source of cohesion, identity, and strength as well as a source of strain, discordance, and strife

Basic to all social work approaches are the values which guide and inform practice.

SOCIAL WORK VALUES

The value base of social work has and continues to be scrutinized. This is as it should be. For social work as a profession is first and foremost committed to people, to their well-being, and to the enhancement of the quality of life. Levy (1973) comments: "The social work profession is well advised to tolerate difference and diversity about some things but not about its ideology. That is too critical a unifying force and one which is essential for its character and role as a profession in society."

Of all the varied statements about social work's value base, the one developed by Levy is particularly relevant to ethnic-sensitive practice. His basic formulations are: (1) values as preferred conceptions of people, (2) values as preferred outcomes for people, and (3) values as preferred instrumentalities for dealing with people.

The first focuses on orientations about the relationships between people and their environment; the second on the quality of life and beliefs about social provision and policy designed to enhance the quality of life; and the third on views about how people ought to be treated.

In respect to the first, emphasis is on viewing people as intrinsically valuable with the capacity to change and grow. People have a responsibility not only for themselves but for others as well. This responsibility involves reaching out beyond the narrow boundaries of one's daily life into the larger society where the need for community may be met. In all of these there is the recognition of the particular uniqueness of each individual. Ethnicity and social class are among those characteristics which make all people "special" in their own right.

The second dimension points to the familiar areas of self-realization, self-actualization, and equality of opportunity. The profession must continually affirm individual and group struggles for growth and development. It is our contention that the ethnic reality sometimes enhances, and sometimes impedes, the struggle.

The working-class Chicano college student expects that going to college will widen his opportunities for personal and professional development, yet he may find that his dark hair, tawny complexion, and native language serve as barriers. For him self-actualization and self-realization are more difficult to achieve.

The final category focuses on the importance of treating people in a way which maximizes the opportunity for self-direction. Stereotyping and prejudgment are destructive.

The consonance of this view with ethnic-sensitive practice is self-evident, as such practice stresses cultural continuity and integrity as well as individuality.

ASSUMPTIONS

The assumptions are delineated and illustrated in some detail. This detailed review is deliberate and based on our conviction that a group's history, values, and perspectives markedly affect the present concerns of individuals and of the group as a whole.

In our view, these factors provide more than background knowledge; together with various theories of behavior they become an integral component of the basic principles which guide practice and serve to shape practice skill and technology.

Past history has bearing on problem generation and solution

Theorists differ in their views concerning the relationship between the origins of a problem and the mechanisms which function to sustain or diminish that problem in the present (Fischer, 1978). Nevertheless, there is little question that individual and group history provide clues about how problems originate and suggest possible avenues for resolution.

Group history. In the review of the persistence of ethnicity as a factor in social life, attention was called to the forces which sustain crucial aspects of human functioning.

The particular history of oppression to which many groups have been subjected was noted; also important is the fact that these groups attempt to develop strategies to protect and cushion their members from such oppression. Culture, religion, and language are transmitted via primary groups to individuals and serve to give meaning to daily existence.

Crucial to a group's past is the history of the migration experience or other processes through which the encounter with mainstream culture took place.

Some, like American Indians and many Chicanos, view themselves as having been conquered people.* Others, including the early Anglo-Saxon settlers, fled religious oppression. Many came for both reasons. These experiences continue to have bearing on how their members perceive and organize life and how they are perceived by others. Thus Howe (1975) suggests that the earlier generations of Jewish immigrants, fleeing oppression and economic hardship, thought it necessary to "propel sons and daughters into the outer world—or more precisely, to propel them into the outer world as social beings while trying to keep them spiritually within the Jewish orbit." The sons and daughters of street peddlers, and of "girls" who had worked in the sweatshops of the Lower East Side, were encouraged to become educated. "The fathers would work, grub and scramble as petty agents of primitive accumulation. The sons would acquire education, that new-world magic the Jews were so adept at evoking through formulas they had brought from the Old World" (Howe, 1975). And so, many Jews went off to school in the mainstream and substantial numbers of them quickly moved into the middle class. Jews' traditional respect for learning, and the particular urban skills in which they had been schooled—a function of anti-Semitism in eastern Europe whereby they were not permitted to work the land (Zborowski and Herzog, 1952)—converged to speed their entry into middle-class America. Education, success, and marriage were the serious things in life. Sensuality and attending to the body were downplayed.

There was a deeply ingrained suspicion of frivolity and sport. "Suspicion of the physical, fear of hurt, anxiety over the sheer 'pointlessness' of play: all this went deep into the recesses of the Jewish psyche" (Howe, 1975).

There may be little resemblance between Jewish life on New

---

*Today, many American Indian tribes view themselves as nations negotiating on a basis of equality with the American Nation (President's Commission on Mental Health, 1978).

York's Lower East Side at the turn of the century and the contemporary urbane Jew. And yet, the emphasis on intellectualism persists, as does the haunting fear of persecution. There is a lingering suspicion of things physical, and a tendency to take illness quite seriously. Jewish men are still considered to make good husbands— steady, kind providers who value their families.

Following the Japanese attack on Pearl Harbor in December, 1941, 110,000 Japanese Americans were removed from their homes and detained in relocation centers. The relocation experience for the first time exposed many to work previously denied. Following the incarceration the Japanese went about reconstructing their lives. As a group they have been highly successful; when patterns of education, occupation, and income are used, they equal "white" groups in the proportion represented in the professions. By 1963 they exceeded many groups in median income (Kitano, 1976).

Despite the horror of the relocation experience, many of the second generation found that they were capable of doing a greater variety of work than they had heretofore recognized. It has been suggested* that the relocation experience speeded up the process of absorption into the mainstream, by turning over the leadership to the second generation at a much faster pace than is usually the case.

Congruity between Japanese and mainstream values with regard to upward mobility converged with the manifestation of a particularly virulent form of racism to affect the experience of this group.

Mexican revolutions early in the 1900s, together with the history of American conquest, generated much family disruption. Conscription of men into the armed forces was common. Poor Mexicans migrating into the larger cities of Texas left behind a history, a way of life centered about homogeneous folk societies. In these societies "God-given" roles were clearly assigned. Women did not work outside home, except in the fields. Each individual had a sense of place, of identity, of belonging. Work was to be found tilling the soil and education in the formal sense did not exist. Rituals of the church were an intricate part of daily life (West, 1980). These new rural immigrants whose language and belief systems were so different from the frontier mentality were not welcomed.

The history of Blacks in this country has become well known.

---

*Interview with Dr. Shozi Oniki.

They were brought in by slavery, an institution of bondage which lasted for 200 years. Yet the astute social worker must know that the history began as Bennett (1964) has stated, "before the Mayflower," on the African continent, where they developed a culture which reflected skill in agriculture, government, scholarship, and the fine arts. Unlike the ethnic groups mentioned earlier, Blacks were unable to openly preserve their customs, religion, or family tradition in this new land. The institution of slavery actively sought to discourage that. The past history of oppression, imposed by the mainstream society, continues to generate problems in the present—oppression continues.

These are but a few examples of how the nature of migration and the values which were brought converge with mainstream America and affect present functioning. Intervention strategies must take these into account.

The collective experience of a group affects individuals differently. Personality and life history serve as filters and determine which facets of ethnic history and identity remain an integral part of a person's functioning, which are forgotten, and which are consciously rejected. It is nevertheless unlikely that any Jew does not emit a particular shudder when reminded of the Holocaust. Japanese Americans, no matter of which generation, recall the relocation experience. In a racist society they can never be sure how they will be received, for their difference is physically visible.

Individual history and group identity. Individual members of groups have a sense of their group's history. For some it is dim and for others it is clearly articulated; for each it provides a sense of identification with the group. Such identification becomes a component, an integral part of the personality. Erikson (1968) suggests that identity is a process "located" in the core of the individual and yet also in the core of his communal culture. The individual maintains a sense of ethnicity, and communal culture, as part of the personality. Events in the present which remind one of a past ethnic history may affect decisions made in the future. Such was the experience of a young Black woman who considered her past and its implications for the future. The memories were dim and called forth in response to a class assignment focused on exploring family origins:

There were always sports persons like Joe Lewis and Jackie Robinson to be proud of but they [the media] never mentioned Paul Robeson or Marcus Garvey. I used to go to the movies and watch Tarzan kill *those* savages. After several movies it finally dawned on me that those savages were actually *my* people. Today, I go out of my way to instill racial pride in my children and make sure they are aware of Third World people.

The same assignment surfaced other dim identifications with a Jewish tradition:

Education was of prime importance to him [my father], followed closely by social class, religion and background. Most of my parents' teachings influenced me in other ways. It was understood that I would attend college. . . . This push toward the pursuit of education and the importance of proper background influenced me in the rearing of my daughters.

In both of these instances the personality of the mothers has been influenced by the core of the communal culture with a connection to a clearly identifiable ethnic history. They recognize that their ethnic experiences influence the way they relate to their children.

A final example highlights the integration of the communal culture into the personality and lifestyle of two generations. In this instance the writer has adult children, who as she states are somewhat removed from their Italian background. Nevertheless, she notes:

My grown son on occasion will request that I 'make one of them ethnic meals.' When my daughter visits she always tries to time her trip to coincide with some ethnic event. She will be coming home this week-end and we will be going to New York to the Feast of San Genaro in Little Italy. We will partake of some Italian cooking specialties and atmosphere. On these occasions I always feel proud of being Italian.

Each individual has an ethnic history with roots in the past. Traditions, customs, rituals, and behavioral expectations all interface with life in America. These aspects of the past have the potential of affecting perceptions of problems in the present. For those Slavics who were raised with the expectation that intergenerational support is or should be available, its absence may be particularly disquieting and in the extreme devastating. The individual and collective history of Blacks suggests that there are resources available in the time of trouble. Families across the social classes respond to the needs of kin, both emotional and financial. The response in either instance may rest upon an awareness, articulated or not, of the past (Stack, 1975; Krause, 1978).

We assume then that in any situation which comes to the attention of the social worker, part of the response to that situation derives from individuals' sense of past as it is intertwined with their personal history. Experience with the ethnic reality is an integral part.

The present is most important

The past affects and gives shape to problems manifested in the present. Social work's major obligation is to attend to current issues, with full awareness that the distribution and incidence of problems is often related to the ethnic reality. Thus alcohol-related problems are extensive among American Indians. A disproportionate number become alcoholics and develop the medical problems associated with chronic heavy drinking. Suicide and homicide rates among some tribes are increasing, as is the incidence of child abuse in urban centers (President's Commission on Mental Health, 1978; Westermeyer, 1974). These problems require attention in the present. Socioeconomic well-being is threatened. The contact with urban America has had particularly negative effects on American Indians. The pride and noble sense of self and tribe so intrinsic to American Indian life must be drawn upon as a mechanism and source of strength for dealing with current problems.

Continued racism has generated a massive Black underclass. Close to 40% of young Black Americans are unemployed or underemployed. Educational deficits persist for this group as well as for many Puerto Ricans and Chicanos.

Understanding and knowledge of the history, customs, and beliefs are required for effective practice, both at the individual and the institutional level. Appreciation for customs and beliefs is essential in response to diverse problems. These are manifest in the wishes of members of many ethnic groups to "take care of their own" in times of trouble. The infant daughter of a paranoid schizophrenic Italian woman needs placement. The schizophrenia is the major problem. It is the grandfather's wish that a cousin adopt the child, thereby keeping her within the family. The ethnic-sensitive worker will realize that the grandfather's effort to keep the infant in the family may well be founded upon the sociopolitical history of Southern Italy. In the midst of that political turmoil the family was the only social structure upon which an individual could depend. Survival depended upon a strong interdependence between family members which influenced all areas of life. It was a bulwark against those who were not blood relatives (Papajohn and Spiegel, 1975). Yet cousins may not be in the position to offer care in the "old country way" envisioned by the father. At the same time, workers must not only recognize this disposition, but make every effort to help the family explore those family resources which will minimize an already traumatic situation.

The current problem must always receive primary attention. However, the practitioner must recognize that ethnic group history may affect present perception of the problem and its solutions.

The ethnic reality is a source of cohesion, identity, and strength or strain, discordance, and strife

In Chapter 1, the effects of ethnicity and social class were sketched in broad outline. Attention is now focused on those specific components of the ethnic reality which serve as sources of cohesion, identity, and strength, as well as sources of strain, discordance, and strife.

The family. As one of the major primary groups the family is responsible for the care of the young, transmission of values, and emotional sustenance. It is a source of the strength, identity, and cohesion mentioned. All families are expected to carry out such tasks.

The value placed on the family and the extent of commitment to involvement in the solution of diverse family problems varies by ethnicity and social class. Attention must be paid to how these same values may produce strain, clash, or conflict with the demands and prejudices of the larger society. Particular cohesive family structures may be observed in the response of Navajo Indians to family problems. It is expected that aunts, cousins, sisters, and uncles all share in the burden of child-rearing and help out with problems. Relatives do not live far away from one another. Old people give guidance to their children and grandchildren (Jimson, 1977). There is strength in this bond. The family becomes a resource when the courts have questions related to child neglect and custody.

Chicanos, Puerto Ricans, Asians, and many Eastern Europeans have similar attitudes toward family obligations.

The sense of family cohesion often diminishes in the second and third generation of immigrants or migrants. The family as transmitter of old values, customs, and language is often seen as restrictive by members of the younger generation.

> Zaidia Perez is a single parent, estranged from her family. She has violated a family expectation by refusing to marry the father of her children. Her Puerto Rican extended family withholds the support usually offered. The result is a life of loneliness and isolation. There is the additional turmoil which comes from Ms. Perez's struggle with her ethnic reality. She is a poor Puerto Rican. It is her conviction that her Spanish heritage and dark coloring have denied her entrance into the middle class. In response she attempts to reject her background by refusal to associate with other Puerto Ricans in the neighborhood.

Zaidia's struggle with the ethnic reality denies her those supports which come from affable relationships with family and neighbors. Some of that support is provided by ritual and other celebrations.

Rituals and celebrations. As Puerto Ricans celebrate "Nuech Buena" (Christmas Eve) there is a feeling of relaxation, of caring, and of temporary retreat from problems. The extended family gathers with close friends to celebrate "The Good Night." The regular diet of rice and beans becomes more elaborate—yellow rice and pigeon peas are most important, as is the *pernil asalo* (roast pork).

The ethnic church—Italian, Polish and Black, and the Jewish synagogue—is where those with similar histories and like problems gather to affirm their identity and beliefs. This is enhanced by feast days, which combine reverence with ethnic tradition.

The Academy Award–winning film, "The Deer Hunter," vividly depicts how rituals and the church serve to buttress and sustain. A wedding takes place in the "Russian Orthodox Church with its spirals that might well have been set in the steppes of the Urals" (Horowitz, 1979). The old Russian women carry cake to the hall for the wedding of one of three young men about to go off to war in Vietnam. There is joyous celebration, Russian folk-singing, and "good old-fashioned patriotism." These second-generation, working-class Russian Americans have strong allegiances to this, "their native land." The wedding provides the occasion for the community's show of love and support as their young men go off to war.

There is excitement in rituals and celebrations. For weeks or days before the event family members in many ethnic groups prepare for Rosh Hashanah, Yom Kippur, Christmas, weddings, and saints' days. Yet, on each of these occasions there is the potential for stress. Each participant does not have the same perception of the event.

Sax (1979) describes his return to his parents' home for the Jewish holidays. No matter what your age, as a child you are assigned a seat at the dining room table. He is a single male and at *shul* fellow worshippers offer condolences to his parents, who try to be stoic on the matter. But it is time he were married. Proud to be a Jew, he returns to his home for the celebration of Yom Kippur. But he has not fulfilled a communal obligation and the strain seeps through, even on this holiest of days.

For, just as the ritual is an occasion for joy and celebration, it is also a time when the young are reminded of transgressions or departures from tradition. Perhaps the David Saxes will think twice about returning for the next celebration.

Ethnic schools and parochial schools. The Hebrew School, the Hungaran or Ukrainian language school, and parochial schools are examples of mechanisms for the preservation of language, rituals, and traditions.

Some, like the after-school language programs, are used to supplement the education provided in secular public schools. Many Jewish children go to Hebrew school sponsored by synagogues in the afternoons and on weekends. There they prepare for the Bar or Bat Mitzvah and learn Hebrew, Jewish history, and the details of ritual. Many Eastern Europeans have after-school programs in which the native language is taught. These often become social centers. Not infrequently these are located in the old city neighborhoods. Second- and third-generation families who have moved to the suburbs provide the financial support by which these schools and the ethnic churches are sustained. The tie to the old generation and its values is often maintained through such schools.*

---

*For example, New Brunswick, New Jersey, is the center of an old Hungarian community. Although the number of Hungarian American families that continue to live there is small, and those who do are aging, there are flourishing Hungarian banks, churches, and schools. The city is viewed as a regional center for Hungarian America in three surrounding states.

The young do not always feel the need for such an experience. While they attend after-school programs, other children are involved in a variety of activities from which they are excluded. The feeling of strain is expressed by a young adult as he recalls his childhood experience: "I went to Hebrew school and felt left out of things that went on in the neighborhood. Hebrew school was two afternoons a week and Sunday morning. So, I couldn't belong to Little League, or play Pop Warner football and do the normal things other kids did."*

Parochial schools in many neighborhoods are expected to transmit ethnic tradition and values, as are the many secular ethnic schools. They assure a continuation of the faith as well as a place in which morality and social norms may be reinforced.

In this design there are inherent conflicts as ethnic neighborhoods change. Gans' (1962) study of the Italians of Boston's West End describes such a neighborhood in which the church and its school were founded by the Irish who slowly moved away and were replaced by Italians. The church, however, retained Irish priests and lay leaders. Dedicated Italian Catholics often complained that the school was indoctrinating their children in Irish Catholicism. Rather than providing the solace anticipated for association with church-related institutions, discordance is quite evident.

An example of the stress that may come from such a conflict is provided by an Italian who attended such a school:

> I like being Italian. I grew up in a mixed neighborhood. But it wasn't mixed in terms of what the authority was in relation to church and school if you were Catholic. It was Irish. . . . I went to a parochial school run by Irish nuns and priests. That is important to mention because there was an insensitivity to our cultural needs at the time. . . . The Americanization of the Italians was a cultural genocide, at least when I grew up. St. Patrick's Day would come and we would all celebrate. . . . Obviously there were other saints who were Italian but the cultural aspects, the cultural pride was not brought in the way St. Patrick was.†

The ethnic church through its schools has the ability to provoke discomfort in students and parents when it does not provide the opportunity for affirmation by all ethnic groups who attend.

---

*Conversation with David Jacobson.   †Interview with Frank Becallo, MSW.

Language. Most immigrant and migrant groups are identified with a past which includes a language other than English. That language is variously used by or familiar to first-, second-, and third-generation children of immigrants. Each language generates a unique ambience and contributes to a group's "Weltanschaung" (Sotomayor, 1977). Although language can serve as a self- and group-affirming function, and the bilingual individual is to be admired, the continued use of the second language often generates problems. This is particularly true in those institutions which refuse to listen to anything but mainstream words. Yet, as has been suggested, the language can function as "solution" in an alien place. For Chicanos, Puerto Ricans, and many others, linquistic identification and affirmation can serve to ease internal stress imposed by political, economic, and social degradation.

The number of Hispanic and Asian immigrants has sharply increased in recent years (President's Commission on Mental Health, 1978; Vidal, 1980). Many groups, especially many Hispanics, reject the notion that they abandon their language and its associated culture. Bilingual education, which facilitates the acquisition of skills needed for participation in the economic sector of society, is strongly supported. Many minorities view this as essential, refusing to relinquish this basis of uniqueness. Nevertheless "talking funny" attracts attention and increases the risk of being called "dumb" wop, polak, spick, or chink.

Language—the sounds of discord. The effect of mainstream negation of native language has already been noted. There are those group members who consciously deny their native language as a way of "losing" their ethnicity. To speak Italian, Polish, Hungarian, Chinese, or Spanish may well cause strain for those who feel this inhibits their efforts to become American.

In the struggle to become American, Rose Mary Posen (1976) did not speak Slovenian, the language of her birth, from the time she entered high school until she reached womanhood. When addressed in that language, more often than not she did not respond.

Names like Franzyshen, Bastianello, and Turkeltaub attract attention. Teachers, employers, and new acquaintances stumble and often resist attempts to learn how to pronounce these names, yet many maintain these names with pride.

Nonconscious phenomena affect functioning

A comprehensive body of literature has developed which addresses the extent to which social workers must attend to or be aware of the nonconscious, unconscious, or preconscious aspects of human functioning. Hollis (1972) points out that there is some confusion about the meaning of the unconscious and the preconscious. There is consensus that in their contacts with social workers people often refer to "hidden" feelings, "vague and obscure thoughts and memories." Turner (1979) suggests that there are significant portions of the personality that are not available to the conscious mind. Hollis' treatment of the subject is thorough. There is little question that matters of which people are unaware or cannot articulate affect their behavior and feelings.

There is a dimension to non-conscious phenomena which is particularly important in relation to the ethnic reality.

In Chapter 1, culture was defined as involving perspectives on the rhythm and patterns of life which are conveyed in myriad ways. Nonconscious phenomena are operative when we speak of the "routine and habitual dispositions to life which become so thoroughly a part of the self that they require no examination." These dispositions, not articulated, go to the core of the self. The rhythm of Polish community life may be conveyed through the sounds heard by children as they grow. The sounds become routine, an accepted part of life; they are not examined for meaning. They may evoke joy or sadness for reasons unknown to the listener. The Polish experience is described: "The sounds emanating from our home were a potpourri of language, music and shouts. . . . We were a rather emotional and demonstrative family. Laughter and tears, anger and affection were fully given vent. . . . We were often headstrong, hasty, sinning, repenting, sinning and repenting again" (Napierkowski, 1976).

Nonconscious factors as identified by certain aspects of psychoanalytic theory do affect individuals. Some culturally induced or derived nonconscious dispositions are an intrinsic component of emotional response.

PRACTICE PRINCIPLES

An eclectic theoretical framework focused on various measures of human functioning has been developed. Particular attention has been paid to those components of theory which serve to heighten attention to the role of social class and ethnicity.

The assumptions on which this model is based generate several perspectives on practice.

The first calls attention to the fact that the paths to social work services are varied. We refer to these variations as "The Route to the Social Worker" and suggest how that route affects problem definition and intervention.

The other relates to the need for simultaneous or sequential attention to individual and collective concerns, as these emerge out of client need and professional assessment. Both reflect the view that "private troubles are examples of public issues, and public issues are made up of many private troubles" (Schwartz, 1969).

The route to the social worker

During the past decade social work theoreticians have increasingly stressed the need to focus on problems as perceived and defined by clients. This is a response to some aspects of past practice where worker, rather than client definitions were given major attention in problem solving. In the view of many theoreticians, psychodynamically oriented workers were particularly prone to emphasize "nonconscious" factors and to minimize those concerns consciously articulated by clients. The following is illustrative: A woman seeks help from a family counseling center because of continuing tensions and quarrels between herself and her husband. An assessment may suggest that she is constantly seeking from her husband the affection she never had from her father, or that her husband is responding in adverse ways to her demands for reconsideration of her traditional woman's role. In either instance this was not the problem as presented by the client. Such problem definition deflects attention from the current aspects of her life situation which may be sustaining the problem. These may derive mainly from emotional tension or concrete problems such as inadequate housing in which to raise a family or insufficient income.

Another area of concern focuses on those aspects of practice wherein a certain degree of paternalism is evident. The assumption is made that the worker's definition of the problem is *more* legitimate, *more* valid than the client's. In this sense problems are attributed to clients which they neither experience nor articulate.

Consider the following common situation: A young woman turns to the public welfare department for Aid for Dependent Children after her husband deserts her and their newborn child. Her request is for financial aid. In the assessment phase the worker assumes that the problem is one of immaturity, and therefore she is unable to care for her infant child adequately. This can be "corrected," however, by participation in a counseling group for young mothers.

This is not an uncommon assumption. Indeed, Mullen, Chazin, and Feldstein (1970) carried out a major investigation based on the assumption that intensive professional casework services would decrease rates of disorganization presumed to be associated with entering the welfare system. Reid and Epstein (1972) have grappled with these and related issues by making the distinction between attributed and acknowledged problems (see Chapter 4). In their view the mother described above should receive counseling services only if she feels in need of them or if her child is in danger. If the latter is the case, a social control, not a treatment function, would be exercised.

This is an important distinction which highlights the need to work with people on issues they define as important. Nevertheless the continuing discussion about the distinction between real and presenting problems and the more current debate about the difference between attributed and acknowledged problems does not fully address the reality. People get to service agencies through various routes. Their problems for the most part are very real. Whether or not they perceive the social worker as a potential source of help in the terms defined by social work practice is another issue. Much of service is rendered in contexts which have a coercive or nonvoluntary component. This is illustrated by what we term the "Routes to the Social Worker." These routes may be plotted along a continuum which ranges from total coercion to totally voluntary request for service. The continuum and examples of types of clients who may fall into each category are shown in Table 1.

As Table 1 shows, whether involvement with social work services is voluntary or coercive is in large measure related to the context in which service is rendered or to what some term the social work "field of practice." This does not negate the fact that there are voluntary and coercive elements in all fields of practice. Parolees do request social work services; by the same token, many people seek family counseling services under duress.

It is suggested that vulnerability to coercive involvement is greater for those who are poor or of ethnic minority status. Not in-

Table 1. Routes to the social worker

Routes to the social worker	Clients	Fields of practice
Totally coercive	Clients assigned by the courts to probation, parole; protective services	Child welfare Corrections
Highly coercive	Welfare clients expected to enter job training or counseling in order to maintain eligibility; person assigned to drug rehabilitation center or Job Corps as an alternative to jail	Public welfare Corrections
Somewhat coercive	Patient involvement with hospital for social worker discharge planning; interview with school social worker to maintain child's presence in school; employer suggests alcohol treatment program	Health services Schools
Somewhat voluntary	Husband enters marriage counseling at wife's request	Mental health Family services
Highly voluntary	Family enters into treatment at the suggestion of the clergy	Mental health Family services
Totally voluntary	Individual presents self to family counseling; psychotherapist	Family services Private practice

frequently, a coercive element is introduced by differences related to cultural or class conflict. For example, the process of institutionalizing mentally retarded children of working-class background is frequently initiated by "official caretakers." Investigation shows that many families with such children do not perceive their children's behavior as sufficiently disruptive to require institutionalization (Mercer, 1965).

There is a significant element of practice which is not subsumed in the "route to the social worker" delineated above. Reference is to "outreach," as exemplified by community development activities, public health, and preventive and educational efforts.

The "route to the social worker" has major affect on the initial approach to the client-worker encounter. If arrival is voluntary, the initial problem formulation is triggered by the social worker's question—"Why are you here?" When coercion has played a major part in the involuntary route the initial question may be posed by the client—"Why am I here?" The burden then rests on the social worker to engage the client.

In outreach the worker poses the question: "Will you come to see me or can we join together?" There is the assumption that people have problems, acknowledged, attributed, or articulated, with which the social worker can help. The client's formulation of the problem has primacy. However, professional practice is based on the assumption that the social worker has a unique contribution to make in assessing, defining, and contributing to problem resolution.

It is clear that many people become involved with social welfare delivery systems whether or not they acknowledge a problem. Given this, the following formulation is proposed:

1. Initial problem definition and formulation is in large measure related to the "Route to the Social Worker"
2. Regardless of that route, social worker's responsibility is to cast the problem in terms of professional values and understanding

This suggests that, no matter who initiates the process of service delivery, the interface between private troubles and public issues is usually evident. The fact that some people are in need of public assistance is in large measure a function of societal forces which contribute to economic inequity. The insistence on job training for some reflects the societal value on work and on economic independence.

Social workers are obliged to be aware of the origins of such problems, as well as the route to the social worker as they function in these various arenas.

Simultaneous attention to micro and macro issues

The interface between private troubles and public issues is an intrinsic aspect of most approaches to social work practice.

All models identify systemic change efforts or "environmental work" as a component of professional function. The integration of individual and systemic change efforts is a basic component of the model of ethnic-sensitive practice presented here. Such integration is essential if practice is to be responsive to the particular needs and sensitivities of various groups and individuals.

Particular attention is focused on the structural source of problems and on those actions which "adjust the environment to the needs of individuals" (Middleman and Goldberg, 1974).

Practice is a problem-solving endeavor (Perlman, 1957). Problems are generated at the interface between people and their environment. Many of the problems with which social workers deal involve economic and social inequity and its consequences for individuals. This inequity is frequently experienced at the individual and small group level.

Ethnic-sensitive practice calls particular attention to the individual consequences of racism, poverty, and discrimination. Examples are internalization of those negative images the society holds of disvalued groups, or learning deficits which are a consequence of inadequate education provided for minorities.

Members of all groups experience some difficulties in their intimate relationships, become ill, and struggle to master the varying tasks associated with different stages of the life cycle. Simultaneous attention to micro and macro tasks focuses the social worker's attention on individual problems at the same time as the systemic source of and possible solution of difficulty is recognized. Support for personal change efforts and help in altering dysfunctional behaviors is crucial.

A useful framework for highlighting the process of simultaneous attention to micro and macro tasks is the one presented by Middleman and Goldberg (1974). They identify practice as bounded by locus of concern (the problem calling for social work intervention) and persons engaged (persons and/or institutions involved as a consequence of the problems being confronted). This formulation suggests an approach to intervention, which in their terms "follows the demands of the client task."

The social worker must look beyond the problems presented by individual clients to see if there are others suffering from the same problem. The perspective also serves to call attention to those community and ethnic networks in which people are enmeshed and which can be called upon to aid in problem resolution.

Problems, as identified by the client or social worker, have diverse sources and call for a variety of systemic and individual action. This may be seen in the following example: A Jewish boy may feel torn between parental injuncture not to become involved in celebration of Christmas and his need to join the children in his public school as they trim Christmas trees and sing carols. The turmoil may result in the child becoming withdrawn and searching for reasons not to go to school. Support and counseling from the school social worker may be needed. This may be particularly true if there are few other Jewish children in the school, and if alternate sources of support and identity affirmation are not available. At the same time, actions may be projected designed to enhance cultural diversity and respect for and knowledge of diverse customs. Suggestions that the school incorporate celebrations unique to various groups as part of the holiday celebration are part of the plan for action. The results provide an opportunity for Jewish children to tell about the tradition of Chanukah and Greek Orthodox children may share the fact that their holiday is celebrated at a different time and in some very unique ways.

Social workers must be attuned to both levels of intervention as they go about the task of helping people who are caught in the clash between varying cultures.

Many of the problems with which we deal involve inequity and discrimination. Systemic actions are often called for by the "presenting problems." If successfully carried out, such action can forestall or minimize similar problems for other people.

A number of cases are presented to illustrate how practice is enhanced when there is simultaneous attention to micro and macro level tasks, coupled with sensitivity to the ethnic reality.

> A Mexican-American woman accustomed to delivering her babies at home, surrounded by family and friends, suffers greatly when placed in the Anglo maternity ward. The sounds are unfamiliar to her and the strangers do not speak her language. She is denied privacy when she is placed in the labor room with other women. Wrapped in a towel, she gets up searching for familiar faces and more familiar sounds. Physical force may be used to return her to bed. She may be termed an uncooperative, unappreciative patient.
> (Brownlee, 1978)

Little consideration has been given to the possibility of adapting hospital procedures to meet the needs of a large Mexican American community in the area. Understanding of Chicano childbirth rituals would enhance the experience rather than induce terror in an alien setting. A variety of actions are required in this situation based on the assumptions and theoretical formulations previously discussed: (1) sociological insights call attention to the ethnic reality and suggest an explanation for the action of wandering out of the labor room—though the possibility of pathology must be explored, (2) the patient needs help to avoid a crisis, (3) alternatives to the alien delivery room structure need to be explored. "Birthing centers" may provide a more comfortable structure—one in which family members participate in the delivery process. This Chicano mother is an "involuntary" social work client. Yet, institutional and individual needs require the social worker's attention. The crisis nature of the situation compels quick action. Subsequent efforts to modify delivery procedures should involve Chicano women in the planning process.

> In the midst of a city, hidden within a Hispanic population, is a community of Russian Orthodox Jews. Their life is barren. Their housing is substandard. The few clothes that they own are threadbare. Many basic necessities of living are missing from their lives. Language separates them even more from the mainstream. A Russian-speaking outreach worker, from a community senior citizen program, discovers that a significant number of the adults are in need of health care. A particular need is in the area of nutrition. They do not get enough to eat. As a relationship develops they are able, with the worker assuming a broker role, to obtain the services of a local Nutrition for the Elderly Program which will respect their dietary tradition. Such an accommodation is accomplished with the rabbi of the community. Together they attempt to work this out, realizing that the nutrition program has no basic stake in providing services for members of this religious group. This response was noted despite the fact that the program's mandate was to meet the nutritional needs of the elderly. Special meals for the orthodox add to the program's work load. However, success means that not only will this group be fed but other ethnic groups will be more likely to have their requests heard.

The activity has provided regular, nutritious meals which meet dietary tradition through work with the elderly, their rabbi, and the various staff members and administrators of the Nutrition for the

Elderly Program. The outreach worker began from a point of sensitivity to the ethnic reality. Application of the principle of "following demands of the client task" was successful in beginning a process of change in the policy of a community service program.

Christine Taylor is a small, thin, Black woman in her middle years. She receives AFDC for herself and her two children, who are 10 and 8 years old. Her sister, Florence Jackson, lives in the same community.

During the past few years Ms. Taylor has had a number of medical problems, including a hysterectomy and a cerebrovascular accident, which caused paralysis of her left side. For some time she was bitter about her condition, feeling that she was being punished for her past wrongdoing, and suspected that the doctors were persecuting her. Her worker has assisted her in getting the resources necessary for her continued therapy and educational programs which meet the children's needs. Although the worker is unable to effect any increase in the family's meager income she is aware that they have sufficient food and the children are well clothed. Suspecting a hidden income the worker probes and discovers that Ms. Taylor is part of a community process known as "swapping." The primary participants are her sister Florence and their close friends. These women have lived on welfare for some time and have had little ability to accumulate a surplus of goods. They share food, clothing, and daily necessities. The limited supply in the community is continually redistributed among family and close friends. Without this system the sisters, their friends, and neighbors may not survive.

The practitioner who is aware of this survival technique which has grown out of the reality of the Black experience would not have assumed that deviance, illicit relationships, and perhaps fraud were at work. Knowledge of the existence of such support systems could have minimized premature suspicion and harrassment.

Hidden in the community is another support which enables Ms. Taylor to cope with the guilt and anger she feels about her handicap. Sister Sawyer is an African healer. She claims to have been born in a little village in South Africa and believes a special blessing has been given to her which enables her to remove evil spells, change luck from bad to good, ease pain, and remove unnatural illness. From Sister Sawyer Ms. Taylor receives comfort, reassurance that she is indeed a special person, as well as potions and scriptures which will assist in her need for affirmation.

In this situation two environmental supports of the type often overlooked or considered illegitimate have been identified. If the principle of maximizing potential supports in the client's environment is to be applied, then ethnic coping practices must be viewed as valid. More extensive knowledge of these practices may enable the practitioner to enhance the established structures. "Swapping" is a well-established custom but may be enhanced if the network is enabled to purchase in bulk from a local cooperative, known to the practitioner and used by the entire community. This would make more commodities available to the group at lower prices, thus maximizing the benefits of a well-established and useful custom.

> A young probationer was under court supervision and had strict orders to remain with responsible adults. His counselor became concerned because the youth appeared to ignore this order. The client moved around frequently and, according to the counselor, stayed overnight with several different young women. The counselor presented this case at a formal staff meeting, and fellow professionals stated their suspicion that the client was either a pusher or a pimp. The frustrating element to the counselor was that the young people knew each other and appreared to enjoy each other's company. Moreover, they were not ashamed to be seen together in public with the client. This behavior prompted the counselor to initiate violation proceedings.
> (Red Horse, 1978)

This counselor is unaware that these young women are functioning as a support system for his client. They are in fact his first cousins, who are viewed in the same way as sisters. He has been obeying the orders of the court and staying with different units within his family network, which includes over 200 people and spans three generations. With this knowledge of this client's ethnic reality the system can be recognized and encouraged. Appropriate family members may be enlisted to participate in plans for the future.

Many additional examples could be given. Individual problems often surface the need for changes in agency policy and administrative practices. Client concerns continually highlight the need for change in existing legislation, the development of new public policy, and research on appropriate service delivery.

The examples have pointed to the need for sensitive awareness of unique cultural patterns whether the service rendered involves one-to-one counseling with individuals or the need to adapt or develop community programs consonant with the ethnic reality. Each of these and other types of services call for an extensive repertoire of skills. The principle of "following the demand of the client task" suggests that client need shall determine the nature of the service rendered. In the example cited earlier of the pregnant Chicano woman who runs out of the labor room searching for a familiar face, a number of interventive tasks are suggested. "On-the-spot intervention" calls for the ability to help her to minimize her fears and avert a crisis. A long-range perspective points to the need to adapt hospital routines in a manner congruent both with the perspective of other Chicano women like her and good medical practice. If practitioners are to respond to diverse consumer needs they must be aware of the range of activities commonly suggested by any one problem.

All of these activities involve extensive skill, which will be considered in the next chapter.

SUMMARY

The basic assumptions of ethnic-sensitive practice are:
1. Individual and collective history have bearing on problem generation and solution
2. The present is most important
3. Nonconscious phenomena affect individual functioning
4. Ethnicity is a source of cohesion, identity, and strength as well as a source of strain, discordance, and strife

In addition to these assumptions, ethnic-sensitive practice is based upon a particular set of principles, which include:
1. Simultaneous attention must be given to individual and systemic concerns as they emerge out of client need and professional assessment
2. Practice skills must be adapted to respond to the particular needs and dispositions of various ethnic and class groups
3. The "Route to the Social Worker" affects problem definition and intervention

REFERENCES

Bennett, Lerone, Jr. 1964. *Before the Mayflower: a history of the Negro in America 1619-1964* (rev. ed.). Chicago: Johnson Publishing Co., Inc.

Brownlee, Ann Templeton. 1978. *Community, culture and care—a cross-cultural guide for health workers.* St. Louis: The C. V. Mosby Co.

Cheng, Eva. 1978. *The elder Chinese.* San Diego: Center on Aging, San Diego State University.

Croog, Sydney, and Levine, Sol. 1977. *The heart patient recovers: social and psychological factors.* New York: Human Sciences Press.

Erikson, Erik H. 1960. *Identity, youth and crisis.* New York: W. W. Norton and Co., Inc.

Fischer, Joel. 1978. *Effective casework practice: an eclectic approach.* New York: McGraw-Hill Book Co.

Fujii, Sharon M. 1976. "Elderly Asian Americans and use of public services." *Social Casework,* March.

Gans, Herbert J. 1962. *The urban villagers.* New York: The Free Press.

Hollis, Florence. 1972. *Casework: a psychosocial therapy* (ed. 2). New York: Random House, Inc.

Horowitz, Irving Louis. 1979. "On relieving the deformities of our transgressions." *Society, 16*(5), July/August.

Howe, Irving. 1975. "Immigrant Jewish families in New York: the end of the world of our fathers." *New York, 8*(41), October 13.

Jimison, Leonard B. 1972. "Parent and child relationships in law and in Navajo custom." In Unger, Steven (Ed.). *The destruction of American Indian families.* New York: Association of American Indian Affairs.

Kitano, Harry H. L. 1976. *Japanese Americans* (ed. 2). Englewood Cliffs, N. J.: Prentice Hall, Inc.

Krause, Corinne Azen. 1978. *Grandmothers, mothers and daughters: an oral history study of ethnicity, mental health and continuity of three generations of Jewish, Italian and Slavic American women.* New York: The American Jewish Committee.

Levy, Charles. 1973. "The value base of social work." *Journal of Education for Social Work, 9,* Winter.

Lum, Doman, Cheng, Lucia Yim-San, Cho, Eric Ray, and Tang, Tze-Yee. 1980. "The psychosocial needs of the Chinese elderly." *Social Casework, 60*(2), February.

Mercer, Jane R. 1972. "Career patterns of persons labeled as mentally retarded." In Freidson, Eliot and Lorber, Judith (Eds.). *Medical men and their work.* Chicago: Aldine-Atherton.

Middleman, Ruth, and Goldberg, Gale. 1974. *Social service delivery: a structural approach to practice.* New York: Columbia University Press.

Mullen, Edward, Chazin, Robert, and Feldstein, David. 1970. *Preventing chronic dependency.* New York: Community Service Society.

Napierkowski, Thomas. 1976. "Stepchild of America: growing up Polish." In Novac, Michael (Ed.). *Growing up Slavic in America.* Bayville, N.Y.: EMPAC.

Papajohn, John, and Spiegel, John. 1975. *Transactions in families.* San Francisco: Jossey-Bass Publishers.

Pincus, Allen, and Minahan, Anne. 1973. *Social work practice: model and method.* Itasca, Ill.: F. E. Peacock Publishers, Inc.

The President's Commission on Mental Health. 1978. *Task Panel Report*, Vol. III, Appendix.

Prosen, Rose Mary. 1976. "Looking back." In Novac, Michael (Ed.). *Growing up Slavic in America*. Bayville, N.Y.: EMPAC.

Red Horse, John G., Lewis, Ronald, Feit, Marvin, and Decker, James. 1978. "Family behavior of urban American Indians." *Social Casework*, 50(2).

Reid, William R., and Epstein, Laura. 1972. *Task-centered casework*. New York: Columbia University Press.

Sax, David B. 1979. "A holiday at home, a widening gulf." *New York Times*, September 27.

Schwartz, William. 1978. In Schulman, Lawrence. *The skills of helping individuals and groups*. Itasca, Ill.: F. E. Peacock Publishers, Inc.

Simic, Andrei. 1978. "Winners and losers: aging Yugoslavs in a changing world." In Myerhoff, Barbara G. and Simic, Andrei (Eds.). *Life career—aging: cultural variations on growing old*. Beverly Hills: Sage Publications.

Sotomayor, Marta. 1977. "Language, culture and ethnicity in the developing self-concept." *Social Casework*, 58(4), April.

Stack, Carol B. 1974. *All our kin—strategies for survival in a Black community*. New York: Harper & Row, Publishers.

Turner, Francis J. 1978. *Psychosocial therapy*. New York: The Free Press.

Vidal, David. 1980. "Living in two cultures: Hispanic New Yorkers." *New York Times*, May 11-14.

West, Richard. 1980. "An American family." *Texas Monthly*, 8(3), March.

Westermeyer, Joseph. 1974. "The drunken Indian: myth and realities." In Unger, Steven (Ed.). *The destruction of the American Indian family*. New York: Association of American Indian Affairs.

Zborowski, Mark, and Herzog, Elizabeth. 1952. *Life is with people: the culture of the shtetl*. New York: Schocken Books.

PART

II

ETHNIC-SENSITIVE PRACTICE

Part II is designed to illustrate the model of ethnic-sensitive practice in action.

In Chapter 6, four stages of social work activity are identified. The basic generic skills associated with these stages are reviewed and defined. For each set of skills, a series of suggestions, termed "adaptation to the ethnic reality," are presented. These are focused on such issues as the information needed before beginning involvement with clients, the importance of understanding the community context, the appropriateness of seeking early self-disclosure and discussion of emotional issues, and the use of contracting, concrete services, community action, and the like.

Each of the following three chapters is focused on work in a particular field of practice: social work practice with families, social work in health care, and social work with recipients of aid to dependent children.

In bringing the model to bear on three fields of practice we suggest how the basic components of the model can be integrated with the body of concepts and themes which have special relevance for any particular arena of practice.

The social worker who is involved with families must be aware of family dynamics, the function of the family in American society, and the way the family is viewed by different ethnic and class groups. The health care social worker needs to understand how health and illness are defined, and the fact that the response to illness is frequently shaped by deeply ingrained cultural dispositions. Those who work with people receiving public assistance need knowledge about how those who are dependent on public support are viewed by the larger society and how these views shape the self-images of public assistance recipients.

In these and other areas of practice, social workers should be familiar with prevailing policies and resources and how services are organized.

Throughout this section, effort is made to highlight the micro and macro tasks generated by specific client problems and by the perspective developed here. Case examples illustrate how understanding of the impact of social class, ethnicity, life cycle stages, self-awareness, and specialized knowledge converge to aid in assessment and suggest directions for intervention.

Implementation of the proposed intervention strategies requires adaptation of skills as was proposed in Chapter 5. Attention is called to how the "route to the social worker" both constrains and enhances practice in the three areas.

David Antebi

CHAPTER

6

Adaptation of skills for ethnic-sensitive practice

In this chapter, emphasis is on social work skills and how those skills most commonly used by social workers in a variety of practice situations may be adapted in order to take into account the various ethnic and class dispositions to seeking and obtaining help.

In introducing the area of skill it is important to note that considerably less attention has been paid to "the what and how" of practice than to the theories and philosophy of intervention. Nevertheless, major strides have been made in filling this gap. Middleman and Goldberg (1974), Eagan (1975), Fischer (1978), Shulman (1979), and others have variously described important components of skill. Most importantly, considerable research has been carried out to determine how the characteristics of worker-client relationships affect problem resolution (Fischer, 1978; Shulman, 1978, 1979; Truax and Mitchell, 1971). Researchers have, however, paid limited attention to how skill and technique need to be modified to conform to cultural and ethnic dispositions. We suggest such modifications derived from the work of the writers referred to earlier. For just as we have not "invented" a new form of social work practice, we do not presume to generate a new body of practice skills. Rather, we present a composite of those skills repeatedly identified in the social work and related literature, and suggest how they might be adapted in keeping with the ethnic reality.

In reviewing practice skills and their adaptation to the ethnic reality, focus is on various stages of the intervention process. All encounters have a beginning and take place in certain contexts. At some point the work proceeds, sometimes falteringly, only to move forward again. Usually, there is a point of termination. These stages of social work activities consist of four phases:

1. The work prior to involvement
2. The work of finding out what the problem is
3. Working on the problem
4. Termination

Identification of these stages of the interventive process does not imply that clearly distinct skills are called for in each stage. Indeed, there is more overlap than uniqueness. However, the skills involved in meeting with an individual or group for the first time do differ from those called for when a relationship has been in process for a while. And the act of termination is not the same as trying to assess what the problem is.

Ethnic-sensitive practice is first and foremost good social work practice. In view of this, the basic skills or guidelines for any one phase of practice are first reviewed and identified as generic skills and principles. Where applicable, these are followed by suggestions for adaptation to the ethnic reality.

WORK PRIOR TO INVOLVEMENT

There is much work to be done before contact is initiated. One level of that "work" involves efforts to learn about the community where service is rendered, acquiring knowledge about the particular types of problems which usually come to the attention of the agency, and developing self-awareness in relation to these problems. Another aspect of the work focuses on the types of data which can or should be gathered prior to meeting with any one individual or group.

Understanding of the community

Knowledge about the community in which services are located is essential. Population characteristics, the availability of resources, the type of government, the availability of transportation, and the prevailing community and neighborhood networks are but a few of the factors which bear on the ability to render service. A variety of tools exist which facilitate the process of becoming familiar with the community. Use of census materials, publications about the community, and interviews with community leaders are but a few of the available resources. It is incumbent upon agencies and practitioners to make use of these in order to develop a community profile.*

Knowledge of human behavior and self-awareness

The social worker has an obligation to draw on the general knowledge of human behavior which has been identified as the first "layer of understanding" and to assess how this interfaces with insight into the particular constellation of problems usually addressed in an agency. Knowledge about the feelings typically generated by the kinds of problems encountered in a setting is crucial.

Practitioners should be familiar with the prevailing trends in family life and with the concerns of those who find themselves in troubled family situations. The daily traumas of marital conflict may be compounded by a sense of personal failure, hostility, the threat of desertion, or economic strain. Work with ill people requires knowledge of the fact that many fear death, desertion, or limits on their mobility. Those who work in schools need to be familiar with theories of learning disability and who is at particular risk for developing school-related problems. These are examples of the kinds of knowledge which social workers must have.

Also important is the effort to learn how others who work in a system think, feel, and behave. This is particularly relevant in interdisciplinary settings. Workers employed in school systems where they function on teams of psychologists, teachers, and consulting psychiatrists must familiarize themselves with the kinds of problems usually brought to the team and how each discipline views its role. They should be clear about the linkage function between school, home, and other resources. They need to be aware of how they may have experienced problems in their own school work. If, as children, they had difficulty, are they likely to "overidentify?" Or, conversely, if their own school careers were extremely successful, how can they use this experience to help those in trouble? How can they *learn* to understand?

---

*See Appendix, which presents guidelines for developing such a profile.

Those who provide service in the criminal justice system need to know something of the adversary system, the law, and how people experience encounters with these awesome institutions.

The young, inexperienced worker with a middle-class background who sets out to organize tenants for better housing services needs to understand the fear of being evicted, the long-standing distrust of authority, and the anger and hostility of landlords who believe they have given "these folks" more than enough for the little rent they already pay.

Such orientation must become part and parcel of workers' thinking, acting, and feeling processes as they embark on work in various contexts.

A *generic* definition of the work which must be carried out before any one client or situation is addressed can now be presented:

> Skilled use of the accumulated knowledge of the types of problems and issues usually dealt with, including the community, the prevailing responses and concerns of people facing certain problems, and workers' own emotional responses to these issues.

What is involved is an emotional and intellectual awareness and readiness to listen and evoke meaningful responses and to draw on diverse resources. This "readiness" is derived from experience, from a conceptual stance that aids in thinking about the problems, and from awareness of the range and types of reactions usually evoked.

Adaptation to the ethnic reality. In approaching the work situation, the particular class and ethnic dispositions related to those issues which regularly surface in the work setting must always be considered. The emotional and intellectual stance referred to above includes a readiness to consider how one's own ethnic and class background affects responses.

If workers are themselves members of the ethnic groups usually served, they may have much "inside" knowledge. At the same time, they must be aware of and guard against the possibility of overgeneralizing from their own experience, or holding out particularly stringent expectations for behaviors they believe are related to their own ethnic group. For example, Puerto Rican workers in school systems may bring particular awareness of the strain and pulls evoked by bilingualism. They may understand the particular comfort the children experience in speaking Spanish to their peers, or know the taunts of teachers who admonish children to speak only English. As young people they may have accompanied their own mothers to the school, the welfare board, or the landlord to serve as translators. They may have experienced the frustration of trying to convey accurate meaning in a different language.

They must guard against approaching the situation by a stance which says "I made it, why can't you?" Such tendencies are not uncommon. Irish social workers have told us that, because they know that alcoholism is a particular problem for some Irish people, they expect Irish alcoholics to "shape up." Also instructive are the experiences of one of the authors of this book (EGS).

> Shortly after beginning practice as a young hospital social worker, I was asked to talk with the orthodox Jewish mother of a child admitted to the hospital because of infected rashes on the leg. The doctors thought that the rash may have begun or been exacerbated by dirt. They thought the child was seldom bathed.
>
> I immediately informed them that I would check—though it was most unlikely because Jews weren't dirty. This was indeed a unique referral involving a Jewish family. I told them that Jewish mothers fussed over and bathed their children a lot.
>
> Subsequent discussion revealed that the doctors had been correct. Not only did I feel chagrined but insulted that Jews should treat their children so.
>
> The initial stance, derived from my perception of "proper Jewish behavior," slowed the process of helping the mother to come to grips with the problem, for her Jewish neighbors and relatives had a similar disposition to mine. To help her to deal with the problem meant that a particular sensitivity to the failure she perceived had to be injected.

When workers are not members of the ethnic and class groups usually served they have the obligation to familiarize themselves with the culture, history, and ethnically related responses to problems.

Just as workers are responsible for learning basic principles of human behavior, they must become self-aware—both in the generic sense and at the level of understanding how their own ethnic background impacts on their behavior. We refer here to the "third layer of understanding."

Gathering data prior to the encounter

Much is usually known about a particular situation before contact begins. The generic work of gathering data prior to the encounter can be defined as the process of reviewing, synthesizing, and ordering information—both factual and emotional—concerning the client(s), the problem, and the route to the agency.

The nature and amount of information available varies. Where "on-the-spot" crisis intervention is rendered, little more may be known than the fact that someone has appeared at the welfare office alone and disoriented. The only information available may be the sex and race of the person and his or her approximate age. On the other hand, there are the extensive referral letters exchanged between agencies and other facilities. Considerable information may be conveyed in cases of neglect or abuse or in a referral from a physician or school for assessment of a child believed to have a developmental handicap. Where much information is available a number of generic skills and processes can be identified: (1) Review of available materials to obtain a picture of the problem. (2) Review of the "route to the social worker"; Chapter 5 contains considerable discussion of the meaning—to both clients and practitioners—of the process involved in getting to the agency. Those people who come on their own may have expressed an eagerness to get to work on a problem. Where the route has been "involuntary," as much information as possible concerning clients' feelings about coming to the agency should be obtained. (3) Efforts to distinguish the client's perception of the problem from the way others perceive it; this involves the distinction between "attributed" and "acknowledged" problems (see Chapter 4; also Reid, 1978). Attention should be paid to such statements by referral sources as: "This child acts out a great deal in school. His mother, Mrs. Jones, insists the teachers 'have it in for him' and find fault readily. Discussion with the teachers reveals that the child comes to school unkempt, looks tired, and on occasion has minor bruises on the arm." Child abuse is clearly implied; whether present or not, the mother does not acknowledge this problem. This difference in perception must be kept in mind by workers in their approach to the mother.

Before beginning the work there is much effort needed in "thinking through," synthesizing, and analyzing available facts and feeling.

Are bruises really indicative of abuse, or does this family consider hitting appropriate punishment for perceived misbehavior?

In processing data prior to the encounter workers inevitably make a preliminary or tentative assessment of what may be operative.

Adaptation to the ethnic reality. In this phase it is crucial that workers integrate and attend to such ethnic and class data as are available and be aware of gaps in the information. Some basic principles can be stated as follows:

1. Information on the ethnic reality should be obtained. Thus, if available information indicates that someone is "white" it is important to have information on the particular ethnic identity. Ample has been said about the differences between Jews and other whites of European ethnic origins, to suggest that the specific group membership may affect disposition to the problem.

2. Social class information should, when possible, be supplemented with information about the nature of the work people do. This is imperative for a number of reasons. In Chapter 1 the relationship between the type of work people do and the way they might feel about their ability to be autonomous and to control their lives was described. The images people have of themselves and those held by others may have great bearing on how they approach problem resolution.

3. In processing information about ethnic and class identity, it is important to be aware of the fact that many people are extremely sensitive on these matters. When the requisite information is not readily available, workers should be careful not to"jump in with all fours" to get it; rather they might wait for clues, asking as it seems appropriate.

4. The fear of racist or prejudiced orientations is never far from the minds of most minority or other disadvantaged people. Practitioners must constantly be alert to this possibility. This is particularly important where the clients are members of minority groups, and where worker and clients belong to different racial or ethnic groups (Brown, 1950; Curry, 1964; Gitterman and Schafer, 1972).

With this work done, attention can be focused on the encounter with the client.

THE WORK OF FINDING OUT WHAT THE PROBLEM IS
Launching the interaction process

Attention is first called to those skills involved in "launching the interaction process" (Middleman and Goldberg, 1974). These may be referred to as "entry skills" and are focused on those activities which are designed to create a comfortable environment for the interview or other form of interaction. These are known as (1) stage setting (Middleman and Goldberg, 1974); (2) "tuning in" (Shulman, 1979); and (3) attending (Egan, 1975).

Stage setting. Stage setting involves attention to the physical setting in which the interaction is going to take place and takes account of positioning vis-à-vis client. The purposive use of space in a sense presumed to enhance comfort and communication is basic.

There is little question that the prevailing norms of American society suggest that privacy is urgent. It is assumed that most people will feel more comfortable discussing their problems if they are not in danger of being overheard by strangers or other family members. By and large people are more comfortable if there is sufficient physical space to permit them to maintain some physical distance from each other; they may move closer together if the situation warrants. Settings which provide at least a minimal degree of physical comfort are thought to be essential. Cushioned, as contrasted with hard chairs, pleasantly painted, cheerful rooms, and a place to stretch one's legs are seen as highly desirable if not essential.

A mental review of many of the places where social workers meet their clients quickly leads to the realization that these generic guides to stage setting are often honored in the breach. Hospitalized patients who are unable to leave their beds usually share rooms with others. A curtain is the most deference to privacy which can be offered. When clients are visited in their homes, relatives, friends, or neighbors may be present. Large segments of the client population—particularly those served by underfunded public agencies—often encounter the worker in large offices occupied by many other people. At best there may be glass-enclosed cubicles in which the partitions do not reach the ceiling. Visits may be made in community center playrooms, libraries of jails, or empty cafeterias of residential centers. Each of these spaces is likely to be frequented by others. Many of these are regrettable structural facts which emerge out of society's low regard and lack of respect for those at the "bottom of the ladder."

Circumstances do exist in which interaction is most comfortable if carried out in "natural" or "convenient" settings. These include seeing the child in the playground or concerned relatives in a parking lot or restaurant during a lunch hour.

Social workers who are sensitive to the facts of space will learn to make adaptations. Where the interview with the hospitalized patient calls for as much privacy as possible, workers will draw the curtain and sit close. This closeness may be a compromise with the desire to maintain a comfortable physical distance, usually important in the early stages of building a relationship. Other compromises with privacy may be seen in the example of talking with youngsters in the community center lounge or with the residents in the institutional cafeteria. Workers will try to gauge to what extent they can create a "do not disturb" ambience by positioning; but by doing so, they must be careful not to embarrass those who are seeking or being offered service. Privacy should be guarded, but not at the expense of avoiding needed contact, or in a manner which publicly singles a person out. A conversation between two or more people in the midst of a crowded room can be more private than one held in a distant but readily spotted part of a public room.

Adaptation to the ethnic reality. The degree to which every effort should be made to adhere to the tenets of privacy will vary considerably by ethnic group membership. Many Eastern Europeans (e.g., Czechoslovakians, Estonians, Hungarians, Poles, and Ukrainians) are particularly "shamed" at having to ask for help (Giordano and Giordano, 1976). For members of these groups and others with similar dispositions, particular effort should be made to assure privacy and/or anonymity. When people who share these feelings are seen in the hospital, it would be wise to take off the white coat if it is customarily worn. After they have engaged in a private conversation with the curtain drawn, they may decide how to answer their neighbor's queries about who that "nice young woman was" who came to see them. They are then free to identify her as a family member, neighbor, *or* the social worker.

When the pain of getting help is almost as intense as the problem which generates it, a number of other concessions to privacy should be considered. Is a prearranged home visit for an intake interview for public assistance feasible? Can workers park their cars "around the corner?" Can workers dress in a manner which does not readily identify them? Can the mother of a disturbed youngster be seen in the school courtyard amidst a crowd? Is the sign on the van advising all that this is the "Senior Citizens' Nutrition Project" or the local "Economic Opportunity Corporation" necessary?

Not all possible concessions to privacy and anonymity can be spelled out. However, it is crucial that workers be aware of these possibilities and behave in a manner which opens up options. Some Slavics, Asians, and others may feel quite comfortable about being interviewed within earshot of their neighbors. However, unless given the choice workers may wonder why, despite sincere offers to help plan for their care, they were most uncommunicative.

There are other people who do not seem to mind discussion of certain private matters when others, unrelated to them, can hear. Many Jewish and Italian people are quite voluble and seem ready to express discomfort and pain publicly; some are given to reaching out for a sympathetic, interested ear (Zborowski, 1952). Dominick and Stotsky (1969) describe Italian nursing home residents who are always ready to converse with visitors about rooms, belongings, "anything at all."

It is possible that people with this kind of orientation may gain some satisfaction from the public visibility which is provided by the social worker's concern and attention. However, the possible satisfaction gained by visible attention to physical problems may not carry over to the situation where an application for public assistance, food stamps, or publicly subsidized housing is to be filed. This may represent loss of face and an earlier status of financial independence. In such situations generic rules of privacy apply. Efforts to learn with which kind of people privacy and anonymity are crucial should be of ongoing concern.

Tuning in

"Tuning in" has been defined as "development of the worker's preparatory empathy" (Shulman, 1979). Citing Schwartz, Shulman suggests that included are the worker's efforts to "get in touch with those feelings which may be implicitly or directly expressed in the interview." Although the process should begin before the encounter, it is ongoing and continues throughout the interaction. Shulman suggests that "tuning in" can take place at several levels. Several of these have been noted in other contexts. They include general knowledge of human behavior, articulation of that knowledge with the problems at issue, and the unique response of worker and client. The following case situation illustrates the articulation of several levels.

> A male school social worker knows that a 13-year-old boy has been referred because he is disruptive in school and is reading several years behind his grade level. The boy has recently transferred to the school as a result of moving into his third foster home this year.
>
> In synthesizing, "tuning in," and processing these facts, the worker draws on his general knowledge about the possible reasons for learning difficulty, family systems and how families absorb new members, and the dynamics involved in foster-parent/foster-child relationships.
>
> In "tuning in" to the situation of this child he should consider the possibility that the reading deficit may be a function of poor education, perceptual difficulty, or emotional distress. He needs to "think and feel" in advance about how alienated, isolated, lonely, and rejected this boy might be feeling. Perhaps the worker can recall an analogous experience he may have had. Did he go to summer camp when he really didn't want to? Was there ever a time when he was afraid his own parents had abandoned him? Did he ever experience a similar school failure?

These and many other examples indicate the varying processes involved in developing preparatory empathy.

Adaptation to the ethnic reality. Similar processes to those described above are involved in "tuning in" to the meaning of the experience to various ethnic groups. In the example cited above it is important to know that the young client is a Black child of lower-class background whose foster parents are Black, middle-class professional people living in a community composed predominantly of white people.

As a white male worker, he needs to review his own knowledge about the Black community and how class differences within that community manifest themselves. He needs to understand the strain which Black people living in a white neighborhood may be experiencing.

At an emotional level he needs to "feel through" his reactions to Black people, particularly adolescent boys. Is he afraid of physical aggression? Does he have a tendency to expect "less" academically from a Black youngster? Is he perhaps feeling that the white middle-class school has been invaded? Does he have a "feel" for how Black children might experience the white world? Does he understand the particular sense of distrust, inadequacy, and fear of not measuring up which many might share?

Many illustrations of the various levels of "tuning in" to ethnic dispositions can be cited. Repeated reference has been made to the frustrations of those whose command of the English language is limited, the feelings of those who sense that their culture and way of life are not respected and who distrust practitioners, particularly those not of their own group. Such matters should always be taken into consideration before an encounter.

Attending

Generically, attending refers to purposeful behavior designed to convey a message of respect and a feeling that what people are discussing is important. Attending skills include the ability to pay simultaneous attention to cognitive, emotional, verbal, and nonverbal behaviors (Middleman and Goldberg, 1974). Included are appropriate use of body language and dressing in a manner which those with whom contact is established consider appropriate.

Egan (1975) identifies the following aspects of "physical attending." He suggests that the other person should be faced squarely, that an "open" posture be adopted, that good eye contact be maintained, and that the practitioner lean toward the other. These aspects of physical attending let the other people know of the worker's active involvement and aids the practitioner in being an active listener. These postures aid in picking up both verbal messages and nonverbal clues. Under most circumstances it is important to maintain a relaxed, natural, comfortable posture and to use those spontaneous head, arm, and body movements which come naturally to workers in most interactive situations. Maintaining comfortable eye contact is customary in many contexts. In professional as well as personal interaction the use of friendly greetings is expected.

Put simply, when the encounter begins—whether with individual clients or with legislators whose aid is sought in supporting an important bill—it is crucial that initial approaches are made in a professional but human manner.

Adaptation to the ethnic reality. There are a number of groups whose members find it difficult to respond to the type of spontaneity and physical posturing described above. Toupin (1980) suggests that even acculturated Asians are likely to consider eye to eye contact as shameful. This is particularly true for women who believe "only street women do that." American Indians view the matter similarly. Eye contact may be indicative of lack of respect.

To the extent that practitioners are viewed as authority figures, and verbal communication about feelings as uncomfortable, some other modification of the physical aspects of attending should be considered. People feeling particularly shamed about needing help and viewing the practitioner as authoritative may be more comfortable when there is an air of formality. It is important, in this connection, that workers understand that for many people failure to respond to eye contact, sitting demurely, or not readily revealing feelings are not necessarily indicative of pathology.

Practitioners who truly attend will modify their behavior according to the knowledge they gain about the disposition of various groups.

At the time of the initial meeting, worker and clients usually have some information about the issue which has brought them together. Such additional data as are needed to proceed must then be obtained.

The nature of questioning

At this point some comments about the nature of questioning and listening are in order. These will be touched on here only briefly. There are many excellent works which treat the matter in detail, including the effects of race on the interview process.*

Two basic types of questions are identified: open- and close-ended. The former are used to explore and get a wide-ranging perspective on an issue; the latter "focus attention on key issues and clarify information provided" (Middleman and Goldberg, 1974).

For example, a client may say: "Things are really awful at home." In an open-ended question, the worker may reply: "Tell me more about that." At some point after a series of complaints have been aired and a lot of feeling ventilated, it may be appropriate to focus on what appears to be a key issue.

---

*See Kadushin, 1972, and Benjamin, 1969.

A male college student who has been doing poorly in his studies tells the worker that his instructors keep asking questions that he doesn't understand; that he studies as hard as any one else but doesn't seem to catch on. With sadness in his voice he says: "My mother was right when she said going to college was a bad idea."

The worker replies, "What's really bothering you is that you think you're not smart enough to go to college, isn't it?"

Open- and close-ended questions are usually alternated in an effort to get a clearer image of what the person is feeling and experiencing.

Adaptation to the ethnic reality. There are no ethnically relevant differences in the nature of questioning other than awareness of the kinds of questions different people can tolerate.

Reaching for facts and feelings

It is difficult, and often inappropriate, to separate the effort to obtain "facts" from that involved in understanding and gauging the associated feelings. In addition, obtaining information about facts and feelings is a two-way street.

Workers need to know what the problem is and how people feel about it. Clients need to know what information and resources are at the worker's disposal in order to try to help them with their problem. Will the worker give them money, help them find a job, tell them how to handle their children? They will want to know how the worker is likely to respond to their fears and aspirations, and to the problem itself. For example, youngsters in trouble with the law, people who have engaged in extramarital affairs, and those suffering from mental illness may be afraid that their behavior will be negatively judged.

In the course of obtaining information about facts and feelings the workers convey a sense of acceptance to the degree that ethics and law permit, and set a comfortable tone.

Reaching for feelings. The process of helping people to express and cope with feelings is an integral part of every professional endeavor. For social workers, the expression of feelings about self, others, and the institutions in which people are enmeshed is a basic and fundamental component of the work. Indeed, there are many situations in which the bulk of the work is devoted to listening to and exploring feelings. When other concerns exist, it is frequently impossible to proceed without first paying attention to feelings. If a neighborhood group is feeling outraged over the closing of a local health service, suggestions that a meeting be planned with the administrator are likely to go unheeded until the members have had the opportunity to express their rage.

Feelings, particularly those of a negative nature, must often be expressed before people can move forward to consider facts or suggestions for action.

Marital partners may not be able to talk about how to improve their strained relationship until they have ventilated their anger. Frustrated tenants may not be able to consider participating in a rent strike until they have "blown off steam" about poor conditions.

There will be many times during the first, as well as subsequent, encounter(s) when people will find it difficult to express what they are really feeling or really want to know. Often they may not know. Many times people do not express feelings which seem appropriate to the situation at hand. Workers need to be sure they understand what is being expressed.

The generic skills of "reaching for" or "obtaining" expression of feeling are encompassed in the core conditions of warmth, empathy, and genuiness. Essentially what is involved is the ability to "hear" and respond to tone, mood, absence of expression of feeling, and the nature of diversionary activities. For example, the hospitalized woman who is uncommunicative when the worker tries to interview her in her husband's presence may be letting the worker know that she does not want to discuss certain matters while her husband is there. The person who fidgets a great deal, fusses about chairs, or makes sure a door is closed may be fearful. The well-dressed young man who tells the child welfare worker matter of factly that he has been sent by his doctor to make arrangements for placement of his newborn mongoloid child may be harboring a great deal of shame and sadness.

In these and like instances it is most important that the worker "reach for feelings," obtain and give information.

Middleman and Goldberg (1974) define reaching for feelings as: ". . . the process of asking others if they are experiencing a particular emotion presumed to be evoked by the situation at hand."

A number of generic skills, focused on (1) obtaining information on facts and feelings, and (2) providing information on facts and feelings can be delineated.

1. *Draw on such information as is available prior to the encounter. Avoid repeating basic questions that have already been asked.* For example, if it is known that a recently widowed woman lives alone, seems depressed, and does not know what to do with her time, it may be appropriate to ask whether she has children. If she says "yes," perhaps she perks up as evidenced by her facial expression; or, she may seem even more sad.

A newly forming group of parents of retarded adolescents may be trying to identify how the group participation might help them. The worker asks them to describe the problems with the children. As the parents talk about their children's disabilities, it is clear from their tone of voice and facial expression that they feel some sadness.

In these types of situations, the alternation of expression of facts and feelings is evident and illustrates a second skill.

2. *Elicit, via appropriate alternation of open- and close-ended questions, as much description and discussion of the facts and feelings of the situation as possible.* The worker may ask the widowed, depressed woman where her children live, how many she has, and how frequently she sees them; or the worker may ask the parents of the retarded adolescents for a description of how the children spend their time, under what circumstances the taunts take place, and the kinds of activities of which they are capable.

3. *Reflect or "get with" the facts and feelings which have been expressed.* Middleman and Goldberg (1974) make some important comments in this connection. They suggest that saying "I understand" is not enough. The worker must try to "step outside his own frame of reference in order to see the world as his client sees it," and "accurately state his own understanding of the client's emotional experience."

If the widowed mother says in a rather strained manner that her children live only a few miles away but are too busy to come and see her, the worker responds to the apparent feeling of rejection. "You wish they weren't so busy, don't you? Sometimes you wonder if they really care." As the parents of the retarded adolescents speak, it appears that they are worried about what might happen should they become ill and unable to care for their children. The worker can help them put this into words. "A lot of you are wondering how you might plan for your children when you can no longer care for them."

4. *Share feelings. This refers to the process whereby workers share,* *with clients, those of their feelings which may be appropriate to the situation.* There is increasing evidence that it is appropriate for workers to share their experiences and emotions when such sharing is thought to contribute to clients' comfort or resolution of the problem. This may involve such "basically human acts" as crying with a person who has experienced a great loss (Shulman, 1979) or expressing frustration about bureaucratic intransigence. "I've had no better luck than you in getting those s.o.b.'s upstairs to budge on those regulations."

In another vein, it must be noted that workers are often placed in a position where clients express prejudiced or racist feelings about groups of people, and assume their feelings are shared by the worker. "You know those 'spics,' they're always stealing."

In our view, the ethics and value system of the profession are such that workers should never convey the impression that they share such sentiments. A comment such as "No, I don't know," or "I know what you're saying, but I don't believe in that kind of prejudice" disassociates workers from such a stance, and allows them to move beyond, by making a comment such as "I think you're really troubled about having things stolen, no matter who does it."

Intergroup tension may be the basis of the problem being considered, as is often the case in schools, community centers, or community action programs. The worker's basic stance on the issue must be conveyed. At the same time, people must be allowed to convey their feelings and to express their perceptions. "What makes you think that all of the white students are out to get you? What happens when you talk to them? Are there times when you've been able to work together, have fun together?"

Sharing facts and giving information. This is such a crucial and essential part of practice that it is frequently not discussed. People come needing information about how to apply for public assistance or housing, or how to process forms. Others have been "told" what their medical problems are but "don't understand." Clear-cut factual statements go a long way toward clarifying the situation:

> "The welfare office is at 310 Main Street."
> "Now here's a list of what you need to take with you when you go to the Housing Authority."
> "Let's be sure you understand what the doctor told you. He says you have hypertension; that means you have a disease involving your

blood pressure. I suppose the doctor told you that taking your medication regularly cuts down the chances of bad side effects."

The basic skill involved here is:

5. *Share facts and offer such opinions or ideas that may increase knowledge of a situation or event* (Middleman and Goldberg, 1974). In beginning the encounter, the principle of "honing in to feelings" and "facts" about the problem at hand is crucial. For the most part, efforts designed to convey warmth and empathy should proceed quickly, on the assumption that people will feel better and more motivated to "move on" with the process if they find the worker to be in tune with their feelings and giving important information.

Adaptation to the ethnic reality. "Reaching for facts and feelings" often means knowing when to move slowly and cautiously; when to concentrate on facts *or* feelings; when to focus on sharing feelings; and when to emphasize the process of providing facts.

It has been noted that some Chinese clients are unlikely to ask for help with emotional problems without at the same time asking for concrete assistance (Chen, 1970). The reluctance of many American Indians to engage in consideration of emotional issues has been observed.

Many people perceive problems less in individual and more in collective terms. Problems are seen as "belonging" to the family and less to the individual. If something is wrong, the family is shamed (e.g., many Asians). A large number of groups tend to perceive emotional problems in physical or other concrete terms. If these kinds of ethnic dispositions are known, the likelihood that certain requests or stances are interpreted as resistance, lack of insight, or inappropriate displacement of feelings is minimized.

Rather, they must be understood in the cultural context and respected. A number of additional skills are offered:

1. *Respect requests for concrete services and be as responsive as possible in meeting such requests.*

2. *Move slowly in the effort to actively "reach for feelings."* People who find consideration of feelings painful need to have time before they can or want to move in this area.

3. *Convey facts readily.* Most people who come for services, despite their reluctance to "engage emotionally," need and want information.

4. *Be imaginative in efforts to learn what the problem is.* We have already addressed the issue of "stage setting," and noted that efforts to talk to people "on their ground" are important.

> Lewis and Hu (1975) describe a situation in which some American Indian school children were brought to the worker's attention because of frequent school absences. Since the worker lived near the family she volunteered to transport the children to school. Sensing some difficulty in the family she simply let the mother know that she was available to listen. After some time had elapsed, the mother sadly told the worker about her marital problems.

Many people view home visiting as an indication of respect and caring. Some people fear visits to the psychiatric clinic because "those people lock you up."

Unannounced home visits are to be discouraged, however, until or unless a situation of trust has been developed. On the other hand, if the worker has been accepted in a community where people freely move in and out of each other's homes, the formality of prearranged visits may strike a discordant note.

5. *Be sure to understand who the appropriate "actors" are.* In many groups some issues are dealt with only by men, others only by women. Frequently matters of housekeeping are "women's work."Among Puerto Ricans it may be appropriate to involve distant relatives in efforts to mediate intrafamilial conflict over matters such as property. Close relationships should not be risked around such issues (Ghali, 1977).

Welfare programs too often exclude Black and other minority men from their dealings with families, except when they "go after them for support payments." Social workers should be ever on guard against activities which reinforce these negative sterotypes, and intensify racist ambience.

It is in these early efforts to find out what the problem is that attention to the ethnic reality is most important, for there may be no further encounter if early efforts are not met with sensitivity.

Specifying the problem

Problems seldom surface in neat, clearly defined packages. At the point when help is sought, or offered, people may be experiencing the cumulative effect of extensive periods of emotional distress, or economic deprivation, or long-standing pain and other physical discomforts. After the initial phase during which workers and clients have talked about the basic problems, a number of other steps follow. These include (1) particularizing or rank-ordering the problem; and (2) identifying the source or locus of the problem.

Particularizing or rank-ordering the problem

Whether practice is approached from a psychoanalytic or a structural stance, it is usually necessary to particularize it into component parts. If environmental pressures are extreme, what are they specifically? Inadequate income? Dissatisfying work? Violence in the neighborhood? Inadequate housing? No place for adolescents to meet? Are the senior citizens depressed and senile, or isolated because they cannot reach the local shopping areas? And, if both emotional strain and inadequate environmental supports are interacting, which can and which should be given prior attention?

Is it impossible for a couple to look at their own fighting and harsh disciplining of their children until their welfare allotments are increased? Or, will they continue to use already meager allowances to punish each other unless they come to understand and change their negative behavior to each other? "I'll show her. I'll go on to play cards and lose money if she doesn't stop nagging me the minute I walk in the house."

Shulman (1979) suggests that one way of tackling complex problems is to break them down into component parts and address them one at a time.

> During the preassessment phase the protective services worker has learned that Mrs. Ignazio's four children were forcibly removed from the family's custody when the young ones were thought to have burns and bruises inflicted by the mother. Further, Mrs. Ignazio had spent 2 years in the reformatory, following sentencing for the death of a fifth child. Although Mrs. Ignazio claimed that the child had hit his head on a table edge, the courts thought there was sufficient evidence that she had inflicted the blow that led to his death.
>
> At the time the new worker sees Mrs. Ignazio she comes in because she wants her children back. In the interview she continues to insist that the removal of the children and her incarceration were unjustified.
>
> She says, "Sure I hit them once in a while, but who wouldn't with five screaming little kids, a husband who spends all his time

and lots of money in the bar, and won't lift a finger even to get a kid a glass of milk. Besides he hits me, and then I take it out on the kids. He says his job is earning the money and protecting me from all of those stray men that hang around this rotten neighborhood."

After this outburst she cries, and says, "I really want to be a good mother. That's all that matters to me."

The worker says: "That's what you really want isn't it—to learn how to become a better mother?" Behind her tears, Mrs. Ignazio nods. The worker asks whether she thinks she's ready yet to have her children back. Mrs. Ignazio, still crying, says "No"—both she and her husband would have to learn to control their tempers. The worker suggests that they might talk about how to decide what needs to be done first. Mrs. Ignazio nods, and says, "Maybe you can help me figure out how to stop hitting the kids when they come to visit."

Of the massive number of problems confronting this family, worker and mother have isolated a major issue. In this or subsequent discussions they may identify other problems to be worked on, including how Mr. and Mrs. Ignazio interact and how the children feel about coming home.

A 12-year-old boy is referred to the court because he has been running away from home. During discussions preliminary to the hearing, the boy is quite uncommunicative. He sits with his eyes averted and says little when court personnel ask him why he's been running away from home, and whether there has been trouble at home. Interviews with the parents evoke a somewhat similar response. He's been running away. They don't know why, they will take care of him. Everything is fine at home. When the court worker suggests that perhaps there are tensions at home, and ways in which the court worker could help, there is minimal response.

With this kind of "resistant client" it is most important to clarify purpose in the process of particularizing. Perhaps a single, gently put statement to the parents such as "We will have to talk, since the judge says that's a condition of keeping your son in your custody," clearly identifies the major issue confronting this family. They may not be ready for more at this point.

In these and many other situations the client's ethnicity may have bearing on how particularization is approached.

Adaptation to the ethnic reality. In neither of the cases described above was the ethnic background of the people identified. The Ignazios are Italian, therefore it is likely that the importance of being a good mother was something Mrs. Ignazio heard about all of her life (Gambino, 1974). She has indeed failed. The offer to try to help her to "stop hitting the kids" is a beginning step toward helping her regain some control over this aspect of her life, crucial to most but particularly imbedded in Italian women.

The 12-year-old boy described before is second-generation Chinese. It is most likely that his particular reluctance to communicate derives from an overwhelming sense that he has shamed his family (Toupin, 1980). The fact that he averts his eyes may be related to the fact that the worker is an authority figure. Even if there is marital strain, the family is likely to feel strongly that this is a matter to be handled within the confines of the home.

The boy and family are in trouble—court action has been taken. The broad-based, exploratory, nondirective interview style has not evoked a meaningful response. The authoritative nature of the setting and the involuntary route to the worker may serve as useful starting points. A clear-cut statement by the worker to the effect that (1) the son is in trouble, (2) he is expected to stop running away, and (3) he is expected to report to the worker regularly, suffices at this point.

Some general principles in adaptation to the ethnic reality are suggested by these and similar cases. Basically they involve the effort to make a connection with the client in terms that are culturally relevant or syntonic. It is through these subtly conveyed nuances that the encounter may begin to have meaning.

Identifying the source or locus of the problem

Both factual information and theoretical perspectives play a part in identifying what the source of the problem seems to be. In the review of approaches to practice (see Chapter 4), divergent theoretical views were summarized. Although these differences exist, a number of basic principles cut across the divergent perspectives.

1. *The client's perspective on the source of the difficulty should be given primary consideration.* Putting this principle into action requires much skill, patience, and holding back. Workers are trained to think in theoretical terms, to synthesize, and to make assessments. It is not easy to "believe" or to "hold back" when people attribute all of their difficulties to external or perhaps supernatural forces. Workers who are eager to "put their knowledge to work" need to be self-disciplined. Sensitive workers will ask, and listen, before they make a judgment.

2. *Where the problem is systemically based, individuals should not be held responsible for the situation.* The list of inadequate resources to deal with problems is endless. When clients complain about welfare budgets, workers must acknowledge the trauma, perhaps even cry with people, before going on to help with budgeting. The budgeting process may be necessary as a survival technique. But to suggest to such people that they are not getting along because they do not know how to budget is "blaming the victim," execpt in instances in which funds are grossly misused.

3. *Effort must be made to ascertain the link between individuals' functioning and the social situation in which they find themselves.* Most people's problems are related to the social structure in which they find themselves and to the coping skills they have developed to function within that structure.

The situation in which increasing numbers of middle-aged women find themselves is instructive. Most women were reared to value the role of wife and mother. With the advent of the women's movement, many have moved out into the world of work, some aspiring to responsible business and professional careers. Not infrequently, considerable conflict ensues. Consider the following situation:

Mrs. Willey, a 35-year-old mother of three adolescents, recently graduated from college and is enrolled in graduate school. One of her children, Mary, is having school difficulties. Mrs. Willey is frequently asked to come to school to meet with the teachers, but her own school schedule interferes. She and her husband spend much time in the evening going over Mary's homework and talking with her about her problems.

Mrs. Willey tells the social worker: "I guess I'll have to give up school. I feel so guilty when I sit there, knowing that Mary's school wants me there."

Much in her own socialization tugs at her to put the needs of her children first. And yet the worker might ask the following kinds of questions:

Is it ever possible to meet with Mary's teachers in the evening?

What is it that has to be done during the day? Could you and your husband consider taking turns going during the day?

This is not an easy conflict to resolve. The system has not yet adapted to the needs of working mothers. But even if schedules were adapted, there are many changes in feeling about oneself and one's responsibilities which go to the core of the personality as people get caught up in the throes of social change.

Both systemic and individual concerns must be balanced.

Adaptation to the ethnic reality. The principles and associated skills discussed above apply in work with all people. They become even more important when dealing with ethnic, minority, and other oppressed people.

The ethnic-sensitive worker has a particular responsibility to be aware of the systemic sources of many problems. Workers are frequently not in a position to change the system. However, they must do no harm. Attributing systematically induced problems—those derived from racism, poverty, and prejudice—to individuals is harmful. It adds to their burden. Helping to identify the links between systemic problems and individual concerns is a crucial component of ethnic-sensitive practice.

Contracting

The literature on contracting is extensive (Fischer, 1978; Maluccio and Marlow, 1974; Middleman and Goldberg, 1974; Pincus and Minahan, 1973; Reid and Epstein, 1977; Seabury, 1976). Implicit in much of this work is the assumption that people can contract to explore their interpersonal relationships, to confront dysfunctional systems, and to make use of health and welfare systems as these are currently organized.

The concept of contracting has evolved from western, rational conceptions of time, reciprocity, and assumptions of trust in formally organized helping institutions. In many ways the concept is viewed as a corrective for that mode of practice where worker and client come together for extensive periods of time, frequently lacking clear focus concerning the purpose of the interaction. Moreover, goals were often imposed by workers.

From many perspectives it is a most useful concept. Nevertheless, when viewed within the context of ethnic-sensitive practice, some of the assumptions inherent in traditional views of contracting must be reconsidered.

Many groups do not share the rational conceptions of problem-solving implicit in the concept. Many lack trust in the available health and welfare delivery systems. Some are particularly loathe to accept the designation of "client," which some views of contracting imply.

Much that is understood about the world view of the various American Indian cultures points to the fact that any seeming act of manipulation or coercion is viewed with mistrust. This applies to psychological as well as physical behaviors. Good Tracks (1973) points out that suggestions concerning appropriate behavior, whether conveyed subtly or in the form of an outright command, are viewed as interference. Interference in others' behavior is considered inappropriate. This holds true for the way parents teach their children, the actions of children, and demands made by organized institutions. Good Tracks suggests that for these reasons many major social work techniques are ineffective with many American Indians.

Contrast this with certain dispositions common to many Asian Americans. Several themes recur in the literature. According to Toupin (1980), some general characteristics of the "modal Asian personality" can be identified. Many are likely to express deference to others, to devalue themselves and their family to others, and to avoid confrontation. Shame—for insensitive behavior, for behavior subjecting the family to criticism, for causing embarrassment—is extensively drawn upon in socialization practices. The family honor is preserved by not discussing personal problems outside. Expression of emotions may not bring relief as it may reflect negatively on the family. There is deference to authority, and therapeutic personnel are viewed as authority figures.

In commenting on the social worker's potential ability to be helpful to American Indians without violating cultural precepts, Good Tracks suggests: "Patience is the number-one virtue governing Indian relationships. A worker who has little or no patience should not seek placement in Indian settings. . . . The social worker's success may well be linked with his ability to learn 'Indian time' and adjust his relationships accordingly." He points out that the workers will be observed, and people may seem indifferent. It may take considerable time, perhaps a year or more, before they are trusted.

Workers' efforts to provide a variety of concrete services will be observed. At some point a member of the community *may* bring a problem of a more personal nature to a worker. Technique alone will not speed up this process—this holds true for many groups.

The principle of contracting is crucial when it is related to client autonomy and self-determination. When viewed primarily as a technique for rapid engagement of clients in the helping process, the danger exists that class and ethnic dispositions will receive insufficient attention.

The approach to contracting which follows is guided by the preceding considerations.

Contracting refers to the process by which workers, clients, and others engaged in problem-solving activities come to some common agreement about the respective work to be done, the objectives sought, and the means by which these are to be attained. By its very nature the process involves clients and others in setting the terms by which the work of problem solving is to be carried out. Various writers have stressed the fact that contracting involves "a partnership" (Compton and Galaway, 1979). When social worker–client interaction is approached from this perspective, workers are less likely to impose their definition of the problem or task on the client.

Many definitions of the contract have been offered. In social work and other interpersonal helping endeavors the contract may be viewed as a consensus, between the involved or concerned persons, about why they are working together, how they will work together, and what they hope to achieve. Translated into the "gut and heart" of day-to-day practice, what does this mean?

It means that workers and clients deliberate—often struggle—to come to decisions about the focus of the work to be done. This is affected by the various contexts in which services are rendered, and the point in time when decisions about the work to be done are made. Some people can make such decisions quickly; others waver, and need considerable time.

The service context and contracting

For the most part, workers and clients meet under the auspices of an agency within the health and welfare delivery system. These differ in many respects and center on the nature of the service offered, on whether people arrive willingly, and on whether social work is an ancillary or primary service (e.g., the welfare office, the protective services agency, or the hospital). Presence in these contexts usually involves coercion and/or fear. The poor tend to predominate among those served. Their socioeconomic circumstances usually leave them little choice about using the services of a social worker. It is in these contexts that the search for consensus should proceed in a forthright manner.

Shulman (1979) makes reference to the "search for the elusive common ground" and suggests that a simple, nonjargonized statement about what the social worker can do is a good starting point. With the prisoner soon to be released, the social worker may say:

> Jim, I'm a social worker. The parole board said that you and I should talk about the things you might do when you get out of here. I've been able to help guys think ahead about what it might be like to get back to the family and friends. Please come down to my office a couple of times a week.

Or, to the mother whose children have been removed because of suspected abuse:

> Mrs. Jones, I'm a social worker. I know you're feeling low right now with the kids going into that foster home. Other women who've been in the same position have found it helpful to talk about that, and after awhile to think about what they have to do in order to have the children returned.

The service is offered and the client is given some options. Nevertheless, the authoritative nature of the worker's role inherent in the setting is not forgotten. The parole board says worker and prisoner *should* talk, the protective services agency sends the message that Mrs. Jones *has to do certain things* if she wants her children back.

These contexts differ sharply from the psychiatric clinic or the family counseling agency. People who come to these types of agencies are also likely to feel stressed or bewildered. Yet the process of getting there may be more volitional.

When people know why they've come to the service center, the social worker can begin to move more quickly to engage the client in contracting on the "how" of the process to be pursued.

> Mrs. White has indicated that she is contemplating separation from

her husband, because they fight a lot over her desire to go back to work. An exchange may go something like this:

> **Worker:** Mrs. White, you've said you want to talk about your plans for separating from Mr. White. Have you pretty much made up your mind that that's the best thing or are you still wondering?
>
> **Mrs. White:** Oh, I'm about 75% decided. But I do want to talk with you a little bit about whether you think there's any way we could make it work.
>
> **Worker:** How would you feel if we spend the next couple of sessions reviewing the bad and the good parts of your marriage? Perhaps you want to review for yourself how you both have dealt with differences in the past, and consider whether there are things you could do which would make it comfortable for you to stay there.

Here much of the focus is on the worker's "enabler role." The worker begins to contract with people to look at their own behavior, their conflicts, and the kinds of changes they can and want to make.

Many of these contexts generate a variety of other roles, which can be contracted early. In the prison, the hospital, or the welfare board, mediating, brokerage, or advocacy roles can be suggested. The new applicant for public assistance may ask whether he/she can be helped to find a job. The prisoner may ask the worker to play an advocacy role. He may suggest that his release is too far off.

> **Jim:** Mr. Brown, they got me staying here another 6 months. Do you think you could help me get a new hearing before the parole board?
>
> **Worker:** I'll look over your record, and we can talk about why you think you should get out sooner. If it makes sense to both of us I'll go to bat for you. I can only do that if I agree and it makes sense to me.

Mrs. White, in conflict about whether to remain in her marriage, may ask the worker whether he/she can play a mediating function.

> **Mrs. White:** You know, if he only wouldn't fuss and fume so when I talk about finding a job I think we could make it. Do you think you could get us both in here, and we could talk about it together? Maybe you could convince him that it's not going to take anything away from him.

The social worker assigned to the outpatient clinic of a hospital is asked to find out why so many people do not keep essential follow-up appointments. In exploring the matter she learns that people are "fed up" with being told to be there at nine in the morning and not being seen until eleven or twelve. They lose time from work, as well as patience. In checking to see what happens elsewhere, the worker finds that the same kind of people come much more regularly if there is a staggered appointment system. In this instance she first contracts with the hospital administration to explore the issue. She then shares her information with the administration and patients. Does the administration want to institute a staggered appointment system? Should she ask her patients how they would feel about it?

In this process, effort is made to maximize the possibility of involvement in problem solving by those concerned—the patients and hospital administration.

In considering the relationship between the context and contracting, a number of generic principles can be stated:

1. Where clients have little or no choice about "being there" a clear-cut statement about the help and the options available, despite the constraints, is essential.
2. The range of services available should be spelled out clearly, with an emphasis on the role the client and worker can play.
3. The contract should not focus on "people changing" where system changing is in order (e.g., only if the staggered appointment system in the outpatient clinic is not successful should the social worker talk to patients about their appointment-keeping behavior).
4. The limitations of time and agency function should be clearly spelled out (Compton and Galaway, 1979).

Adaptation to the ethnic reality. There is little doubt that minority groups, those who do not speak English, and those who have a long history of negative experience with health and welfare institutions are particularly sensitive and fearful about what might happen. These need not be repeated here. What needs to be stressed is that continuing attention and sensitivity to these matters must be evident. The skill of helping people who feel particularly defeated to recognize and believe that they can play a part in determining why and how something is to be done is one which needs to be continually sharpened.

The injustice done to American Indians by massive removal of children from their homes to "boarding schools" has been repeatedly documented (Byler, 1977). The assumption that minorities and the poor are not articulate and cannot constructively engage in therapeutic encounters involving active verbalization has been challenged. The difficulty of conveying affect and sensitive factual information through an interpreter is well known. Despite this, some American Indians abuse their children, and some poor minority people need help with basic survival needs before they can engage in the process of examining interpersonal relationships. Bilingual or indigenous workers are not always available.

The basic rules of contracting must then be *expanded* to include the following kinds of considerations:

1. Consider the basic meaning which involvement with this setting is likely to have for different people. For instance, the American Indian family may be quite ready to consider placement of a child with someone in the extended family, once assured that the child is not going to be torn from the fold of the community.
2. Consider the implications of what is being suggested, given the client's ethnic reality.

Groups respond differently to deviant behavior by their members. While all experience some sense of shame, or of being disgraced, some Poles, Asians, and Chicanos find it particularly difficult to deal with the assault to group pride represented by delinquency or crime (Lopata, 1976). In contracting with the Polish prisoner Jim Jablonsky about planning for his release, recognition of this aspect of his life may be extremely important. Efforts to engage him in contracting must take this into account.

As one plans for care for the elderly, it should be remembered that institutional care is anathema to many Blacks and Puerto Ricans.

Studies have shown that working-class people are less prone to institutionalize their retarded children than are middle-class people (Mercer, 1972). In suggesting institutionalization to such families, this must be borne in mind.

Turning *compadres* into paid foster parents may help Puerto Rican families to feel more comfortable about out-of-home, publicly paid child care.*

---

*Study the practice of using parafoster parents, developed by the Division of Youth and Family Services, State of New Jersey.

Contracting, then, must take account of the particular sensitivities generated by the problem and the context where service is rendered.

The timing of the contract

When the social worker and client begin to talk and the relationship is being developed, an ongoing, albeit shifting, consensus about the nature of the interaction is being established. Timing in contract development is a shifting and extremely variable process that will depend on a number of factors. The way in which these factors converge has major impact on *when* the process of contracting is used or initiated.

Many services are time-limited and by their nature focus on the provision of concrete services. Most welfare clients need money. Some people require information about their eligibility for Medicaid or food stamps. Services such as these do not call for extensive contracting. At the same time, in order to make use of these services, people must fill out forms and give permission for release of information.

Even for the provision of such seemingly simple services the principles of contracting—and the implication that worker and client are working together on something—apply. Such contracts are usually arrived at early and quickly.

If the major basis for the contact is for public assistance, day care services, homemaker services, or other concrete services, contracting is usually done early in the encounter. As is always the case, careful attention must be paid to the previously identified skills of stage setting, attending, tuning in, and finding out what the problem is.

In many instances, people in need of concrete services are also in need of supportive casework or group work services. Those who apply for public assistance may feel defeated or fearful that they will not be able to obtain sufficient food, pay their rent, or manage their bills.

The process of offering and contracting for services beyond those of a concrete nature is delicate and requires much skill. On the one hand, there is the danger of "seeing" and "looking for" emotional problems where none may exist. On the other hand, people requiring supportive services are frequently troubled. In weighing these issues, skillful workers will first attend to the problem presented before attempting to contract for anything beyond.

In many situations, the concrete service, courteously and warmly rendered, may be all that the client wants or is able to deal with at that point.

There are many differences in the nature, duration, and intensity of the service. Parents may come to a school social worker or those in child guidance clinics expecting workers to provide discipline for unruly children. Other may come distressed about the embarrassing behavior of a psychotic family member. Tenants may ask the social worker to intervene with the landlord to get them more heat or needed repairs. A group of institutionalized children may come and ask the social worker to get cottage parents "to change their nasty ways."

In each of these situations people may expect the social worker to intervene on their behalf to effect a change in others' actions. Frequently they do not perceive their own role in attaining the desired changes: parents may become defensive when effort is made to explore how they discipline the children; tenants feel powerless with the landlord; families coping with an emotionally distressed member feel fatigued and hopeless.

"Facts and feelings" about these matters have usually been expressed in the problem identification stage. There is evidence that if people are to move from a sense of distress and powerlessness to the point of some resolution of the difficulty, their active participation in goal setting is crucial (Seabury, 1976).

The various approaches to social work (see Chapter 4) differ in their view as to how quickly clients are to be engaged in contracting, setting priorities, and defining tasks. Some generic rules can be set forth.

1. *When appropriate, suggestions should be offered early as to how client and worker might proceed.* For example, when there is beginning understanding of the circumstances which trigger the child's difficult behavior, the worker may suggest that he/she could talk with the parents about how to modify their behavior. Early in the contact the worker may suggest that parents try firmness rather than a wavering "No" in the face of a seemingly unreasonable demand. This begins the contracting process, and sets into motion the idea that all have an obligation to examine their actions.

2. *The second generic rule suggests that early evidence of what might be accomplished by working together be provided.* In the situation of the complaining tenants, workers must express verbally and nonverbally their understanding of the frustration engendered by poor services. If the tenants can be helped to see the potential of their own strength, perhaps they can move to the next stage of acting on their own behalf.

3. *Be specific in the goals set at any one point in time.* If the child's unruly behavior is the presenting problem, action should be targeted to accomplish change in this area. Only if and when the parents arrive at some agreement that the tensions in their own marriage contribute to the child's behavior should contracting focused on the relief of these tensions be considered.

When people who have cared for an emotionally ill person at home come asking for help in managing that person, they may or may not be considering the possibility of institutionalization. Their request should be taken at face value. They may need supportive services (e.g., day care, homemaker service) and the opportunity to ventilate. An early suggestion to institutionalize may well prove a barrier to further help. Should the situation continue to prove difficult, and when a trusting relationship has been developed, a family may consider the possibility of alternative care, including institutionalization.

In sum, the generic skills of contracting involve an ongoing effort to "tune in" to the dynamic, shifting situation, and recontracting for specific, manageable goals. A mutual effort, consonant with clients' perception of the problem, is projected.

Adaptation to the ethnic reality. We defined the contract as "a consensus between the involved or concerned persons about why they are working together, how they will work together, and what they hope to achieve."

The discussion on timing and contracting has focused on the need to remain "tuned in" to client perceptions of problems, and the effort to come to agreements on action.

The work of Good Tracks (1973) and others strongly suggests that the rules of speedy contracting as defined here may need to be suspended unless initiated by clients. Similarly, highly focused efforts to suggest behavioral changes or introspection are likely to be viewed as interference. The process of building a relationship, and of showing sensitivity to the culture and problem, in the hope that trust will be developed, is ongoing. The reliance on authority, and the fear of shame and self-disclosure shared by many Asian Americans, suggests time might need to be viewed somewhat differently for this group. According to Ho (1976), many Asian Americans are not used to "functioning with ambiguity." Agency functioning should be clearly spelled out in first contacts; the respect for the deference to authority suggests that clients should be politely informed of what is expected of them. If return visits are anticipated, this should be clearly stated. If this is not done, clients may fear that they are imposing on someone in authority by returning. By contrast, contracting for expression of feeling may need to be deferred. For "just being in therapy" may generate such extensive anxiety that the process of verbalization may bring no relief (Toupin, 1980).

The situation is not dramatically different for many "blue-collar ethnics." Giordano (1977) suggests that many avoid seeking help—particularly in the mental health arena—until problems have reached crisis proportions. The role of client is viewed as "stigmatizing." Emphasis should not be on pathology but on "problems in living."

Many techniques for contracting have been proposed. These include written agreements specifying the workers' and clients' obligations, writing out suggestions for avoidance or carrying out of specific behaviors, and time limits by which certain goals are to be accomplished (Fischer, 1978; Reid, 1978). These are undoubtedly useful under some circumstances. There is no evidence, either in the literature or based on our own work, whether or not these are helpful in furthering ethnic-sensitive practice.

WORKING ON THE PROBLEM

Recently one of the authors visited an agency to review a student's progress. In the course of reviewing the student's process recording it seemed that there were any number of times that the student deflected a client's attention from the problem at hand. As soon as her clients seemed ready to discuss an emotionally sensitive matter, the student changed the subject. When this was pointed out, this insightful student said, "I know, but if they really tell me I might have to do something about it. And I don't really know how. Those people have terrible troubles, and they won't go away. I can't really change anything for them." This is a common dilemma, not only for the student but also for the more seasoned practitioner.

Some of the dilemma arises out of the seeming intractability of the problems for which help is sought, some is related to lack of skill, and some to the inherent difficulty entailed in forging ahead, on a sustained basis, with efforts to help. These sustained efforts call for extensive commitment, skill, and continuing attention to the diverse helping roles that can be played.

Much of the "bulk of the work" is a continuation of the processes set in motion in the course of problem identification and contracting. And yet, there is a distinction between the preparatory phase and the ongoing work.

Once the work is begun, workers and clients truly become involved in the work of problem solving. The phases of this process can be identified. With some variation, these phases obtain whether work is focused on problems of interpersonal relationships with individuals or groups, on planned community or other systems change efforts, or on a variety of planning endeavors, including: (1) ongoing reassessment of the problem; (2) partializing the problem into manageable parts; (3) identifying obstacles; (4) obtaining and sharing additional information; (5) reviewing progress or setbacks; and (6) termination.

No single work can possibly do justice to the various facets of skills involved in the problem-solving process. We approach the matter by suggesting, for a number of select areas, how the *work* of problem solving may differ from the beginning phases.

Ongoing reassessment of the problem

The process of ongoing reassessment calls attention to many facets of the situation. External changes may take place that can dramatically alter the course of events. Life can be measurably altered if a job is lost or obtained; if the child of a couple experiencing marital difficulty becomes seriously ill; if the neighborhood that is organizing for better service is scheduled for demolition. All that need be said in this connection is that we must be sure to listen and to review. Too often, workers become so caught up in the preparatory work that upon seeing people they forget to review. Setting aside some time to learn what happened this week, yesterday, or an hour ago is an essential component of interaction.

Partializing the problem

In the discussion of contracting, several illustrations were given of how workers begin to help people to identify problems that might be considered. The reader will recall the situation of Jim Jablonsky, soon to be released from prison. In contracting with him the suggestion had been made that he consider his future living and working plans. Mrs. White, the woman who was considering separation from her husband, agreed to review the positives and negatives of the marriage; she also asked for a joint session with herself and her husband to see whether such discussion would alter his perspective on her wish to find a job. In these, and many other types of situations, multiple problems present themselves. In the contract phase, it was possible to delineate these—and to propose some priorities. As the work proceeds, the initial contract needs to be reviewed. Is it possible for Jim Jablonsky to consider what type of work he might do until he decides whether he can return home to live with his family? Opportunity and financial need may vary considerably, depending on where he goes. He seemed most troubled about how his family might receive him. Earlier it appeared as if discussion of job possibilities was a first-order priority. But as the work progressed he kept returning to his fear about how his family would act when he was released. The earlier plan needed revision, and discussion had to be refocused.

Mrs. White may be unable to "see" any positives in her marriage unless there is some indication that her husband will take a positive attitude toward her taking a job. The joint interview with her husband may have priority. If he is adamant about his refusal to "let her" find a job, the discussions may focus on what she needs to do to terminate the marriage. Will she move out right away? Can she afford to do so? What will the financial settlement be? This is a generic phase of the process applicable to all people.

Identifying obstacles

Obstacles come in the form of emotions, entrenched behavior patterns, discrimination, language barriers, environmental deficits, and so on. Despite this, understanding of barriers or obstacles can help to overcome or minimize them. The tenants and workers who agreed jointly to plan a strategy for the meeting with the landlord around heat and services may find that the landlord is "not available." This may be an absentee landlord off to distant parts. Does that mean that the plan must be abandoned? Or is there a legal recourse? Is it possible to subpoena the landlord? Are there responsible public agencies?

If Mrs. White cannot afford to leave until she has enough income, what might she do? Is she sufficiently determined to go ahead with the separation so as to tolerate living with her husband while she pursues a job and manages to save some money?

Adaptation to the ethnic reality. Plans made in the privacy of the worker's office, or in locales in other ways removed from the network of church, community, and kin may flounder when others become aware of what is going on. A Catholic woman planning a divorce may talk to her priest, who suggests she reconsider. The members of a Black neighborhood improvement group encounter explicit and implicit racism as they meet with the mayor and other city officials. A Chicano woman who obtained employment encounters the wrath of her husband who feels his very being threatened by her action.

These and like obstacles derive from deeply ingrained attitudes. Where cultural dispositions serve as obstacles to moving ahead, the following principles are suggested: (1) explore the source and nature of the difficulty carefully and gently; (2) consider whether the obstacles are of an individual or a collective nature. For example, is the Catholic woman devout and basically committed to staying in any marriage, or is she simply reporting the question raised by the priest? Were the racist slurs encountered by the neighborhood improvement group of such a nature as to warrant investigation and action by the agency? Is the Chicano woman the only one in her community to have taken a job? If not, have other women encountered similar problems? Is it possible to organize a Chicano women's support group?

Obtaining and sharing additional facts and feelings

Throughout the worker-client encounter, both give each other factual and emotional feedback. When Mrs. White reports happily that she has a job, the worker gets a clue as to whether this is something she really wanted. If, on the other hand, she finds a job and seems depressed, this is a different kind of fact. The worker may share her own feeling: "I'm pleased that you seem so happy. It seems as if this really is something you've been wanting a long time." If Mrs. White is depressed, a feminist worker may find it difficult to hide her disappointment. Perhaps this woman is not a "free spirit" after all. How does the worker "use" her feeling of disappointment? It is here that the process of "tuning in" must again come into play. How did the worker feel when she first "defied convention" and sought a career instead of or along with marriage? This can help her to explore some more. Has Mrs. White really changed her mind? Or does she need more support to get her through a difficult transition? Where is she in the life cycle?

Adaptation to the ethnic reality. It is quite possible that ethnicity or culturally sensitive matters may not have surfaced earlier in the helping process. This may be related to (1) the worker's lack of knowledge, (2) the client's reluctance to trust at an earlier stage, (3) different ethnic backgrounds of worker and client, and (4) lack of awareness by both that ethnic factors have bearing on the problem.

> Mr. Capella, an Italian group worker, has been working with a group of young, underclass men who were enrolled in a training program to upgrade their job skills. The group's objectives were to share experiences and feelings about the program, and to anticipate problems they might have as they try to get jobs. The men, all in their late teens and early twenties, come from varied backgrounds—Hispanic, Black, Italian.
>
> They readily shared common experiences and talked about the particular problems of discrimination the Black and Hispanic men might encounter.
>
> During the fourth session, one of the young Black men started the discussion by saying he wanted to thank Mr. Capella, and make a confession. He said he's had his doubts about what a "white dude" would know about how he felt. He almost wasn't going to come, but he thought he'd give it a try. Mr. Capella, though, he "really had a feel for where it's at."

There are other situations in which the basis for lack of progress may finally be shared, as it is related to ethnicity. Only when the matter is shared and aired does the work progress. A young Slavic woman was assigned a Black worker to help her think through her job troubles. The young woman was working at a semiskilled clerical job and was quite dissatisfied. The worker's efforts to try to find out what the problem was yielded a very fuzzy picture. One day the young client blurted out in a rather embarrassed manner: "You know what's really bothering me on the job is my supervisor. But I never told you about that because she's Black like you, and I thought you'd get mad at me." Only when the worker accepted her feeling and told her it was acceptable not to like any particular Black person were they able to move on to realistically consider the young woman's situation.

Ethnicity as a variable in the problem being considered may become evident during a later phase of contact.

> Mrs. Miller, a 25-year-old college graduate, had crossed out all sections bearing on background on the form requesting service for marital counseling. The worker, respectful of her right to privacy, did not ask. The conflict as originally presented revolved around the couple's differences about having children. Mrs. Miller wanted to have children, Mr. Miller did not.
>
> One day Mrs. Miller came in particularly distraught, and said: "I thought we had it all worked out before we got married. But yesterday he told me he doesn't want children because I'm not Jewish. He'll have children if I convert. I told him before we were married I couldn't do that."

Sometimes people are not aware of how important their ethnic background is until such basic issues as childbearing arise. And so the client shares a bit of information not heretofore known, perhaps even to herself.

The phasing out of the worker-client encounter

Strean suggests that the termination of any meaningful worker-client relationship will induce strong and ambivalent feelings (Strean, 1978). Others (Compton and Galway, 1979; Fox, Nelson, and Bolman, 1969; Shulman, 1979) variously address the dynamic generated by the separation process, the sense of loss or support that can be experienced in transfer or referral, and the heightened affect sensed by both worker and client as the end of the relationship approaches.

Shulman (1979) suggests a number of principles to be considered in the termination phase: (1) identifying major learning; (2) identifying what is to be done in the future (3) synthesizing the ending process; (4) considering alternative sources of support to those obtained from the worker. For the ethnic-sensitive worker the latter has particular significance. The alternative sources of support are often lodged in kinship and neighborhood networks, in the church, or in a newly heightened sense of ethnic identity. These and others are major considerations, requiring particular sensitivity to the possibility that clients may view termination as rejection or that they may be fearful about going on alone.

Most of the skills reviewed—stage setting, attending, tuning in, and identifying areas of concern—continue here. The stage is now set for departure, and all need to articulate what that means.

> Will Mr. and Mrs. Jones sustain their efforts to minimize their fighting?
>
> Has the community action group acquired the skills to work alone on new projects as the need arises?

In "tuning in" to these kinds of concerns, workers again need to pay attention to the three levels of understanding—the broad area of concern within which the functioning takes place (e.g., the strain on marriages in general; the way people feel who have experienced marital counseling; and the kinds of strains *any* Mr. and Mrs Jones are likely to experience). Workers need to think and feel through their own concerns about the termination. Supposing contact was abrupt, and no progress was made? What went wrong? What did they learn? If the encounter appeared successful, are they also losing a valued relationship? In either case, when possible, workers should share their satisfaction, their appreciation of the people involved, or their regrets.

> "I'm going to miss talking with you every week. I like you a lot, and I've learned a lot."
>
> "I'm sorry it didn't work out. Perhaps someone else will be able to help you more."

The fears and joys which surround termination are universal. They will be variously expressed. Some will bring gifts, others will say their polite farewells, others will want to embrace the worker as a friend. Within the limitations of that which is possible, we must respond with grace and sensibility, in this as in all other phases of the work.

SUMMARY

The practice skills presented represent a composite of many identified in the social work literature. Ethnic-sensitive practice requires adaptation or modifications which are in keeping with knowledge about prevailing group dispositions to issues such as privacy, using formally organized helping institutions, stances concerning self-disclosure, discussion of intimate matters outside of the family, and the context in which service is or should be offered Flexibility is necessary in determining where service is to be rendered and the speed with which workers seek to engage clients in contracting.

REFERENCES

Aguilar, Ignacio. 1972. "Initial contacts with Mexican American families." *Social Work, 17*(3), May.

Benjamin, Alfred. 1974. *The helping interview* (2nd ed.). Boston: Houghton-Mifflin Co.

Brown, Luna Bowdoin. 1950. "Race as a factor in establishing a casework relationship." *Social Casework, 31,* March.

Byler, William. 1977. "The destruction of American Indian families." In Unger, Steven (Ed.). *The destruction of American Indian families.* New York: Association on American Indian Affairs.

Chen, Pei-Ngor. 1970. "The Chinese community in Los Angeles." *Social Casework, 51*(10), December.

Compton, Beulah Roberts, and Galway, Burt. 1979. *Social work process.* Homewood, IL: The Dorey Press.

Curry, Andrew 1964. "The Negro worker and the white client: a commentary on the treatment relationship." *Social Casework,* March.

Dominick, Joan R., and Stotsky, Bernard. 1969. "Mental patients in nursing homes IV. Ethnic influence." *Journal of the American Geriatric Society, 17*(1), January.

Egan, Gerard. 1975. *The skilled helper: a mode for systematic helping and interpersonal relating.* Monterey, Calif.: Brooks/Cole Publishing Co.

Fischer, Joel. 1978. *Effective casework practice: an eclectic approach.* New York: McGraw-Hill Book Co.

Fox, Evelyn F., Nelson, Marion A., and Bolman, William M. 1969. "The termination process: a neglected dimension in social work." *Social work,* October.

Gambino, Richard. 1974. *Blood of my blood—the dilemma of the Italian-Americans.* Garden City, N.Y.: Anchor Press/Doubleday.

Ghali, Sonia Badillo. 1977. "Culture sensitivity and the Puerto Rican client." *Social Casework,* October.

Giordano, Joseph. 1977. *Ethnicity and mental health: research and recommendations.* New York: American Jewish Committee.

Giordano, Joseph, and Giordano, Grace Pineiro. 1977. *The ethno-cultural factor in mental health—a literature review and bibliography.* New York: American Jewish Committee.

Gitterman, Alex, and Schaeffer, Alice. 1972. "The white professional and Black client." *Social Casework, 53,* May.

Good Tracks, Jimm G. 1973. "Native American noninterference." *Social Work,* November.

Ho, Man Keung. 1976. "Social work with Asian Americans." *Social Casework,* March.

Kadushin, Alfred. 1972. *The social work interview.* New York: Columbia University Press.

Lewis, Ronald G., and Ho, Man Keung. 1975. "Social work with Native Americans." *Social Work, 20*(5).

Lopata, Helen Znaniecki. 1976. *Polish Americans: status competition in an ethnic communiy.* Englewood Cliffs, N.J.: Prentice-Hall, Inc.

Maluccio, Anthony N., and Marlow, Wilma D. 1974. "The case for contract." *Social Work,* January.

Mercer, Jane R. 1972. "Career patterns of persons labeled as mentally retarded." In Freidson, Eliot, and Lorber, Judith (Eds.). *Medical men and their work—a sociological reader.* Chicago: Aladin-Atherton.

Middleman, Ruth, and Goldberg, Gale. 1974. *Social service delivery: a structural approach to social work practice.* New York: Columbia University Press.

Pincus, Allen, and Minahan, Anne. 1973. *Social work practice: model and method.* Itasca, IL: F. E. Peacock Publishers, Inc.

Reid, William J. 1978. *The task-centered system.* New York: Columbia University Press.

Reid, William J., and Epstein, Laura. 1977. *Task-centered practice.* New York: Columbia University Press.

Seabury, Brett A. 1976. "The contract: uses, abuses and limitations." *Social Work,* January.

Shulman, Laurence. 1978. "A study of practice skill." *Social Work, 23,* July.

Shulman, Laurence. 1979. *The skills of helping individuals and groups.* Itasca, IL: F. E. Peacock Publishers, Inc.

Stack, Carol B. 1974. *All our kin—strategies for survival in a black community.* New York: Harper & Row, Publishers.

Strean, Herbert. 1978. *Clinical social work practice.* New York: The Free Press.

Toupin, Elizabeth Sook Wha Ahn. 1980. "Counseling Asians: psychotherapy in the context of racism and Asian-American history." *American Journal of Orthopsychiatry, 50*(1), January.

Truax, Charles B., and Mitchell, Kevin M. 1971. "Research on interpersonal skills in relation to process and outcome." In Bergin, Allen E., and Garfield, Sol L. (Eds.). *Handbook of pschotherapy and behavior change: an empirical analysis.* New York: John Wiley & Sons, Inc.

Zborowski, M. 1951. "Cultural components in response to pain." *Journal of Social Issues,* 4(8).

David Antebi

Jewlee Bryant

CHAPTER
7

Ethnic-sensitive practice with families

While social work is practiced in many different settings, most practice involves work with families, whether work is carried out in the voluntary family service agency, the juvenile justice system, the schools, the health care system, and many others. Whether a marriage is tottering or a child is ill or in trouble with the law or at school, the family as a system is or should be involved. Problems are frequently traced to the family at the same time as the family is sought as source of support and solution. It is within the family that many life cycle tasks are carried out.

Understanding of family dynamics, of intergenerational struggles, and of how the ethnic reality impinges on the family's capacity to play its varying roles is crucial for the ethnic-sensitive social worker.

In this chapter, prevailing views of family functioning are reviewed. These are related to the model of ethnic-sensitive practice developed.

Case examples serve as the vehicle for illustrating how the perspectives of ethnic-sensitive practice are brought to bear on work with troubled families.

The family is a major primary group; its tasks, though universal, are interpreted in diverse ways by each ethnic group and at each social class level.

Family functions have been and continue to be discussed in the literature. Analysts continue to concern themselves with the changes that have come about as America has moved from an agricultural to a technological society. In earlier days the family performed economic, status-giving, educational, religious, recreational, protective, and affectional functions. Other institutions such as the school and the church have assumed greater responsibility for education and religious development of family members. Much family-centered recreation has been replaced by sports events in which individuals may be participants or spectators; and by social clubs, movies, and concerts. Many activities are related to life cycle stage (Cub Scouts, Pop Warner Football, business womens' clubs, senior citizens' clubs).

The family continues to have major economic and affectional functions—generally known as the *instrumental* and *expressive* functions.

An alternative interpretation of the functions of the family has been presented by Ackerman (1958). It is a more contemporary view of the major social purposes served by the family that focuses on the development of the expressive function. Ackerman stresses (1) the provision of opportunity for "social togetherness," the matrix for the affectional bond of family relationships; (2) the opportunity to evolve a personal identity, tied to family identity; (3) the patterning of sexual roles; (4) the training for integration into social roles and the acceptance of social responsibility; as well as (5) the cultivation of learning and support for individual creativity and initiative. Ogburn's perspective (1938) in relation to the economic and affectional function and Ackerman's expansion of the latter form a base from which to consider the family in relation to the ethnic reality.

The definitions of family are as varied as are the delineation of its functions. The one selected here is particularly useful for our purposes since it encompasses the varied family constellations which are encountered in the course of social work practice. Papajohn and Spiegel (1975) developed a framework for family analysis intended to detect family states or conditions conducive to "good" or "bad" mental health. Their framework is universal, in that it imposes no boundaries, except those determined by families themselves. Among their reference points for defining family are two that are useful for our purposes:

1. The family is a major unit of the social system. Its structural

and functional characteristics extend into other subsystems such as the occupational and educational system.

2. The family is an agency for the transmission of cultural values.

In its form and function the family is connected with the values of a given ethnic group (Papajohn and Spiegel, 1975). These ethnic values are the core of ethnicity which has survived through many generations in various forms.

In presenting our model of ethnic-sensitive practice we called attention to the importance of relating the past history of ethnic groups to the contemporary situations which they confront. The exploration of that history will reveal that the values held by various groups are a product of that history, and that these cannot easily be separated from sociopolitical events. For example, the interrelatedness between the "Polish character" and its past history is clarified by this statement made by Edmund Muskie, a prominent Polish American (1966). "There is much of glory in Poland's past—glory which was the product of the love of liberty, fierce independence, intense patriotism, and courage so characteristic of the Polish people." The past to which Muskie referred included guarantees of religious freedom laid down in 1573, and the development of a constitution in 1791 which considered individual freedom as essential to the well-being of the nation. The Polish family of the present is a product of that history and may be expected to hold many of the values that Muskie identifies. Fiery independence continues to characterize many Poles. As we have noted over and over again, such values seep into the dispositions to work, to child-rearing, and to the role of women. As Polish and other ethnic families encounter mainstream America, struggles may ensue as values begin to shift or take on a different shape. Social workers must be aware of the delicate balance which sometimes ensues. The third-generation Italian father is less distrusting of the outsider than was his grandfather and may allow his daughter to date outside of the immediate ethnic circle; but at the same time he may maintain a traditional view on premarital sex (Kephart, 1977). This shift accommodates to the realities of present-day society but maintains a position in which women are held in high regard and effort is made to protect them from the outside world, which is "not to be trusted." The consequence of this evolution of values is often intergenerational conflict. Daughters in Italian families cannot appreciate the effort it may have taken for their fathers to permit them to date non-Italian men; their fathers cannot understand a changing code of sexual morality which does not condemn a bride who is not a virgin.

Each ethnic family, as a major unit of the social system, is influenced by the various aspects of the larger society. These influences serve to throw into question values which have been treasured for generations and have sustained the family for several generations in America. The resulting tension between resistance and accommodation may cause family turmoil, some of which may eventually come to the attention of a social worker.

These are but some of the kinds of family issues of which the ethnic-sensitive social worker must be particularly aware.The model for ethnic-sensitive practice presented in Chapter 5 presents a basis for attention to these aspects of family tensions.

In order to highlight how the various components of the model are brought to bear in practice, a variety of cases are presented here. Each case is distinctive in relation to the ethnic reality and how it influences the ways in which families and workers respond to the problems presented. In all cases social workers are expected to draw on the various layers of understanding and to adapt the various skills and techniques used to the ethnic reality.

To achieve the goal of ethnic-sensitive practice, social workers must be continualy aware of the second layer of understanding, which relates to awareness of their own ethnicity, recognizing that such awareness is incorporated as part of the "professional self." Social workers are not immune to the feelings of ambivalence about the fact of ethnic diversity and their own location in the ethnic geography. Greeley (1974) suggests that we are all torn between pride in our heritage and resentment at being trapped in that heritage. He speculates that the ambivalence is probably the result of the immigrant experience of shame, and defensive pride in an unappreciative society. No matter what the origin or nature, social workers must be aware of their own feeligs about their ethnic identity.

The case of Clyde Turner

When Clyde Turner saw the social worker at the Mental Health Unit of the hospital he said that he had come because he needed "a rest to get himself together." He was self-referred, but had been in mental health treatment centers before. The diagnosis made was schizophrenia. The tension and anxiety that he felt were evident in his behavior. Problems seemed to be generated by internal and external stresses.

Clyde is Black; he is 20 years old and a sophomore at a university near his home. His father, Roland, is on the faculty of another university in the area; he is working on his doctoral dissertation. Eleanor, his mother, is not employed outside of their home. His sister Jeanette, age 17, is a high school student who gets excellent grades.

Clyde said that family pressure is a part of his problem. He feels that he has not had a chance to become an independent person. The family upsets him and he becomes very argumentative.

His father has urged him to take five "profitable" courses in the next semester. Clyde had planned to take three such courses and two in the humanities, which would lessen the burden of school.

In an effort to "move away" from his family Clyde joined a fraternity but when the "brothers" learned of his problems they began to ridicule him and became patronizing.

School, family, friends all became "hassles" and Clyde sought refuge in the mental health unit for a rest.

Clyde's tensions and anxieties are in the present. The diagnosis of schizophrenia is not in question. There is sufficient evidence from previous admissions to other mental health centers to confirm the schizophrenic assessment. Relief of his tension and anxiety are of primary concern.

As the model for ethnic-sensitive practice is applied, consideration must be given to the first layer of understanding, knowledge of human behavior. This knowledge provides the data that begin to explain Clyde's disease. His natural struggle for independence at the emerging adult stage is hampered by the nature of his illness. The symptoms confound him and his parents, who at middle age, have begun to look forward to a life without child care responsibilities. One of their children, however, continues to need care, which they seem unable to provide.

The Turners are a middle-class Black family; that is their ethnic reality. Mr. Turner's thrust for advanced education for himself and his son are among the dispositions that often flow from that position. Unlike many Black middle-class families, that status is achieved with the employment of only one adult; Mr. Turner's salary as an educator provides sufficient income to maintain their middle-class position in appropriate style.

In other ways, however, the Turners are characteristic of the

Black middle class as delineated by Willie (1974): (1) one family member has completed college and attends graduate school on a part-time basis after adulthood; (2) they want their children to go to college immmediately after high school so that they will not need to struggle as long to attain their goals as did the parents; (3) there is little time for recreation because of intense involvement in work. Mr. Turner teaches at the college and works on his dissertation; Mrs. Turner works hard at housekeeping activities. They are socially accepted and respected in their own community. There are many adults who pursue graduate degrees in their adulthood, but for Blacks there has been the continual resistance by racist institutions which were reluctant to admit them. This is part of the experience of Blacks in America of which Clyde's social worker must be aware.

As Clyde and his father disagree about his selection of courses for the coming term they respond to an unconscious, unspoken, value of the Black middle class. Education will enable Black people to change their position in society; it will move them upward. There is no discussion about *whether* Clyde will return to school; the discussion is about *what* he will study when he returns.

In the struggle for independence Clyde sought out peers and as a result became a member of a Black fraternity. It is in peer groups such as this, whose membership is comprised of one ethnic group, that one often finds comfort. These groups affirm identity through special social projects and recreational activities undertaken. For Clyde, however, they intensified stress because of their inability to respond in comforting ways to his incapacities. But, like Clyde, they too are emerging young Black men seeking a place for themselves in the larger society. They may, however, be enlisted by the social worker to serve as a support group for Clyde. Efforts to provide them with a clearer picture of Clyde's difficulties may well enable them to refrain from ridicule and include Clyde more completely in the group activities.

Although there is no mention of extended family, further inquiry may uncover a kinship network that is available to give emotional support to the entire family. Although middle-class Blacks may sever connection with family members as they move upward, there is significant evidence that many retain a family support system mainly because of the vulnerability of their middle-class position (McAdoo, 1978).

As a young college student Clyde is subject to the stress of academic life, even without the extreme stress of his illness. How many other students at the university suffer? What resources in counseling are available? How adequate are those that exist? How may the services of the mental health unit be expanded or adapted to meet the needs of students from any college who reside in this suburban community? How does the stress of Clyde's illness disrupt the family as they struggle to maintain middle-class status?

These are among the questions that may be raised by social workers as they work with college students of any ethnic or social class group. Attention is focused on practice which moves from dealing with individual client need to modifying those larger systems which influence, positively or negatively, the client's day-to-day activities.

It is not the intention of this discussion to suggest a specific course of action which Clyde's social worker might take—that will depend upon many aspects of this case not presented. The activity will, however, be related to the route Clyde took to the social worker. It was totally voluntary and based upon previous successful experiences in mental health settings. The mental health unit is one of the services provided in a suburban general hospital. A majority of patients, of all ethnic groups, hold middle-class status. In such a setting there is often little involvement with larger systems. Yet evidence of systemic failure as it relates to the Turner family may be seen in the pervasiveness of racism. The energy invested in overcoming the obstacles required to attain a middle-class position may have some relationship to Clyde's problems; the specifics have to be determined by the worker and family.

The ethnic-sensitive worker, having applied the perspective of the model, now has more data available that will give a wider view of the Turner family as it struggles to cope with their schizophrenic son.

The case of Michael Bobrowski

It was Jean Bobrowski who took her husband Michael to the Family Counseling Association. It seemed the only way to help him. Since he lost his job he sat around the house or wandered aimlessly. She was very worried and went to see Father Paul, who suggested that she take her husband to the Association. The priest spoke to him also and encouraged his cooperation.

Mr. and Mrs. Bobrowski are Polish. When he was employed Mr.

Bobrowski was a truck driver. His work record was poor. When he backed a truck over a gasoline pump and failed to report it to his employers, he was fired. Because he was a member of the union, Mr. Bobrowski had expected that the union would help him find other employment but this did not materialize. He is ineligible for unemployment due to the circumstances of his dismissal. Mrs. Bobrowski now takes care of other people's children; his job had been the sole source of their income. They have lost their home due to nonpayment of the mortgage.

The Bobrowskis have been married for 30 years. He is presently 55, she is 50. Their son Michael, Jr., is 28 and lives in California with his wife and young son. Debbie, their daughter, is 24, married, and lives nearby. She has two children.

Both of the Bobrowskis are members of the Polish American Home, a social club, and the American Legion. They get a great deal of pleasure from the activities of each group, but they are less active since Mr. Bobrowski lost his job.

A major problem for this family is financial; the strain is becoming evident in this couple's relationship. The lack of employment is devastating to this Polish working-class family. While difficult for most people, this particular kind of devastation is to be expected in the case of a Polish family. To the Slavic work is the reason for living; if one cannot work then one is useless.

The work of Stein (1976, 1978) suggests that this attitude cuts across all social classes. In addition, essential goals of life are to own one's own home and to amass cash wealth as a cushion for security. Mr. Bobrowski has failed in all areas. His behavior has deprived him of work and, although he wishes to work, his union has not supplied employment as he expected. He has lost his home due to his failure to pay the mortgage. There are no cash reserves set aside. His application for unemployment insurance has been denied. The independence of character referred to by Muskie cannot be exemplified when there is no work, no home, no reserve. He is unable to protect his wife, who must now take care of other people's children in order to support the family. In their later adulthood, when there is the universal expectation of less responsibility because the children are emancipated, the Bobrowskis find themselves dependent and may need to seek resources from public agencies. The task of coping with a diminishing work role usually executed at old age must be accomplished earlier than expected. Although Mr. Bobrowski resists, it is unlikely that he will ever have steady employment again due to his poor work history.

Despite the emphasis on hard work and building up a cash reserve, the chances of attaining the security envisioned are fairly slim for Polish and other working-class families. Their income may appear to be substantial; the hard work that they do pays well. But they, as do many working-class families, have attempted to find the "good life" through the acquisition of consumer items. Many of these items are purchased "on time" and so the family income that appears to be "good" is spread out to make payments on the car, appliances, mortgage or perhaps a truck, camper, or small boat— before the purchase of food or medical care. Rubin (1976) has identified this precarious position on the edge of financial disaster as one contributor to the "worlds of pain" of the white working class.

An understanding of the realities of Michael Bobrowski's ethclass position, in which he suffers from the pain of a working-class position and failure to meet ethnic group expectation, enables the ethnic-sensitive worker to go beyond the problems of finance and depression.

An awareness of community resources will provide a direction as the worker seeks to help the family. Other resources must be enlisted by the ethnic-sensitive worker committed to simultaneous activity at micro and macro levels.

The couple is active in two secondary groups: the American Legion and the Polish American Home. Both are sources of strength in their lives. In each there is a sense of patriotism, which has been identified as a distinctive Polish characteristic. They are able to affirm their "Polishness" among other Poles at Polish American Home gatherings. Their present problems in living have caused them to become less active. They feel the stigma of unemployment and the depression which followed. Yet, this group may be able to help to diminish the sense of stigma. Mr. Bobrowski is not the only member who has problems leading to tensions and anxieties. Others may have marital conflict and problems with their children or parents. The nature of interpersonal relationships are such that similar problems may surface in many families. Is it possible for the Polish American Home to become an outreach center for the Family Counseling Association?

The Polish association could, with joint effort by the social worker and community leaders, become a part of the effort to minimize the stigma attached to mental health problems and to seeking service, which often plagues white ethnic communities (Giordano, 1973). Programs and services may be encouraged that span the life cycle, from day care services to senior citizens' activities, centered about the home and located in community-based institutions.

Mr. Bobrowski's route to the social worker was highly voluntary. He followed the suggestion of his priest, a significant person in his life. At the family association he may expect to be active in the plans for the solution of his problems. If he chooses not to continue services, he may be encouraged to continue until the work is completed but he will not be "punished" for this decision.

As social workers consider the route to services as well as the other aspects of the model for ethnic-sensitive practice, many components of Mr. Bobrowski's life are revealed that may have been overlooked in the past.

The case of Bobby Ramirez

Bobby is 15 years old, the fourth of five sons in the family of Luis and Berta Ramirez. He was referred to the child welfare agency by the family court after episodes of delinquent behavior. The charges included truancy and automobile theft. On one occasion he stole a truck and demolished it. He is believed to be incorrigible at home, having little regard for the expectations set forth by his father. It is the expectation of the court that the child welfare agency will find a place for him outside the community: a foster home or, as a last resort, a residential treatment center.

The Ramirez family is Mexican American. Mr. Ramirez was born in Mexico but came to the United States as an infant; his wife Berta was born here but her parents were born in Mexico. Their eldest son, age 23, is self-supporting and lives outside of their home. The second son lives at home but is partially dependent upon his parents. The work that he finds is of an unskilled nature and does not provide him with an income essential for living. The other sons at home besides Bobby are 17 and 13; both attend school.

Mr. and Mrs. Ramirez have completed high school and are employed. Luis is a sanitation worker for the city; Berta is a domestic worker. They live with their sons in a two-bedroom house, which they rent. At one time they owned a house but lost it when they were unable to keep up the payments. There is never enough money to save for the down payment on another house, even though that is their wish.

They have barely enough money for clothing. In order to stretch the food budget, their diet often includes rice and beans prepared in the Mexican way. There is no money for recreation and so leisure time is spent with friends and family. Parties are often spontaneous. Friends, whose circumstances are similar, bring food and beer. There is dancing, drinking, eating, and a great deal of happiness in just being together.

Bobby Ramirez's route to the social worker was totally coercive; it is the decree of the court, which has also suggested a solution. In addition, he is in a state of dual marginality, that involving his ethnic minority status on the one hand and adolescence on the other (Long and Virgil 1980): the universal tasks of coping with puberty and a growing sexual awareness, seeking for independence from parents, and developing the skills for that independence (Chapter 2) are compounded by his ethnicity. Exposure to the Mexican American and Anglo worlds may well have produced pressures which force him to make a choice rather than make a decision; internal ambivalence develops. Garcia (1971) suggests the kinds of questions which confront Bobby and many other Mexican American youth and which may generate ambivalence: Should I reject my parents and accept the culture, ideals, and aspirations of the Anglos? If I do, will my family reject me? But, if I claim my cultural identity will I eliminate the possibility of admission to the Anglo world that offers success and escape from poverty? The temptation is to choose the Anglo way.

This beginning knowledge of Bobby's adolescent dilemma comes from the layers of understanding focused on a (1) general knowledge of human behavior and (2) an awareness of the ethnicity of others. The problem identified by the court is juvenile delinquency—a place must be found for him. As the worker begins this task, the model for ethnic sensitive practice aids in developing insights that may make this transition less painful for all involved. Although the parents seem to concur with the decision of the court there is pain, for Bobby has brought the honor of the family into question.

Although Bobby has ignored the authority of his father by breaking the family rules (a major transgression among Mexican Americans), Luis as the head of his household will nevertheless take part in the planning for Bobby's future. Some Mexican American fathers feel so shamed by this kind of behavior on the part of their sons that they will offer no support (Murillo, 1976). Failure in the adult policing roles does not deny him the role of representing the family in the community and in association with other systems, in this instance the child welfare department. The roles of policing and representing the family are among the activities associated with *machismo*.

In his analysis of *macho*, the masculine role, Paz (1961) sees it as one which incorporates superiority, aggressiveness, insensitivity, and invulnerability subsumed under one word—*power*. The history of this position of honor, strength, and masculinity lies in associations which lead back to a history of the"warring, sacrificing Aztecs and their medieval Spanish conquerors" (Queen and Haberstein, 1974). In the present, *machismo* calls for an aloof authoritarian head of the family who directs its activities, arbitrates disputes, polices behavior, and represents the family in the community and society.

The social worker may expect Mrs. Ramirez to be devoted to her husband and children, including the eldest son who has moved away. Children, family, and a few friends are the core of life for Mexican American women (Murillo, 1976). Even though she works as a domestic, she does not do this every day; she must leave some time for her family responsibilities.

Her employment, along with that of her husband, provides barely enough income for the family to survive. Domestics and sanitation workers clean up after others. They carry out the most menial of tasks. The completion of high school has not provided access to higher positions; racism and discrimination have limited their opportunities. Although all family members speak English fluently, their surname and physical appearance provoke attitudes which diminish them in stature and attack their self-esteem.

A smaller family would require fewer resources but a smaller family would deny a tradition which supports large families. This tradition, however, serves to diminish the opportunity to attain the ordinary material rewards of American life. Mexican Americans are much more marginal in this respect than most other populations (Moore, 1970); they have few new clothes, a limited diet, and little recreation. The ethnic reality involves a life of near poverty, but at the same time there is much pride in their ethnic heritage; this is certainly true for the adults. Support comes from ethnic associates, who in an informal way share resources. This activity is not limited to the parties mentioned earlier but may be a regular occurrence, in respect to daily needs.

The decree of the court gives the social worker and the Ramirez family little choice; Bobby must be placed outside of the home. The court, however, is representative of those macro systems which appear to be blind to the needs of those most vulnerable: the poor, ethnic minority families. To remove Bobby from the community protects automobile owners from his larceny; it does nothing to address his adolescent conflict as he is trapped between two cultures of almost equal force.

The ethnic-sensitive worker has a heightened awareness of the need to promote change in the judicial system which will recognize the larger world of Bobby Ramirez and others like him. Perhaps efforts may be made to seek out *compadres* (godparents) of offenders, as a matter of policy, to assess their ability to lend support to their godchildren and become part of the process in planning for their care. The community in which the Ramirez family lives has few recreational resources for children and teenagers, a complaint that has often been expressed by the Ramirez boys and their friends. A study of the community will determine the accuracy of their statement. If their claim is indeed true, what efforts may be made to organize the various kinship groups in the area so that together they may press for funds from the city recreation budget to provide the supervised recreation needed by all of the children in this poor ethnic neighborhood?

The model for ethnic-sensitivity practice focuses the social worker's attention on how ethnicity and social class impact on the daily life of families. Bobby's acting out behavior has led him to a social worker, who with patience and greater awareness may begin to change his life and the lives of other young Mexican Americans with similar problems. In so doing the worker also takes into account the unique family dynamics involved.

SUMMARY

Each of the families presented in this chapter (the Turners, the Bobrowskis, and the Ramirezs) is attempting to carry out the functions of family presented early in the chapter. Sometimes they succeed, sometimes they fail. The potential for success or failure is related to their social class position and their ethnicity. Willie (1974) concludes (1) that all families in America share a common value system and (2) that they adapt to the society and its values in different ways, largely because of racial discrimination. Discrimination has intensified Mr. Turner's efforts to gain more education in order to maintain and enhance his middle-class position; on the other hand, it has kept Luis Ramirez in a near poverty position, denying him power over the destiny of his family. The Bobrowskis' expectations of working-class prosperity are denied as income is used to "pay the bills" for minor luxuries.

In each family, however, there are the joys of ethnicity that come from associations with others who are like them—this is a source of comfort and power of peoplehood. These relationships will continue as will the family; as a collection of individuals; as a group; as a major unit of the social system; and as an agency for the transmisson of cultural values (Papajohn and Spiegel, 1975). It is in the family that the stresses and strains of daily life are played out; children are born and reach adulthood; men and women love and hate; interpersonal and intrapersonal conflicts develop and subside as men, women, and children struggle with the demands of the larger society and with their own needs for sexual and emotional fulfillment. This is the base from which the ethnic-sensitive worker involved with families begins. The particular approaches to practice may vary.

Some may choose a broad-ranging psychosocial approach with the Turners, Bobrowskis, Ramirezes, and others like them. Others may find task-centered, structural approaches useful as a way of helping them to struggle with the problems presented. Others may help them to focus primarily on the external, structurally induced sources of their problems. Whichever approach they choose, ethnic-sensitive workers will be aware of how the route to the social worker constrains problem definition and work to bring those definitions into line with social work values. Essential also is simultaneous attention to how micro and macro systems impinge on family functioning, and attention to those macro task which will enhance such functioning. Always crucial is awareness of the layers of understanding and a recognition that techniques and skills may need to be adapted in order to respond to the families' ethnic reality.

REFERENCES

Ackerman, Nathan A. 1958. *The psychodynamics of family life: diagnosis and treatment of family relationships.* New York: Basic Books, Inc.

Garcia, Alejandro. 1971. "The Chicano and social work." *Social Casework,* *52*(5), May.

Giordano, Joseph. 1973. *Ethnicity and mental health—research and recommendations.* New York: American Jewish Committee.

Gordon, Milton M. 1964. *Assimilation in American life: the role of race, religion and national origins.* New York: Oxford University Press.

Greeley, Andrew M. 1974. *Ethnicity in the United States: a preliminary reconnaissance.* New York: John Wiley & Sons, Inc.

Kephart, William M. 1977. *The family, society and the individual* (4th Ed.). Boston: Houghton-Mifflin Co.

Long, John M., and Vigil, Diego. 1980. "Cultural styles and adolescent sex role perceptions." In Melville, Margarita B. (Ed.). *Twice a minority: Mexican American women.* St. Louis: The C. V. Mosby Co.

McAdoo, Harriet Pipes. 1978. "Factors related to stability of upwardly mobile Black families." *Journal of Marriage and Family, 40,* November.

Moore, Joan. 1970. In Queen, Stuart, A. and Haberstein, Robert W. (Eds.). *The family in various cultures.* New York: J. B. Lippincott, Co.

Murillo, Nathan. 1976. "The Mexican-American family." In Hernandez, Carrol, Haug, Marsha J., and Wagner, Nathaniel N. (Eds.). *Chicanos: social and psychological perspectives* (2nd Ed.). St. Louis: The C. V. Mosby Co.

Muskie, Edmund. 1966. "This is our heritage." In Renkiewicz, Frank (Ed.). *The Poles in American 1608-1972: a chronology and fact book.* Dobbs Ferry, N.J.: Oceana Publications, Inc.

Ogburn, William. 1938. "The changing functions of the family." In Winch, Robert F.and Goodman, Louis Wolf (Eds.). 1968. *Selected studies in marriage and the family* (3rd Ed.). New York: Holt, Rinehart and Winston, Inc.

Papajohn, John, and Spiegel, John. 1975. *Transactions in families.* San Francisco: Jossey-Bass Publishers.

Paz, Octavio. 1961. Quoted in Queen, Stuart, A. and Haberstein, Robert W. (Eds.). 1970. *The family in various cultures.* New York: J. B. Lippincott Co.

Queen, Stuart A., and Haberstein, Robert W. 1970. *The family in various cultures* (4th Ed.). New York: J. B. Lippincott Co.

Rubin, Lillian Breslow. 1976. *Worlds of pain: life in the working-class family.* New York: Basic Books, Inc.

Stein, Howard F. 1976. "A dialectical model of health and illness—attitudes and behavior among Slovac-Americans." *International Journal of Mental Health,* 5(3).

Stein, Howard F. 1978. "The Slovac-American 'swaddling ethos': homeostat for family dynamics and cultural continuity." *Family Process, 17,* March.

Willie, Charles V. 1974. "The Black family and social class." *American Journal of Orthopsychiatry,* 44(1), January.

David Antebi

CHAPTER
8
Ethnic-sensitive practice with recipients of Aid to Dependent Children

The Other America—Poverty in the United States was published in 1963. Its author, Michael Harrington, discussed the poor as "invisible people" who were to be found off the beaten track in "valleys of Pennsylvania," along rutted roads in cities and towns, or on farms. He described them as undereducated, underprivileged, lacking medical care, and in the process of being forced from the land into life in cities where they were misfits. This poverty, he declared, "twists and deforms the spirit." The move to the city often proved Harrington's prediction to be correct; they *were* misfits, without skills for jobs above the most menial level. Many soon looked to public agencies for financial support. For others the poverty was transitory— they were able to overcome with education, ambition, or the sheer refusal to remain suppressed (*Time*, 1977). The remainder soon became the core of the present American under class; a population of poor Blacks, Hispanics, Whites, Asians, and American Indians concentrated primarily in large urban centers.

The groups who fell readily into the "invisible poor" population were those most often the victims of racism, discrimination, and prejudice. The physical appearance of Blacks, Hispanics, American Indians, and Asians immediately set them apart. For many, language was an additional burden. Mainstream institutions denied ac-

221

cess to adequate education or housing and offered few opportunities for employment in positions with dignity.

The discovery of poverty in the 1960s was not its first appearance as a political issue. The poor and the response to their need have surfaced continually in our sociopolitical history. The response has developed at all governmental levels—federal, state, and local. The result is a vast, pervasive network of social services designed to provide financial help and a variety of services which enable people to obtain the essentials for living: food, clothing, and shelter. These services now range from day care centers for children to nutrition programs for older Americans. The largest of the many governmental programs is for dependent children. Known as Aid to Families with Dependent Children (AFDC), it is supported by federal and state funds. Its vastness has become a concern for those who would reform the welfare system.

THE WORK ETHIC

The call for reform is based upon the American ethic which requires *able-bodied* adults to work for their own subsistence rather than rely upon the public for support. This was not the case, however, when the Social Security Act of 1935 was introduced. This act enabled mothers to remain home with their children to raise them without the need to seek employment. But, as the numbers of mothers in the work force grew, a thrust for reform arose which was to induce welfare mothers to seek work (Rein, 1972). The mothers and fathers were subject to value judgments which questioned their *worthiness* for public support. Many of the children were born out of wedlock; fathers abandoned their children, legitimate and illegitimate, leaving them to bear the stigma of being "on the welfare."

In a society that adheres to the *residual* conception of social welfare, which expects the individual to look to institutional supports only after the "normal structures of supply, the family, and the market" have broken down, those who look to welfare programs are less valuable (Wilensky and Lebeaux, 1950). The poor in ethnic minority groups continue to look to government for assistance; the needed response is not readily provided. A reason may be found in the following observation: "The laziness and immorality of the lower classes were constantly referred to and alleged to account for their inferior standard of living. At no stage were the lower classes considered full members of society with rights in any way comparable to other classes" (Mencher, 1974). Although this reflects seventeenth-century British attitudes, twentieth-century American mainstream attitudes are similar as they label the poor: lazy, immoral, unappreciative, unable to manage their lives, and a general blight on the nation. Assistance becomes attached to acceptance of the work ethic.

The ethnic-sensitive worker must be aware of these attitudes which demand work instead of relief. At the same time there must be a recognition that the needs of the poor must be met. Their lives are continually judged by others. Although some ethnic groups are judged more harshly than others, all are judged.

The "feeling" of being a poor child is expressed in this poem:

> It's not so bad being poor,
> If you don't mind,
> That you can't really help the way you are
> 'Cause you haven't had the proper socio-
> Economic upbringing.
> Your skin's too dark, your hair is too curly
> And your father never married your mother.
> (Sermabeikian, 1975)

The child who speaks in this poem recognizes the barriers of ethnicity and social class and the powerlessness of an underclass status.

Poor men who attempt to provide the essentials for their wives and children are often frustrated in that effort by unemployment. There are a variety of solutions which will provide the needed income. He may abandon his family, which will make them eligible for AFDC, or he may remain and apply for assistance as an unemployed father. In either instance he may be expected to be judged, particularly if he does not belong to a poor ethnic minority group. Feelings of frustration and the resulting questions are expressed in this excerpt from a long poem about white urban poverty:

> The Black
> Welfare woman says,
> "Don't you know that you're
> White and
> Blond and
> Blue eyed?

Don't you know that you can
Get a job easily?
You can't get on welfare
No way!"
So,
How come I can't get work?
So
How come I can't get work?
So,
How come I have no money for
Bread and mustard
Sandwiches?
For milk and baby-food for
The babies?
How come?
I'm white . . . but I'm poor.
(Brown, 1974)

SELF-AWARENESS IN THE PUBLIC WELFARE SETTING

The poet feels the attack of the social worker, who makes assumptions that in his position as a white male he should have no problem finding the employment which he so sorely needs. This worker and others who find themselves in similar positions must begin to look closely at attitudes and assumptions which they hold that may interfere with the helping process.

In Chapter 3 the layers of understanding were introduced; they call for an understanding of human behavior and of the ethnicity of others and of oneself. The examination of self in this setting poses many questions; among them is the pervasive welfare question, "Why can't they get jobs?" Why are there so many Blacks when there are so many more opportunities than there were in the past? When are "they" going to learn to speak English and stop using their children and friends? With all the birth control available, why do they keep having babies? Some of them are only babies themselves. I'm like them (Black, Puerto Rican, Asian, American Indian) and I'm working, why aren't they? Why are there grandmothers, mothers, and daughters all without husbands?

As the social worker considers these questions again and again, there must be a recognition of the individual recipient's responsibility for his or her own behavior, and at the same time an understanding that there are indeed systemic failures which perpetuate the welfare system. To engage in coercive activities which attempt to get adults to go to work in many ways blames the victim. The answers are to be found as each social worker develops a greater understanding of each level of understanding. The final question becomes—how do *I* help to make a difference?

ORGANIZATION OF THE WELFARE SYSTEM

Making a difference in a large complex system is not an easy task. A developing self-awareness must encounter the realities of the welfare system. Although applicants and recipients are viewed as persons with particular needs and desires, the conditions for their eligibility for assistance are established outside of the local welfare agency where applicant and social workers meet. The rules and procedures are determined by a state division of public welfare. All assistance allowances are made in accordance with federal law and regulation, which permit a wide variation in assistance payments throughout the United States. Welfare is not limited to AFDC; it includes related services such as the Food Stamp Program, administered by the Department of Agriculture. Cities maintain general assistance programs; some states have Medical Assistance for the Aged, most may have Medicaid. The latter is a benefit which covers medical assistances for all financially eligible individuals and families. Special programs have addressed the needs of recent immigrants in the form of Cuban Refugee Assistance and the Indochinese Refugee Program, which provide financial assistance to individuals and families from Cuba, Vietnam, Cambodia, and Laos.

Payments of grants and the provision of social services are administered at the state and local level. The organizational structure, however, begins at the federal level in the office of the Secretary of Health and Human Services. Such elaborate and large systems always face potential problems in coordination of the individual components and effective communication (Federico, 1980). The smallest component of this system, the client, seems to be powerless in the face of such complexity. A welfare recipient who receives assistance for two sons comments upon her feelings of powerlessness:

I had no other choice but to apply for assistance. My family was no help when my husband took off. I was five months pregnant. If I ask my Income Maintenance Worker for help with a personal problem I get referred to my case worker. Sometimes I don't know who my case worker is. I had an IM worker who I never met at all.*

Another comments:

> The system is not set up to help you. It's set up to pull you down and keep you down. They tell you they are there to help you help yourself, . . . it's not true. They are out there to keep your face in the dirt.
> (Mauch, 1972)

The social worker caught up in the vastness may have a sense of powerlessness that begins to equal that of the clients. Questions begin to form about the real purpose of the welfare system and the ability of any one social worker to make changes. The frustration of work in a seemingly noncaring organization is expressed by a social worker in a large urban welfare agency: "No one would work if they knew what the policy is; if it was explicitly stated that we are here to pacify people so that they won't cause trouble, to let some people barely subsist so that other people can live the good life" (Mauch, 1972). This realization is often hard to take, as is the grueling work load. The result in many agencies is a constant turnover of professional staff.

The ethnic-sensitive worker who remains must understand the complexities of the organization and seek to enforce the values of the profession, which recognize the worth and dignity of all people and their capacity to change, their responsibility for themselves and others, and their need to "belong" (Morales and Sheafor, 1980). The importance of these values may be lost in the maze of the public assistance structure, but they must be remembered. Persons who apply for or receive assistance are among our most vulnerable citizens. They are questioned continually about their worthiness by the mainstream society as well as by other agency staff members. "Why don't you have a job?" is repeated again and again.

In our explorations we have found no ethnic group whose members refuse to work; indeed the perspectives on work may be different, but people *do* work. In the American Indian tradition work is not a good thing in itself, and so many Indians work only as much as they need to (Peretti, 1973). The Mexican American may view

---

*Conversation with an AFDC mother.

work as necessary for survival but not as a value in itself (Murillo, 1971), while the Japanese have a reverence for hard work and achievement (Kitano, 1976). The work ethic takes on its own form in relation to ethnicity. Each form must be respected for its own uniqueness in a setting that provides help when a person is without work.

THE WORK INCENTIVE PROGRAM (WIN)

> When your youngest child is six years old you have to apply for the WIN program. You have no choice. If you don't do it they will hold your check. You may want to stay with the kids but you have to go to apply for WIN . . . . They favor practical nursing and secretarial programs . . . . people seldom get jobs after they take WIN training . . . . but if you don't sign up, they hold your check. You sign up but you don't get a job.*

This is a welfare mother's comment on the Work Incentive Program. Introduced as a program to provide training and jobs for welfare recipients, WIN has not been able to fulfill that goal to any significant degree. Those who promote welfare reform through employment assume that jobs can be generated for those who are able to work, that training can be provided for all those who can be made employable. But job opportunities are not always available, as was the experience of this trainee: "Jobs just aren't available and it is a lie to say they are. Every time they offered me training I took it, although you can't do much with it. . . . I went to school for key punch, clerical training and nurses aid" (Mauch, 1972).

A study of the Work Incentive Program in Chicago, Detroit, and Cleveland conducted by Reid and Smith (1972) revealed that some recipients who claimed to be pleased by the referral to WIN held negative feelings about it; they felt that pressure might have been exerted if they refused, including being cut off from assistance. The women in the sample wanted jobs as a result of this experience, jobs that were unlike the low-level work they had done in the past. The final assessment, 21 months after the beginning of the study, revealed that in time only 11% of the original sample had found jobs through WIN. The remainder had found jobs on their own or had dropped from the program. In their conclusion Reid and Smith suggest that the program become voluntary; coercive efforts have failed

---

*Conversation with an AFDC mother.

and women might apply for training or educational programs as openings occur. Even though these suggestions are reasonable, we must recognize that those persons for whom jobs are sought are mostly ethnic minority women who are likely to be "peripheral workers" who need to work part-time or intermittently because of ther children (Lowenthal, 1972).

Lowenthal suggests that if we assume that no major economic interventions are forthcoming to make jobs available and increase wages in low-wage sectors, then the ability of most AFDC family heads to earn their way off assistance is low.

What then is the position of the ethnic-sensitive worker? There must be an examination of personal attitudes about individuals and their behavior, and perceptions about the value of work. In addition, there must be a commitment to simultaneous work through individual and systemic change efforts.

THE MODEL FOR ETHNIC-SENSITIVE PRACTICE

It might seem that, in this massive system burdened by rules, regulations, and procedures, ethnic-sensitive practice would not be possible—not only is it possible, it is *urgent*. The large number of ethnic minority recipients has been recognized. At times when they are most vulnerable, without power to control events about them, a social worker who is attuned to the impact of the ethnic reality and its various dispositions is important.

The route to the social worker

To be a recipient of AFDC suggests failure in a society that expects self-sufficiency. Eligibility for assistance requires that there be an absent parent; if both are present, then one must be disabled or unemployed. In each instance there is deficiency, an inability to provide for children in the expected way. Given this requirement, who wants to be on public welfare? The route may be called voluntary, yet the circumstances suggest pain from illness or failure. Husbands and lovers walk away, leaving women to ask, "Why?" Death comes to a young father, leaving his wife and children alone. An unfortunate automobile accident leaves a mother physically handicapped. Each of these events may create eligibility for AFDC, but who would invite such pain? The trip to the agency is a response to the need to provide food, clothing, shelter, and medical care for the children. Applicants do not choose a relationship with a social worker—it is part of the procedure. Social workers must recognize this as a possibility when recipients seem to be "uncooperative." Unnecessary coercive activity must be avoided if the rights of recipients are to be respected. The directive which insists upon pushing adults to work makes this difficult to achieve. In the cases which follow there is an undercurrent of coercive activity that appears to be unavoidable due to agency policy. Nevertheless, social workers must be aware of the values and assumptions of the model for ethnic-sensitive practice as well as the layers of understanding. Whenever possible, attempts must be made to work simultaneously through individual and systemic change.

The case of Marie and Hector Padilla

Marie and Hector Padilla are a young Puerto Rican couple with a 6-week-old baby girl. They are eligible for Aid for Dependent Children (AFDC) because Mr. Padilla has been on strike.

They do not want any services offered by the agency, only the grant.

Although they are polite, friendly, and straightforward in their answers to questions, they do not respond to any attempts to discuss any problem areas such as child care, particularly because the baby is so young, nor do they have any interest in training programs. Mr. Padilla insists that they have no problem other than the fact that he is not working.

After the company went on strike Mr. Padilla asked his family, his friends, neighbors, and *compadres* for help before he applied for public assistance (Ghali, 1977). The welfare department was his last resort. He needs to maintain his *machismo,* authority role, as husband and father; unemployment has put a strain on those relationships (Papajohn and Spiegel, 1975). However, if he does not present this potential stress as a problem, it is inappropriate for the social worker to assume that it must exist or that they are unable to care for their child. To insist that they "accept" counseling is viewed as coercive. Lack of cooperation may threaten eligibility. A large family network is available for support in child care; in fact, as their daughter grows she will be disciplined, when misbehaving, by any number of relatives, with her parents' approval (Papajohn and Spiegel, 1975). The strength of this ethnic family system is available to Marie and Hector. The model for ethnic-sensitive practice suggests that this strength be recognized and counted as an available resource. No further direct efforts are called for, except for the continual payment of the monthly allowance of \$336.* Considering the inadequacy of this allowance, it is suggested that the social worker give considerable thought to entering into alliance with other social work professionals, community service agencies, the Urban League, Puerto Rican Action groups, and any others who may choose to join. These professionals, along with the recipients, may organize to work toward legislation that would increase grants to a level which allows for a standard of living with some dignity.

One of the tasks assigned to welfare social workers is to assist clients in the management of their finances; often recipients are accused of irresponsibility because the money never lasts a whole month. One AFDC mother explains how she budgets each month:

> I get \$336 each month. First I pay the rent. I never keep the money from the landlord. Then I buy the food with the food stamps, I pay the phone bill and the electric. Last month my son needed sneakers. . . . No sneakers. . . . I take anyone's leftover furniture and even curtains. If they don't fit my window I may give them away or keep them in case I move to another apartment. We eat good at the first of the month but by the end it's really bad. Sometimes I have to borrow money from a friend.

The case of Sally Jackson

Ms. Jackson is a burden to her social worker. No matter how she tries, Ms. Jackson is never able to learn how to manage her money. She is always running out. She is always on the brink of disaster. Like other recipients she receives her grant of \$386 for her family of four, plus food stamps and Medicaid, but she still cannot seem to manage.

Sally Jackson is Black and a recipient of Aid for Dependent Children. Her eligibility is based on the fact that she has three minor children. She was married at one time, but her husband deserted after the birth of their first child. Soon after she established a relationship with Ray Evans, and they began to live together. They had two children. He had been employed in a local factory. Unfortunately, he was abusive and Sally left him, taking her children with her.

She is 32 years old. Her children are 12, 10, and 8 years old. On occasion Ms. Jackson works as a cleaning woman in a hospital. When she works her grant is reduced in relation to her income. The

---

*AFDC grant, June 1980, New Jersey Department of Public Welfare.

procedure is very complicated but in the end she seldom has more than $386 and so she does not pursue work heartily, although she enjoys being away from the house and with other people during the day. Work, the desired activity, is not worthwhile.

If Ms. Jackson were to work full time her income would be marginal, and she may lose her Food Stamp privileges as well as Medicaid benefits, so important when there are growing children subject to colds, contagious diseases, and broken limbs. As Ms. Jackson attempts to change her life, she finds her efforts fruitless. She feels powerless and impotent. This feeling of powerlessness may be found in Blacks at all social class levels, as society places *all* Blacks in the same single category regardless of attainment or income. The fruits of the impotence Ms. Jackson feels are a "loss of autonomy, a diminished sense of self-worth, and low self-esteem," which are even more debilitating at her underclass level. Leon Chestang (1972) in a discussion of "character development in a hostile environment" adds that the emotional effects originating from impotence are feelings of fear, inadequacy, and insecurity. Again and again the literature alludes to the history of Blacks in this country as an experience of degradation and humiliation which affects present attitudes of society and the availability of educational and occupational experiences.

The model for ethnic-sensitive practice calls for attention to Ms. Jackson's problem in the present, recognizing the effects of the history of Blacks upon her situation. But like Mr. and Mrs. Padillo, Ms. Jackson's problem is financial. As she looks to her siblings for support, as is often the custom in the Black under class, she finds that they too are struggling with barely enough to cover their own needs. Her tenth-grade education limits her job opportunities (Willie, 1976); she is "stuck" in the welfare system.

It is primarily through systemic change that Ms. Jackson's life will become less oppressive. The change must provide a reasonable income, employment with dignity, and training programs which do not carry a coercive overtone. These changes come about slowly and Ms. Jackson's problems with money are overwhelming today. But, the problem is not hers alone. The monthly allowance is not budgetable, yet families seem able to survive; how do they do it?

A group of AFDC mothers who meet together regularly may be able to share their "survival techniques" with Ms. Jackson; indeed, she may have some to contribute herself. Such a gathering recognizes the strength in families and provides an opportunity to visit and be among friends. Ms. Jackson's attempts at employment were largely motivated by a desire to be among other adults. While efforts are made toward systemic change, Ms. Jackson's need for immediate help in making the money last as long as possible can be found among other AFDC recipients.

The grants Ms. Jackson and others receive are provided to give support to dependent children, a powerless, helpless group. They remain powerless and helpless as the program responds continually to the problems of adults (Federico, 1980). Social workers must not forget that the assistance is for children and must begin to organize for change that affects their life more directly. This effort may be as small as negotiating with the neighborhood school administration to open the gymnasium for a few hours on weekday evenings and on Saturday mornings, thereby providing a recreational resource previously unavailable for Ms. Jackson's sons and the other children in the neighborhood.

The case of Marie Santangelo

Marie Santangelo is 37 years old. She receives Aid for Dependent Children for the support of her son Mike, who is 17 years old. He is a high school senior and will graduate in a few months.

They have lived with Jerry Rossi for most of Mike's life. Jerry is unemployed but receives social security disability benefits due to a work injury. He is 40 years old.

Their life together has been one of striving to make ends meet. Mr. Rossi says that he would marry Miss Santangelo but it would be too expensive; the grant from AFDC would be decreased. In a few months, however, Mike will be 18 and no longer eligible for assistance. When it is suggested that Miss Santangelo begin to consider employment, Mr. Rossi becomes very agitated, claiming that it is not right for her to work away from home. Both Miss Santangelo and Mr. Rossi are Italian.

The reality of lost income is a threat to the Santangelo-Rossi family. But, the eligibility criteria are clear. Children are eligible for AFDC from "birth to eighteen or to twenty one if in school, college, vocational or technical training."* Mike's eighteenth birthday and

---

*New Jersey Department of Human Services—Department of Public Welfare, July, 1978.

graduation from high school are only a few months apart. He expects to find employment in one of the small industries in the area. His earning will no doubt exceed the $255 that his mother receives for their support, but neither will be eligible for food stamps or Medicaid any longer.

Adherence to the model for ethnic-sensitive practice will alert the social worker to the possibility that Mr. Rossi's agitation when employment is suggested for Miss Santangelo may be the response to an ethnic disposition. The family has continued to be the central focus in Italian interpersonal relations. Women are expected to "take care" of their men. A majority of Italian women in Krause's study (1978) agreed that women do best as wives and mothers and that *true* women are happiest with their husbands and children. If this is the feeling of Miss Santangelo as well, then resistance to employment is not as irrational as it seems in a system that is beginning to consider the employment of women to be a major determinant of worthiness.

The dilemma may be compounded. Miss Santangelo, like the respondents in Krause's study, may feel that women are too emotional for some jobs and that they are different from men. If this is so, then social work efforts to steer Miss Santangelo toward training and/or employment may meet with minimal success.

Miss Santangelo does have two resources immediately available—her son and Mr. Rossi. Is it possible that they are willing to assume the responsibility for the support of their "wife" and mother. Since Mr. Rossi insists that work is not appropriate for his friend, then he must recognize the consequence of his position. He has been a part of this family for most of Mike's life; his discussion of marriage suggests a commitment to Miss Santangelo. To insist that she enter training or find employment is coercive activity which does not take into account the wishes of this AFDC family.

A study of community resources may reveal social service agencies, churches, or women's groups that will be able to assist the Santangelo-Rossi family when the AFDC grant has been discontinued.

In our present society it does not seem to be unreasonable to expect high school graduates to seek employment if they do not intend to continue their education. Mike, in fact, looks forward to the independence that will come with a job. As an Italian male adolescent moving toward emerging adulthood, he has become more involved with friends at school and in the community. He has done without many of the "extras" that are important as children grow, but he now looks forward to independence.

Solutions that please the system are not always forthcoming. The social worker must respect Miss Santangelo's decision not to work and provide her with knowledge about community resources which may be helpful to her in the future.

SPECIAL PROGRAM
Example: The Indochinese Refugee Program

Among the special programs supported entirely by federal funds is the Indochinese Refugee Assistance Program introduced to provide financial assistance to individuals and families from Vietnam, Cambodia, and Laos. This new group of refugees has problems with language, employment, and adaptation to a new country. Special centers have been established to aid them as they learn to speak English, seek employment, and learn to solve problems in a strange environment. They are eligible for public assistance programs as individuals, couples, or parents with children.

The case of Mr. and Mrs. Dinh Nguyen

Mr. and Mrs. Dinh Nguyen are Vietnamese. They have a 4-month-old child. Mrs. Nguyen's brother Pao lives with them. They are all quite young. Mr. Nguyen is 24. His education in Vietnam was extensive and he holds what could be called a baccalaureate degree. At present, however, he is not employed but attends the county vocational school to learn new skills. In the evening he attends an adult program for newly arrived refugees from Indochina.

Pao is 19. He is employed as a maintenance person in a local supermarket. In the evening he too attends school to learn English. Some evenings he goes to the vocational institute to learn a new trade. In Vietnam he was a factory worker.

Mrs. Nguyen is 25. Her primary task is to take care of the baby.

The family was sponsored by a local church. The congregation assumed responsibility for locating housing when they arrived. The house was furnished with secondhand and new items supplied by the church. Members have assisted with shopping for household supplies and food. They were most helpful when the baby was born, providing the necessary clothing and furniture.

The family receives public assistance. Their grant of $336 is based on AFDC allowance standards. Months before the Nguyens arrived, the church began its efforts to sponsor a Vietnamese family. Contacts with the denomination headquarters and Church World Service led to the assignment of the family. The congregation agreed to help in the ways described earlier and have continued to do so. This initial institutional response to need is supported by the legislation which gives financial support to the Nguyens and Pao.

As social workers apply the model for ethnic-sensitive practice in work with the Nguyen family they realize that history has had an immediate impact upon their lives. Past and present history of war and its aftermath have caused their migration to a new country. Their ethnicity causes immediate strain as they confront an entirely new environment in which they are dependent upon the church and the welfare system for support. Strength and support may be found in relationships formed with members of the church, but the most comforting are found among other participants in the refugee assistance program. The bilingual and bicultural counselors understand the tensions that are present as the Nguyens and Pao find their way.

In the public agency workers must be aware that Asian recipients are most responsive if at initial contact agency functions, services, and the kind of assistance available are made very clear (Ho, 1976). Ho suggests that short-term service with concrete goals is usually needed. This has been the experience of social workers in public agencies who have worked with Vietnamese families. Their experience suggests that Mr. Nguyen and Pao will complete their training programs, find employment with the help of the refugee assistance program, and request that assistance be discontinued.

The system has designed a special program to meet the needs of this special group of Asians; however, there are countless Asian Americans who are without the many resources available to new arrivals. Elderly Japanese, Chinese, and Koreans are hidden in many "Chinatowns" of our urban centers. Japanese families have problems with alcoholism, mental illness, and retarded children, as do other American families; yet there is a negative attitude toward mental illness in the Japanese community (Mass, 1976). Chinese youth are faced with the tensions common to adolescence as well as cultural value conflicts that may arise with their Chinese-born parents (Chen, 1970). At each stage of the life cycle Asian families are in need of various services, including public assistance. The need for systemic support is evident but is lacking. The tendency of Asians to hide problems because of their sense of shame and pride makes work difficult, but efforts must be pursued. Chen (1970) has presented steps which need to be taken in working toward change in the Chinese community. They are useful in other Asian communities as well: (1) inform the general public and the Chinese community; (2) develop community resources to cope with the existing problems by initiating social programs; (3) promote social action; (4) initiate constructive legislation; (5) develop leadership; (6) educate bilingual social workers; and (7) conduct research and surveys into the changing Chinese American family structure. These steps enable the ethnic-sensitive worker to move in an organized fashion toward change in neglected Asian communities; the effort may well begin with an Asian recipient of public assistance.

SUMMARY

This chapter has considered the application of the model for ethnic-sensitive practice in the public welfare setting. We recognize that recipients for the most part do not wish to be a part of this system. They are continually negatively viewed for behavior that is acceptable at other social class levels. There is continual coercive activity which provokes a sense of powerlessness, and a budget allowance which barely meets minimal requirements for survival. Many recipients are women and their children; often they are members of ethnic minority groups and are judged more harshly than other recipients. The ethnic-sensitive worker must recognize these factors and work continually for systemic change that will support voluntary employment training programs and provide grants to enable parents to provide their children with nutritious meals all month, appropriate clothing as the seasons change, and a few of the extras that make childhood a joyful experience.

REFERENCES

Brown, Sam Ervin. 1974. From "Poetic expressions of a white urban family." Submitted in partial fulfillment of course requirements for the Urban Family, Rutgers University School of Social Work. Fall.

Chen, Pei-Ngor. 1970. "The Chinese community in Los Angeles." *Social Casework*, *51*(10), December.

Chestang, Leon. 1972. "Character development in a hostile environment." Chicago: The School of Social Service Administration, The University of Chicago.

Federico, Ronald C. 1980. *The social welfare institution—an introduction.* Lexington, MA: D. C. Heath and Co.

Ghali, Sonia Badillo. 1977. "Cultural sensitivity and the Puerto Rican client." *Social Casework,* October.

Harrington, Michael. 1962. *The other America—poverty in the United States.* Baltimore: Penguin Books.

Ho, Man Keung. 1976. "Social work with Asian Americans." *Social Casework,* March.

Kitano, Harry H. L. 1976. *Japanese Americans* (2nd ed.). Englewood Cliffs, N.J.: Prentice-Hall, Inc.

Krause, Corinne Azen. 1978. *Grandmothers, mothers and daughters.* New York: American Jewish Committee.

Lowenthal, Martin. 1972. "Work for welfare clients: a nonreform." *Urban and Social Change Review,* 5(2), Spring.

Mass, Amy Iwasaki. 1976. "Asians as individuals: the Japanese community." *Social Casework,* March.

Mauch, Joan. 1972. "Voices never heard/faces seldom seen." *Public Welfare,* 30(3), Summer.

Mencher, Samuel. 1967. *Poor law to poverty—economic security policy in Britain and the United States.* Pittsburgh: University of Pittsburgh Press.

Morales, Armando, and Sheafor, Bradford. 1980. *Social work—a profession of many faces* (2nd ed.). Boston: Allyn and Bacon, Inc.

Murillo, Nathan. 1970. *The Mexican American family.* In Hernandez, Carrol, Haug, Marsha J., and Wagner, Nathaniel N. (eds.). *Chicano—social and psychological perspectives,* St. Louis: The C. V. Mosby Co.

Papajohn, John, and Spiegel, John. 1975. *Transactions in families.* San Francisco: Jossey-Bass, Inc., Publishers.

Peretti, Peter O. 1973. "Enforced acculturation and Indian-White relations." *The Indian Historian,* 6(1), Winter.

Reid, William J., and Smith, Audrey D. 1972. "AFDC mothers view the work incentive program." *The Social Service Review,* 46, September.

Rein, Martin. 1972. "Work incentives and welfare reform." *Urban and Social Change Review,* 5(2), Spring.

Sermabeikian, Patricia. 1975. "What's so bad about being poor." In *A little piece of the world.* Submitted in partial fulfillment of course requirements for the Urban Family, Rutgers University School of Social Work, Fall.

Time Magazine. *The American underclass.* August 29, 1977.

Wilensky, Harold L., and Lebeaux, Charles N. 1958. *Industrial society and social welfare.* New York: Russell Sage Foundation.

Willie, Charles V. 1974. "The Black family and social class." *American Journal of Orthopsychiatry,* 44(1), January.

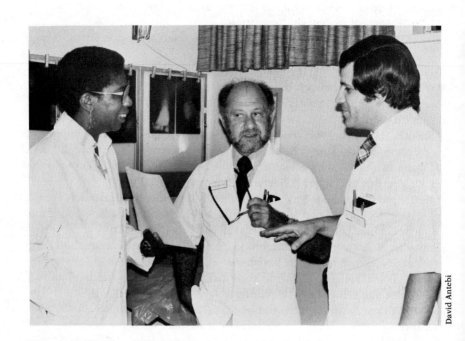

Ethnic-sensitive practice in health care

Social work's involvement in health care has a long and honorable history. Indeed, it has been suggested that the roots of social medicine, medicine that looks beyond the diseased body to the social antecedents and consequences of illness, are to be found in social work in health care (Rosen, 1974).

"Medical social work," a term more commonly used in the past than in the present, was introduced at Massachusetts General Hospital by Dr. Richard Cabot, a physician of vision who suggested that: "The average practitioner is used to seeing his patients flash by him like shooting stars—out of darkness into darkness. He has been trained to focus upon a single suspected organ till he thinks of his patients almost like disembodied diseases" (Cabot, 1913).

Cabot looked to social work to help identify and intervene in those social factors which were behind "individual suffering." He recognized that work pressures, political organization, and inadequate income are factors which affect health and illness. His vision was far-reaching. He understood early what has become more evident and intensified since the days when he invited Ida Cannon to begin a social work department at Massachusetts General Hospital. Since then medical and health care has become more complex, more specialized, and more fragmented. Unprecedented advances in technology continue to hold out hopes for cure and relief of distress.

At the same time, specialization intensifies the likelihood that health care practitioners will focus on the diseased organ, having limited training and time to look beyond that organ at the person suffering from the disease.

Social work in health care is fast-paced and frequently crisis-oriented, and involves work with people experiencing acute pain, dealing with frightening procedures which they may not understand, and fearing threat of loss of their own lives or those of others near and dear. Whether they work in hospitals, ambulatory care centers, health departments, mental health centers, or planning departments, social workers are obliged to be aware of and work with the facts that: (1) health problems have a social component, and (2) the psychologically and culturally induced responses to pain and illness affect responses to treatment.

Importantly, they need to understand how the health care system responds to these "social facts," which form the basis for the social work role in health care. Social work is committed to function as a professional, humane link between patients, families, health care providers, and the political and social system which shapes how care is rendered and what care is available. Included is attention to prevention and intervention.

> Physicians care for ailing organs. Hospitals provide facilities for testing and for acute care. A variety of rehabilitation specialists assist in the development of occupational *or* physical *or* other faculties. No one seems to be able to deal with the whole person and all of that person's complex needs. . . . These tasks have in the past and will in the future be carried out by social workers"
> (Dinerman, Schlesinger, and Wood, 1978).

There are a number of conceptions which must be understood by the ethnic-sensitive social worker in health care. These include (1) self-awareness; (2) health and illness behavior; (3) illness as deviance; (4) the sick role; (5) the cultural roots of illness behavior; (6) prevailing patterns in the organization and financing of health care; (7) the relationship between socioeconomic status and illness; and (8) the role of social and community networks in curing and caring.

We begin the discussion of the kind of issues which confront the ethnic-sensitive social worker in health care by examining the issue of self-awareness as it pertains to practice in this area.

SELF-AWARENESS

Social workers in health have a particular obligation to be aware of their own feelings about physical suffering, pain, disfigurement, and death.

The array of life-saving drugs and equipment currently available makes it possible to prolong life. Concerns about the quality of life thus sustained receive increasing attention. Holden (1980) suggests that the ambience in renal dialysis centers does not offer patients a true choice between life and death. Unable to live without dialysis or a kidney transplant, some choose to die, despite the resistance of the staff. Recent decisions by the Catholic Church (as in the case of Karen Anne Quinlan) suggest that recourse to religious precept no longer serves as an unswerving guide. American Indians do not always seek to prolong life (Coulehan, 1980). Workers must guard against imposing their own feelings about prolonging life on the choices patients make. The hospice movement and other developments in oncology suggest that our awareness in these matters is heightening.

The legalization of abortion has created a moral dilemma for those workers whose own belief systems are at variance with the view that women have the ultimate right to make decisions affecting their own bodies. Social workers who view abortion as sinful will need to be particularly on guard against imposing their values on those who seek their help in this area. Some workers who do not believe in the right to abortion ask to be excused from working with women having abortions. This reflects appropriate self-awareness. Workers who feel strongly that having an unplanned child is a mistake are similarly obliged to be sure that their own biases do not intrude on the client's decision-making process.

Changing life-styles in the area of sexuality sometimes offend social workers whose own background has not exposed them to sexually active teenagers, homosexuals, and people living together without benefit of wedlock. We have seen many students struggle in the effort to present a nonjudgmental stance when working with poor teenagers who are having their second or third out-of-wedlock child.

It is not uncommon for social work students, particularly those of middle-class background, to describe their first exposure to ghetto clients as involving culture shock. On closer questioning, we find that their shock is not infrequently related to adolescent sexuality. Extreme sensitivity to the way these kinds of problems affect the workers' own sensibilities is needed.

For those who do not call on God, or other supernatural beings, for help, the type of faith expressed by others is sometimes unsettling.

The case of Mrs. Brown

Mrs. Brown, an elderly Black woman, was admitted to the hospital in a severe state of malnutrition.

Review of the record revealed that Mrs. Brown and her husband, a childless couple, had no assets other than their fully paid-up house. Neither was able to work any longer; they were not eligible for Social Security. Their eligibility for public assistance was contingent on their willingness to sign over their house to the public assistance agency. Having steadfastly refused to do this, they literally had no money to buy food. Old and isolated, they were not part of a community network.

After several days of trying to speak to Mrs. Brown, who was drowsy, the worker was finally able to identify herself and offer help. Mrs. Brown responded, "I knew God would help."

The worker, a Jewish woman with few religious beliefs, was startled and chagrined. Lacking the deeply ingrained religious commitment which Mrs. Brown had, the worker was tempted to offer a lecture on the workings of the public welfare system. Workers need to understand how faith can sustain others through much trauma.

Social work in health care is interdisciplinary; social workers in hospitals, clinics, and health centers are not as autonomous as they would like to be. Considerable attention must be given the feelings invoked by the physicians' authority. Importantly, social workers in this practice arena need the self-awareness and self-confidence required to advocate and to assert professional expertise. This is not easy vis à vis doctors and hospital administrators. "Clinging vines" who like to sit behind their desks waiting for people to come to them do not do well in the fast-paced, traumatic, multidisciplined settings in which health care is delivered.

Advocating for the poor, for those who do not speak English, and for those who have greater faith in the spirits than in modern medicine requires a great awareness of self and of one's professional identification.

BASIC CONCEPTUAL FORMULATIONS
Health and illness behavior

We begin this discussion by presenting two case examples. The context in which the care is rendered, the health problems presented, and the class and ethnic group membership of the involved people vary considerably. Despite this divergence, it shall become evident that some common themes emerge.

The case of Mr. Mangione

Mr. Mangione, a 55-year-old Italian man, is referred to the Hospital Social Work Department by the Department of Physical Medicine. They find him to be uncooperative in treatment and ask the social worker's help in eliciting Mr. Mangione's cooperation in the treatment plan.

Victim of a stroke, Mr. Mangione has undergone considerable rehabilitation therapy. His speech, though still slightly slurred, is readily understood. He walks quite well, though he still has a slight limp.

He thinks he is ready to return to his job as a clerk in a local hardward store. He is refusing to undergo any more rehabilitation therapy, feeling he has had enough.

In exploring the situation the worker discovers that Mr. Mangione's employer agrees that Mr. Mangione is now capable of working in the store. However, he has let Mr. Mangione know that he does wish that he "would speak just a little better so that the customers don't know there's anything wrong with him."

The staff in physical medicine is frustrated. They know that with just a bit more effort he could improve considerably. "We've put in so much time, we don't want him to let us down now."

Coulehan (1980) cites the case of Tommie Chee, a 38-year-old Navajo man who lives on a 25,000–square mile reservation.

The case of Mr. Chee

Mr. Chee, a married man, employed at a boarding school dormitory, left his job, feeling too sick to work. He had chronic low back pain and insomnia. His appearance deteriorated, and he would not return home for several days at a time. At one point he was found wandering aimlessly in the desert, near the family camp.

On hospitalization a diagnosis of endogenous depression was made. Antidepressant medication was prescribed, and he was referred to a mental health clinic in a town 65 miles away from home.

He did not keep clinic appointments or take his medication. Over the next period of time he got worse.

Following this the family engaged a "shaker."* He thought Mr. Chee had married into the wrong clan, was possessed by the ghost of his mother's brother, and thought too much, thus lowering his resistance and allowing the ghost to gain possession. After a Nine Day Sing† Mr. Chee was cured of possession. Following this he returned to work and was relieved of symptoms.

These examples illustrate the diverse expectations and prescriptions related to illness. Mr. Mangione considers himself "cured" when he feels able to function. This is at odds with the view of others close to him. Mr. Chee does not get better until traditional healers help him. In both situations, social workers are obliged to be aware of these divergencies. Illness behavior varies in other respects.

In some groups people are expected to be stoic when experiencing pain (Zborowski, 1952). In others, distress is vigorously expressed. A set of symptoms—which may consist of tearing off one's clothing in public, screaming and falling into a semiconscious state while twitching—is considered a culturally recognized cry for help when people are experiencing a lot of strain. This set of symptoms, described as an *ataque*, is not uncommon among Puerto Ricans on the mainland (Garrison, 1977). Mechanic (1978) suggests that: "Illness, illness behavior and reaction to the ill are aspects of an adaptive social process in which participants are often actively striving to meet their social roles and responsibilities, to control their environment, and to make their everyday circumstances less uncertain and, therefore, more tolerable and predictable."

Mr. Mangione, Mr. Chee, and people who experience *ataques* are responding to personal stress. They are all seeking means to relieve stress in ways which are consonant with their personal histories and with how the ethnic and class group in which they are enmeshed tend to deal with that stress.

Italians are said to be particularly concerned with the immediate relief of discomfort (Zborowski, 1952). Many American Indians attribute disease to a variety of extrahuman forces which must be dealt with if the "causes of the illness" are to be removed (Coulehan,

---

*A folk diagnostician who is believed to be able to ascertain the cause of disease.
†A ceremony that recounts myths of creation, emergence, and salvation.

1980). Analogous beliefs are held by many Hispanics (Garrison, 1977; Samora, 1978; Stenger-Castro, 1978).

The problems of all of the people described above can be diagnosed and understood in varying terms. *Ataques* are variously diagnosed as schizophrenia, as the function of being possessed, and as hysteria (Garrison, 1977).

The examples cited suggest that they must be viewed within the cultural context of people's lives, which must be understood by those working with them. How these conceptions aid in assessing and developing intervention strategies will be considered in various sections of this chapter.

Illness as deviance and the sick role

With few exceptions, all groups view illness as a negative phenomenon. Whether it is perceived in purely physical terms—as pain and injury—or at an emotional level—as in the case of extreme anxiety, depression, or disorientation—illness involves discomfort and disruption. When people are sick, they are usually totally or partially unable to go about their daily business.

For these reasons, illness has been characterized as "legitimated deviance." Because of its disruptive effects all societies and social groups define the rights and obligations associated with being ill, and develop mechanisms to control illness and its social consequences.

Closely related to the concept of illness behavior and illness as deviance is the concept of the sick role. Parson's (1958) initial formulation, though considerably extended and critiqued, is incisive. There are four key elements: (1) since people do not choose to be ill, they are usually not held responsible for their illness, but "curative processes" independent of their desire to get well are essential for recovery (e.g., penicillin, not motivation, will "cure pneumonia," and only an appendectomy will serve to prevent the negative consequences of appendicitis); (2) while ill, people are excused from carrying out their obligations; (3) this exemption is contingent on the "sufferer's recognition that illness is an undesirable state not to be maintained"; (4) the sick person is obliged to seek competent help.

Some of the criticism and extensions of these formulations are particularly relevant for social workers in the health arena. Freidson (1970) suggests that the view is limited to western conceptions of the doctor-patient relationship and that not all groups share the view that all sick people are to be exempt from carrying out their ordinary responsibilities. He suggests that Parsons' perspective focuses on acute illness, asumes the availability of cure, and does not allow for analysis of what happens to those who are chronically ill. Important is the notion of stigma (a spoiled identity) (Goffman, 1963). Those with visible physical handicaps, with incurable illness, or with illness for which they are held accountable (e.g., venereal disease) develop a negative sense of self and are often treated negatively.

Rehabilitation efforts are frequently targeted to minimize the discomforts of the nonafflicted, who want the disabled person to conform to their vision of normality. Rehabilitation agencies are in the business of "defining" what is proper recovery (Freidson, 1972).

The relevance of these conceptions for social work practice in health care are illustrated by the cases presented above.

The situation in which Mr. Mangione finds himself points to differing views on what it means to be "well" and what "competent help" means. He considers himself sufficiently well to sell hardware. But in the view of his employer a slight limp or slurring of speech may be discomforting to customers.

The staff of the Department of Physical Medicine wants to do "their thing" and, by refusing further treatment, Mr. Mangione is preventing them from showing what they can do.

What is the social worker's obligation? First and foremost, workers must assess the basis of the client's wish. Is Mr. Mangione fearful he will lose his wife's respect as head of the household if he continues to be dependent? Is the worker aware that the medical opinion is only one among many? Can the staff be helped to recognize that Mr. Mangione has fulfilled many of the obligations of the patient role? Keeping in mind these kinds of considerations will likely help Mr. Mangione arrive at a decision which is congruent with his sense of himself, his need to continue work, and how his disability is perceived by his own ethnic and class group. Perhaps he cannot economically affort to withstand the pressure to continue treatment. As a 55-year-old, semiskilled, working-class man, his chances of finding another job are slim. Social workers have obligations beyond helping the individuals who find themselves in this position.

First, they need to be aware of how their own ethnic and class dispositions affect their position on these issues. If they have internalized the view that "total rehabilitation" or recovery is a desired goal, they are likely to characterize Mr. Mangione's reaction as "pathological"; perhaps in their view he is really trying to get out of working, hoping he'll be fired and eligible for disability payments. How do they really feel about incorporating the handicapped into the work force? How have they felt about and dealt with handicapped people in their own work settings? And, importantly, is there a way that they can sensitize other staff members and other patients with problems similar to those which Mr. Mangione is experiencing? Is the staff aware of different ethnic and class dispositions? Can efforts to enhance such understanding be built into staff seminars? Would patients of varying ethnic and class groups benefit from group counseling?

And what of employers? Is there a way in which the social worker can reach them to explore the problems they experience when the handicapped return to work? Perhaps Mr. Mangione would be too embarrassed to have the social worker contact his employer. But the ethnic-sensitive social worker might think about joining with physiotherapists, other rehabilitation specialists, and representatives of such groups as the Chamber of Commerce in organizing educational and discussion sessions.

In the case of Mr. Chee, both Western physicians and native healers viewed his illness as disruptive. Marked differences prevailed on "who the appropriate healers are." The fact that mental helth clinics, removed from the core and center of the community, are perceived as alien has been frequently documented, as has the positive role played by folk healers. Social workers who view folk ministrations as "mumbo jumbo" or, even worse, fail to inform themselves of their existence, will not gain the trust required for work with people who hold strong adherence to such belief systems.

Many health beliefs and behaviors—both those which are congruent with Western medicine and other systems—have ethnic, class, and cultural roots.

The cultural roots of illness behavior

It has been suggested that: "Culture exerts its most fundamental and far-reaching influence through the categories we employ to understand and respond to sickness" (Kleinman, 1978). Considerable evidence exists to support this assertion.

The American health care system is in large measure an outgrowth of our reverence for science and technology, and the conviction that nature can be mastered. It is secular, rational, and based on the premise that those who use and deliver these services share that perception (Parsons 1951). There is substantial evidence to suggest that the belief systems of middle-class people of all ethnic groups are reasonably congruent with this view (Greenblum, 1974; Zborowski, 1952). This is particularly true of Jews, who have a long history of extensive concern with matters of health, a concern attributed to "the sense of precariousness" and fear concerning survival related to centuries of dispersal and persecution (Howe, 1975).

Zborowski (1952) and others (Greenblum, 1974) have suggested that these cultural themes manifest themselves in a volatile, emotional response to pain accompanied by a concern about how the illness would affect the future. Medical specialists of all sorts are highly valued and their advice sought extensively.

Consider the following example as a case in point.

The case of the Jewish adolescent

A 15-year-old Jewish boy has been diabetic since early childhood.

The son of parents who are both professionals, he was a good student who knew that he was expected to go to college.

His parents were solicitous and highly attuned to every nuance of the disease. His mother was particularly solicitous, fussing a lot about the diet as well as the mildest symptoms.

He was seen by the "best" internists and frequent consultation was sought. His good adaptation to the illness was frequently noted by doctors, relatives, and friends alike. He was a good athlete, affable and outgoing. While admiring of this, his parents did let him know that he should not "overdo"; at the same time, grandparents, while visiting, were admonished not to remind him of his illness or suggest that he restrict his activity.

During his sophomore year in high school he began to neglect his school work and found many excuses not to go to school. He seemed somewhat distracted and anxious, despite the fact that symptoms had considerably abated and the disease was well controlled.

When the anxiety increased to the point where he virtually stopped going to school, psychiatric care was sought.

The evaluation revealed that the young man was extremely worried about how he would be able to function in a year or two, when he would be expected to go off to school and care for himself.

In addition to the disease itself, the cultural heritage, together with adolescence—a stage of the life cycle when the assertion of independence assumes great importance—converged to precipitate a crisis.

Could an ethnic-sensitive perspective on the part of health care professionals have helped to avert a crisis? Perhaps the parents could have been helped to minimize the "shopping" for specialist care, thus reducing the ongoing attention to the illness. And how about their expectations for achievement? Could they have been helped to reduce the mixed messages? "You're so sick my dear, but we expect you to excell anyway!"

There are other views of illness. Illness is variously viewed as a punishment for sin (Samora, 1961; Stenger-Castro, 1978), as a function of supernatural forces, as "disharmony" (Coulehan, 1980), as a force to be mastered, or as a fact which is passively accepted. Many tribal cultures make no distinction between religion and medicine. Healing experiences are an integral part of community life. Harmony—of people with nature, with each other, and with the gods—is the desired state. Symptoms or disease states as conceived by the western mind are viewed as reflections of underlying disharmony. This disharmony may be caused by witchcraft, spirits, storms, or animal contamination (Coulehan, 1980).

Analogous beliefs and related health practices are found among Puerto Ricans and Chicanos. These groups also use non-western healers. In fact, among Puerto Ricans, American Indians, and Chicanos, there is a marked tendency to use both folk and western healers simultaneously (Fuchs and Bashshur, 1975; Garrison, 1977; Lazarow, 1979).

Puerto Ricans use healers known as *espiritistas*, who have supernatural inspiration which they can bring to bear on health and illness. "The essential belief is that any individual jealous of the achievement, advantages or abilities of another, whether in love, business or politics can arrange to have an evil spell cast on the adversary" (Wintrob, 1973). Spiritist treatment procedures focus on exorcising harmful spiritual influences and strengthening benign spiritual influences.

Many Mexican American health beliefs relate to the view that God, the creator of the universe, is omnipotent. Personal destiny is subject to God's judgment, and suffering is a consequence of having sinned and a punishment (*castigo*) for disobeying God's law (Stenger-Castro, 1978). Witchcraft also plays a part in this belief system.

The practice of *curanderismo* invokes the belief that the natural folk illnesses that commonly afflict people within the Mexican American culture can be cured by a *curandero* (folk healer), who has been chosen for this mission by God (Stenger-Castro, 1978).

The extent to which these types of belief systems intertwine with western health care systems and the social worker's role is of major concern here.

Interviews with Anglo social workers in Colorado suggested how closely related these are. The following type of situation is illustrative.

> A Chicano woman who uses the services of a neighborhood health center for routine care for herself and her children one day voiced the opinion that a lizard had entered her stomach. The social worker, though attentive, did not assume that extensive pathology was present, though she did not rule this out. On subsequent visits, she talked some more with the woman. She seemed well and no further mention was made of the lizard.*

In explaining this situation to us, the worker noted her awareness of Chicano health belief systems, and the fact that many clinic patients used *curanderos* to rid themselves of the visits of the spirits. She also knew that, by and large, Anglos were not privy to the information she obtained, and so she "stayed out of that area." Mexican American patients fear ridicule when they express such beliefs. Further, in some areas *curanderos* are subject to prosecution for practicing medicine illegally, despite the fact that folk healers have in many places been invited to join the health care team.

The ethnic-sensitive social worker has many options when working with such populations. Our informant respected the client's belief system and did not impose a definition of pathology. The "joining" of traditional and western healers has been proposed in many contexts. Some have suggested a role for the "culture specialist" in crisis intervention (Podell and Campos, 1979). They describe such a specialist as someone "trained in a model of cultural universals and variations who is able to discover the relevant cultural factors in the interface of the psychiatric institution with any patient from any

---

*Conversations with Jane Collins, Director and Staff, Department of Clinical Social Work, Denver General Hospital.

culture and to communicate these to the clinical staff responsible for the patient's treatment." They point out that social workers have traditionally interpreted cultural factors in team deliberations, and suggest that whether such a distinct role merits the cost needs further examination. We do not negate the need for such examination. However, it is clear that ethnic-sensitive social workers, attuned to the cultural roots of illness behavior, will themselves play such a role and attempt to effect administrative and attitudinal changes which facilitate attention to these matters. In Chapter 5 we presented the case of a Chicano woman who fled the deliver room, fearing alien surroundings. We suggested how some alteration in delivery room practices could accommodate the needs of this woman and others who are likely to have similar fears.

Intervention at the systemic level can be crucial. Cultural sensitivity training can alert emergency room personnel who see Hispanics suffering from *ataques;* mental health staffs serving American Indians about the suitability of recommending treatment modalities that do not include the family and community networks; and psychiatrists who may interpret the behavior of the Jewish diabetic boy as a manifestation of pathological, infantile dependency needs. While these may be a part of the picture, their origins in the disease itself, which generates some realistic dependency, must be understood. The ambivalence about dependence and independence, spurred by the Jews' particular fear that illness will affect survival and achievement, must also be understood. These considerations all require extensive knowledge of human behavior, understanding of how the culture shapes illness behavior, and the social context in which care is rendered.

Health care organization: providers and financing

Volumes have been written on each of these topics (e.g., Freeman, Levine, and Reeder, 1979; Fuchs, 1974; Mechanic, 1978). The following case situations, though by no means illustrative of all of the complexity of our delivery system, exemplify some of the dilemmas.

The case of the Jankowitch Family

The Jankowitches are a Polish working-class family. Mr. Jankowitch is employed as a semiskilled laborer in a small factory. Mrs. Jankowitch is a housewife. They have three children, ages 3, 6, and

9, and live in a suburban community about 50 miles from the near-est big city.

John, the 3-year-old, developed a high fever, sore throat, aching limbs, and generally felt ill. His parents noted that he bruised easily. After a week of persistent symptoms, they took him to see the family doctor, who said John had to be hospitalized immediately for a di-agnostic work-up.

Tests results confirmed what the doctor had feared. John had leu-kemia. Treatment for this condition has progressed considerably. However, he needed extensive ongoing treatment—both in- and out-patient. The nearest hospital equipped to render the care he needed was 50 miles away.

These processes set into motion a round of trauma. First, there was the confirmation of a dreaded diagnosis. Will the child live and for how long? The treatments (usually chemotherapy) may produce nausea, hair loss, and other complications.

The horror of the diagnosis is compounded by involvement with a maze of specialists in a distant city. The hospital is a research center, and so most of the actual cost of care is covered. There is, however, the cost of travel and of babysitters for the other children, and time lost from work when Mr. Jankowitch accompanies his wife and child to the hospital.

The social worker and medical staff at the hospital are kind and caring. But distance precludes their making home visits, or main-taining close ties with the family physician, whom the family had come to trust.

The social worker understands their difficulty. Despite the reluc-tance of many Poles to share intimate feelings with "formal caretak-ers," she is able to help them to communicate their fear and hurt. She is aware that the "noncovered costs" are a burden and offers to find sources of help. This proud Polish family, accustomed to taking care of themselves and not asking for help, is burdened with this additional insult to their integrity.

The case of Mrs. Owens

Mrs. Owens, a Black childless widow in her early seventies, lives with a widowed sister. Her husband was a postal worker. She was accustomed to a comfortable working-class life-style. She has a small pension and, although eligible for health services under Medi-care because of her age, her income does not make her eligible for services available to Medicaid recipients.

Mrs. Owens has hypertension, arteriosclerotic heart disease, and mild diabetes. Although able to carry out minor chores, she tires easily and can no longer shop for herself. Her sister, somewhat younger than Mrs. Owens, is also frail but continues to do domestic work several times a week. Some nieces and nephews who live nearby help out by taking the women shopping and to church.

Mrs. Owens' medical condition is not considered acute. This disqualifies her from receiving regular homemaker services under the Medicare program.

On her regular visits to the hospital outpatient clinic she shares her concern about needing some help at home with the social worker. Unable to locate a source of funding for ongoing home health services, the social worker asks whether Mrs. Owens would consider going to live in a home for the aged. Mrs. Owens vigorously rejects this suggestion.

Both families suffer because of the organization of the health care system, which is now briefly discussed.

Health care is provided in a variety of organizations and contexts. Most Americans still receive the bulk of their care from private practitioners, working alone or in small groups, who provide services for a fee.

Other modes of practice are on the increase. These range from health maintenance organizations, to neighborhood health centers, to hospital-based practice. Some (e.g., neighborhood health centers) are primarily designed to serve the poor.

Hospitals vary in complexity, function, and auspice. They range from the large university-affiliated research centers, like the one to which John Jankowitch was sent, to community hospitals such as the one attended by Mrs. Owens, to those focusing on care in one problem area.

The sources of funding are complex, ranging from voluntary contributions, to such publicly sponsored programs as Medicare and Medicaid, to reimbursement through private insurance carriers (e.g., Blue Cross/Blue Shield, Major Medical). Medicare covers approximately 40% of health care costs incurred by those over 65 years of age. Medicaid financing is uneven and contingent on state matches. There are many categorical programs (e.g., services for maternal and child health, renal dialysis).

There is no question that availability and accessibility of care

are worse for the poor and many minority groups than for others in the population. The United States is the only major industrialized nation without a comprehensive system of national health insurance.

Specialization is extensive. Twenty-two approved medical specialties have been recognized (Mechanic, 1978). In addition there are the nurses, physiotherapists, social workers, technicians, physicians' assistants, and many others. The availability of folk healers has already been noted.

Negotiation of this complex, fragmented system, where the availability and quality of care is in no small measure related to residence, social class and ethnicity, can be highly problematic. This has been suggested by the problems faced by the Jankowitch family.

It is unlikely that any country could make the specialized care needed for this illness available in every community hospital. But a program of national health insurance, and community networks of families with like problems, could ease the burden. Our model suggests that workers assigned to working with such families can move beyond the traditional counseling role for such families, though that role is basic and essential.

People who view illness as an "act of God" must be helped to express this, or to utilize their churches and their community networks to work out their grief. When older children afflicted with leukemia and like diseases return to school—possibly bald and frightened—they, their teachers, and their fellow students need some help in adapting to these differences. Education programs designed to help the schools to deal with these issues are most helpful.*

The case of Mrs. Owens illustrates many of the absurdities of our present delivery system, its emphasis, and the neglected areas. Mechanic (1978) states the case succinctly:

> While aging is experienced as a personal crisis, it is largely socially caused. Since it is unlikely that we have the capacity or will to set back social trends, remedies must lie in developing group solutions that build the resources, coping capacities, supports and involvement of the aged. While the United States invests vast resources in the medical care of the aged, these are devoted almost exclusively to

---

*Conversation with Judith Ross, MSW.

staving off the infirmities and disabilities of old age or to long-term institutional care. Only meager resources are invested to maintain the social integration of the aged, to protect them from loneliness and inactivity, to insure adequate nutrition, or to assist them in retaining a respectable identity. Quality of life of the aged could be enhanced if some of the resources now wasted on relatively pointless technological efforts were invested in programs to repair old social networks among the aged or to devise entirely new ones. The population of retired people have enormous resources of their own that would be valuable assets once such a program were initiated. What is needed is the construction of a basic model; the aged themselves could then do the rest.

Mrs. Owens' rejection of placement in a home for the aged was quite appropriate, given her physical and mental state, her age, the availability of caring relatives, and her participation in the church.

Prevailing emphases, such as those noted by Mechanic, constrain the potential for humane attention to her needs. Aside from offering Mrs. Owens the opportunity to ventilate, what is the social worker's responsibility?

Our model calls attention to the need to pursue simultaneously or sequentially micro and macro tasks as they are identified by the client, by professional assessment, and by the client's ethnic reality.

Ongoing efforts, via professional associations and the legislative process, to bring health care policy in line with the needs of population groups such as the elderly chronically ill must be ongoing. If appropriately revised, such policy would not tie eligibility for home health to "acute" medical conditions but to social need. "Following the demands of the client task" (see Chapters 4 and 5) at this level is an ongoing obligation. Mrs. Owens' ethnic reality suggests additional tasks. In exploring alternative sources of home health care, was the Women's Association of her church contacted? Is it possible that the church or other neighborhood groups—perhaps other Black senior citizens themselves—could provide such service? This would enable them to play a useful role. Many groups reject institutional care for their elderly. Blacks are underrepresented in nursing homes (Lowy, 1979; Wolf, 1978).

By the same token, these services when needed must not be denied because of discrimination. Lowy (1979) suggests that a battle must also be waged on this front. The plight of Mrs. Owens is to some extent shared by many Asian Americans, Chicanos, and other groups. Many elderly Chinese and Japanese live in poverty and alone (Chen, 1970; Kitano, 1976). The old Asian benevolent societies are losing ground as the young move away and become assimilated. Yet there is an upsurge of ethnic consciousness. Social workers would do well to take up the challenge of "repairing old social networks," as proposed by Mechanic.

The relationship between socioeconomic status and illness

Repeated studies have shown that the highest rates of mental and physical illness are to be found in those groups which are in the bottom socioeconomic strata (Dohrenwend and Dohrenwend, 1974; Fried, 1975; Hollingshead and Redlish, 1958; Kosa and Robertson, 1975). The disproportionate rates of hypertension in the Black community are well known; while not all agree with the view that these can be partially explained by oppression, this matter warrants ongoing inquiry (Eyer, 1975).

The fact that on most indicators of health American Indians fall below the rest of the population is well known, as is the fact that infant mortality rates for the Black community are considerably higher than those for whites (United States Health, 1976-77). These matters call for intervention at all levels.

The case of Mrs. Green

Mrs. Green, a 40-year-old, friendly, hypertensive, obese Black woman is told she must take her pills regularly or she might have a stroke. She's also advised to reduce her salt intake and to lose weight. She feels well and is employed at night as a nurse's aide. Her husband takes over with their three children when she goes to work.

Review of her dietary habits indicates that one of her great pleasures—in a hectic schedule—is to stop at the local fast food store for hamburgers, french fries, and soft drinks. She also snacks a lot on the job.

Weekends are happily spent with gatherings of the family, where all bring food.

As a nurse's aide she sees many sick people; she has little trouble understanding the consequences of her disease and takes her medication regularly. But to lose weight and reduce salt intake takes a lot of the pleasure out of her life. "What am I going to do?" she asks the social worker, in a half-joking, half-dejected manner.

Together she and the social worker arrive at an idea. A lot of people in this community eat at the fast food store. How about asking them to reduce the salt in their food? And what about a family discussion on the weekend? For Mrs. Green has discovered that many of the other people also have hypertension.

Both efforts were successful and involved family and community cooperation. These have a major bearing on illness and the role which the ethnic-sensitive social worker in health care must play.

The role of the social and community networks

Our review of the literature revealed a persistent theme. Over and over again the importance of family and community as a source of caring and healing was stressed. The clients of *espiritistas* receive advice about interpersonal relations, support, encouragement, and physical contact such as stroking or massage; treatment typically takes place at public meetings of spiritist groups. The patient's family is often required to be present in the healing process (Harwood, 1977; Lazarow, 1979).

The Navajo sing is a public event, which draws in the entire community in behalf of the afflicted person:

Sings are group ceremonials, which involve the patient, the Singer, his assistants, the immediate and extended family of the patients, and many friends. Family members contribute both money and other resources, such as sheep. When the time comes, all drop their ordinary duties and gather together for the event. The patient becomes the center of interest. The support of the whole community is lavished freely. The community recognizes that by restoring harmony to one person the ceremony improves the harmony of the people as a whole. It relates person to environment, past to present, and natural to supernatural. The Sings involve "an interplay between patient, healer, group and the supernatural, which serves to raise the patient's expectancy of cure, helps him to harmonize his inner conflicts, reintegrates him with the group and spirit world . . . and, in the process, combats his anxiety and strengthens his sense of self worth."
(Coulehan, 1980)

This vivid description gives powerful credence to the notion that family and community support systems can and do play an integral part in the healing process.

This is true not only for groups which share "nonWestern" belief systems. Giordano and Giordano (1977), Fandetti and Gelfand (1977), and Krause (1978) all point to the fact that "extended family is seen as the front-line resource for intensive advice on emotional problems" (Fandetti and Gelfand, 1977).

That is not to say that these resources always serve cohesive, caring functioning. The rejection of old practices by the young is frequently noted. There is a risk that folk healers will deal with matters in which they are not expert, or that the "Sing" will delay emergency treatment. Most importantly, these resources are not always available, particularly as American Indians leave their community or younger generations move away from the ethnic communities described by Gans (1962), Krause (1978), Fandetti and Gelfand (1978), and others.

People who are enmeshed in these community networks need and do use the range of prevailing mental and physical health services. There is considerable evidence that these facilities, particularly mental health services, are underused. This is particularly true for Asians (Kitano, 1976), for Mexican Americans (Martinez, 1978), and for many Eastern Europeans (President's Commission on Mental Health, 1978). This pattern of underuse is attributed to many factors. Included among these is the system's failure to provide services congruent with the values, belief systems, and support networks available within these communities. Language differences often pose a major barrier.

In addition to the other roles played by social work in health care, crucial in this connection is the function of interpreting, serving as a cohesive source. Most importantly, skills must be used to marshall and organize ethnic and class-based sources of support. Effective medical care cannot be rendered—particularly to people who mistrust or do not understand the system—without such interventions.

Population at risk

The concept of "population at risk" and related epidemiological perspectives basic to public health concerns provide a useful frame of reference for the practice principles proposed here, particularly as they pertain to community networks. Emphasis is on identifying those aspects of group life which generate health and which generate illness.

Public health principles thus serve to specify and clarify the objectives and concerns of ethnic-sensitive practice in health care. Some of these are supported by the "Task Panel on Special Populations" which submitted reports to The President's Commission on Mental Health (1978). The reports focused on Asian Americans, Blacks, Americans of European ethnic origin, Hispanic Americans, American Indians, and Alaska Natives. Without exception, the various reports stressed the need (1) to train personnel who clearly understand and are sensitive to the needs, values, beliefs, and attitudes of these special population groups, and (2) to increase the number of mental health professionals who themselves are members of these groups.

The preventive components are stressed throughout (e.g., day care, recreational facilities). The provision of services in the context of the group's own definition of their community, with funding made directly available to settings as part of the community's natural support system, is stressed by the report on Americans of European origins. The subpanel on American Indians points to the need for developing Family Resource Centers on the reservations. Mechanisms designed to assure the preservation of the cultural heritage and the protection it offers are emphasized by all the reports.

Yet the ethnically sensitive social worker cannot wait for enactment of legislation—designed to enhance ethnic diversity and minimize the effects of oppression. There is much that workers can do from the vantage point of their assignments to a home health agency, the medical surgical services of a general hospital, the community mental health center, and many others.

The underutilization of mental health services by the Asian American community is frequently noted. Among the reasons are the Asians' "notion that one's capability to control expression of personal problems or troubled feelings is a measure of maturity" (President's Commission on Mental Health, 1978). Given this, mental health services which emphasize self-revelation are anathema to many members of this population group. Culturally relevant mental health services are essential. These may involve inclusion of folk healers (e.g., acupuncturists, herb healers) and services based in and organized by the community. This community is highly protective of its own; many Asians do not come to the attention of public facilities until mental health problems have reached the stage of psychosis (President's Commission on Mental Health, 1978). Benevolent societies and the church might well be drawn in; young Asian students who have a renewed sense of ethnic identity could be called upon to help develop culturally relevant mental health programs.

In many of the case examples we cited, there was the need to move from micro to macro tasks, and to consider how community networks could be drawn in.

Mrs. Green was helped to control her diet by calling on the family to cooperate in a common concern about hypertension. Mr. Mangione, the Italian man recovering from a stroke, may need the support of the Italian American Club; his employer may need positive sanction from fellow employers before he can feel comfortable about having Mr. Mangione work in the hardware store again. Mrs. Owens needs her church, and the Jankowitches may derive some strength and sustenance if they meet with parents of other children who have leukemia. None of these people, or for that matter most others who have contact with the health care social worker, are voluntary clients.

Throughout this chapter, reference has been made to the fact that minority groups are at particular risks for certain health problems; that the very nature of our health system makes for fragmentation and pays too little attention to ethnically derived health beliefs; and that supporting, caring networks are an essential component of health care practice. For all these reasons, simultaneous attention to micro and macro issues is critical.

People who face the prospect of nursing home placement may be experiencing *the* major crisis in their lives. Those who are diagnosed as having cancer or severe heart disease must make major changes in the way they live and love. Diabetes and hypertension are insidious diseases. Constant care is required, often in the absence of symptoms. People with these and similar problems often do not quite know whether to view themselves as ill or well. They fear whether others will withdraw their love, or jobs will be lost.

Those who, by cultural disposition, are prone to reject the sick role will experience such illness as a particular threat to their integrity. Those who have always worried about illness may have their worst, perhaps nonconscious, fears realized.

The illustrations given so far are all focused on chronic illness. While there are many other health problems, chronic illness is on the increase. Medical treatment can provide some relief from distress, but there are few cures. Social work involvement is essential if the caring, linkage function is to be expanded.

THE ROUTE TO THE SOCIAL WORKER

With few exceptions, people do not choose to be ill, to go to the doctor, or to be hospitalized. When they do require health services, they usually do not choose to see the social worker. They come because of injury or pain; to deliver babies; or to obtain relief from depression, frightening hallucinations, or overwhelming anxiety. While social workers are increasingly perceived as professionals who have the skill to intervene and be helpful, involvement with the social worker is often somewhat coercive.

The case of Mrs. Slopata

Mrs. Slopata, a 35-year-old Slavic woman, is in the hospital because of severe abdominal cramps, extensive vomiting, and diarrhea.

Although very weak, this Slavic woman insists she can go home and take care of her children. The doctors have advised her that unless she has help at home and stays in bed for a few weeks, these episodes will recur.

The social worker goes to talk with her to help her to make a decision and tell her about available services. Grimacing with pain the whole time she spoke, Mrs. Slopata nevertheless insisted she needed no help.

Understanding the Slovaks' need to prove stamina and independence (Stein, 1976), the worker supported Mrs. Slopata for her past and future efforts in caring for her home and family. Mrs. Slopata did agree to have her sister-in-law come in to help her out; a formal homemaker would be too difficult to accept.

Coercion is illustrated by the highly progressive practice known as "high-risk screening" or open access. On the assumption that early social work intervention can forestall some of the psychosocial problems related to illness, social workers assess patient records and see those patients and families who, in their view, might benefit from social services. This practice permits social workers to use their own expert judgments about who might need service, rather than wait for physician or self-referral. While patients are free to reject social work services thus offered, it is important to remember that the hospitalized patient is in a vulnerable and dependent state. Many such patients are members of populations at risk for psychosocial crisis; for example, the young underclass married and unmarried mothers who are at the beginning of a critical life cycle stage. All of these groups require extensive social care. Such care consists of the availability of counseling services, and adequate nutrition, home health services, and humane administrative practices.

In characterizing these services as falling on the "coercive" end of the "route to the social worker," we do not imply that they are negative. Rather, this highlights the fact that problem definition is likely constrained by the context. Elderly, chronically ill people may prefer to stay in the hospital rather than be transferred to nursing homes or to homes where they have no one to care for them. The hospital, constrained by high costs, the need for the bed, and the view that it is set up to care for the acutely ill, views the problem differently.

Given this, social workers have a particular obligation to help patients frame the problem in terms they understand and in the way they perceive them. The patient who does not want to leave the hospital, and is simply put in an ambulance, is somewhat like the mother whose child is being taken from her because of her abusive behavior. The social worker who participates in such actions is carrying out a social control function. How much better to anticipate and attempt to forestall such a tragedy! While this example is extreme, there are many poor, chronically ill, minority people who face these kinds of dilemmas. Fearing the fate which would await them in nursing homes, they do not want to go home. If they are alone, with insufficient resources, their eligibility for publicly financed home health services will vary with their age, whether or not they are eligible for Medicaid and/or Medicare, and the supply of home health aides.

Teenage mothers about to take their newborn babies home from the hospital may not define their problems in psychosocial terms. Outreach is needed—to help them to anticipate and plan for the day-to-day vicissitudes of caring for the demanding newborn.

These are but a few examples to illustrate the importance of outreach, using our skills in helping people to articulate their concerns; at the same time it must be recognized that institutional constraints have an effect on how these problems are articulated.

In the process of "high-risk screening," those population groups at particular risk for the social consequences of illness are seen without their request. They are often the poor, minorities, the elderly, and those bereft of community networks. Ethnic-sensitive social workers would not be carrying out their responsibilities if they faulted on these tasks.

SUMMARY

This chapter has considered the application of the model for ethnic-sensitive practice to social work practice in health care. People who encounter health care social workers are, for the most part, involuntary clients. Their problems are pressing—usually involving serious illness, the fear of death, disability, or discomfort, and the need to change life styles in keeping with their illness.

The social worker serves as a link between troubled people and the complex, often fragmented health care system.

The response to illness is in large measure governed by cherished ethnic and cultural dispositions. These affect the way people experience pain and the kind of healers to whom they turn when physical or mental illness strikes.

Caring as well as curing functions are essential. Effective care requires simultaneous attention to micro and macro tasks. The ethnic-sensitive social worker must be knowledgable about the diverse responses to illness, and call upon community-based caring networks in the effort to generate a more humane health care environment. Public health principles specify and clarify the objectives and concerns of ethnic-sensitive practice in health care.

REFERENCES

Cabot, Richard. 1915. *Social service and the art of healing.* New York: Moffat, Yard and Company—NASW Classic Series.

Campos, Daniel, and Podell, Judith. 1979. "The role of the culture specialist in crisis intervention." Prepared for Annual Meeting of the Society for Applied Anthropology, Philadelphia.

Chen, Pei-Ngor. 1970. "The Chinese community in Los Angeles." *Social Casework, 51*(10), December.

Coulehan, John L. 1980. "Navajo Indian medicine: implications for healing." *Family Practice, 10*(1).

Dinerman, Miriam, Schlesinger, Elfriede G., and Wood, Katherine. 1978. "A framework for the evolving role of social work practice in health care." Paper presented at the APHA Annual Meeting, Los Angeles.

Dohrenwend, Bruce P., and Dohrenwend, Barbara Snell. 1974. "Social and cultural influences on psychopathology." *Annual Review of Psychology, 25*, 417-452.

Eyer, Joseph. 1975. "Hypertension as a disease of modern society." *International Journal of Health Services, 5*, 539-558.

Fandetti, Donald U., and Gelfand, Donald E. 1978. "Attitudes towards symptoms and services in the ethnic family neighborhood." *American Journal of Orthopsychiatry, 48*(3), July.

Freeman, Howard E., Levine, Sol, and Reeder, Leo G. 1979. *Handbook of medical sociology.* Englewood Cliffs, N.J.: Prentice-Hall, Inc.

Freidson, Eliot. 1972. "Disability as social deviance." In Freidson, Eliot, and Lorber, Judith (Eds.), *Medical men and their work.* Chicago: Aldine-Atherton.

Freidson, Eliot. 1970. *Profession of medicine.* New York: Dodd, Mead & Co.

Fuchs, Michael, and Bashshur, Rashid. 1975. "Use of traditional Indian medicine among urban Native Americans." *Medical Care, 13*(11).

Fuchs, Victor R. 1974. *Who shall live? Health economics and social change.* New York: Basic Books, Inc.

Gans, Herbert J. 1962. *The urban villagers.* New York: The Free Press of Glencoe.

Garrison, Vivian. 1977. "The Puerto Rican syndrome in psychiatry and *Espiritismo.*" In Crapanzano, Vincent, and Garrison, Vivian (Eds.). *Case Studies in Spirit Possession.* New York: John Wiley & Sons, Inc.

Giordano, Joseph. 1973. *Ethnicity and mental health: research and recommendations.* New York: American Jewish Committee.

Giordano, Joseph, & Giordano, Grace Pirreiro. 1977. *The ethno-cultural factor in mental health: a literature review and bibliography.* New York: American Jewish Committee.

Goffman, Erving. 1965. *Stigma.* Englewood Cliffs, N.J.: Prentice-Hall, Inc.

Greenblum, Joseph. 1974. "Medical and health orientations of American Jews: a case of diminishing distinctiveness." *Social Science and Medicine, 8.*

Harwood, Alan. 1977. "Puerto Rican spiritism: Part II. An institution with preventive and therapeutic functions in community psychiatry." *Culture, Medicine and Psychiatry, 1*(2).

Health—United States—1976-1977. DHEW Pub. No. (HRA) 77-1232.

Hyattsville, Md.: U.S. Department of Health, Education and Welfare, Public Health Service, Health Resources Administration, National Center for Health Statistics and Health Services Research.

Holden, Mary O. 1980. "Dialysis or death: The ethical alternatives." *Health and Social Work,* 5(2), May.

Howe, Irving. 1975. "Immigrant Jewish families in New York: the end of the world of our fathers." *New York,* 8(41), October 13.

Kitano, Harry H. L. 1976. *Japanese Americans* (2nd ed.). Englewood Cliffs, N.J.: Prentice-Hall, Inc.

Kleinman, Arthur. 1978. "Clinical relevance of anthropological and cross-cultural research: concepts and strategies." *American Journal of Psychiatry, 135*(4), April.

Kosa, John, and Robertson, Leon S. 1975. "The social aspects of health and illness." In Kosa, John, and Zola, Irving K. (Eds.). *Poverty and health: a sociological analysis.* Cambridge: Harvard University Press.

Krause, Corinne Azen. 1978. *Grandmothers, mothers and daughters: an oral history study of ethnicity, mental health and continuity of three generations of Jewish, Italian and Slavic American women.* New York: American Jewish Committee.

Lazarow, Cynthia. 1979. "Puerto Rican spiritism: implications for health care professionals." Submitted in partial fulfillment of course requirements for Survey of Health Care, Rutgers University School of Social Work.

Lowy, Louis. 1979. *Social work with the aging.* New York: Harper & Row, Publishers.

Martinez, Ricardo Arguigo. 1978. *Hispanic culture and health care.* St. Louis: The C. V. Mosby Co.

Mechanic, David. 1978. *Medical sociology* (2nd ed.). New York: The Free Press.

Parsons, Talcott. 1972. "Definitions of health and illness in light of American values and social structures." In Gartly, E. Jaco (Ed.). *Patients, physicians and illness: a sourcebook in behavioral science in health.* New York: The Free Press.

Parsons, Talcott. 1951. *The social system.* New York: The Free Press.

President's Commission on Mental Health. 1978. *Task Panel Reports,* 3, Appendix.

Rosen, George. 1974. *Medical police to social medicine.* New York: Science History Publications.

Samora, Julian. 1978. "Conceptions of health and disease among Spanish Americans." In Martinez, Ricardo Arguijo (Ed.). *Hispanic culture and health care.* St. Louis: The C. V. Mosby Co.

Stein, Howard F. 1976. "A dialectical model of health and illness attitudes and behavior among Slovak Americans." *International Journal of Mental Health,* 5(2).

Stenger-Castro, Earl M. 1978. "The Mexican American: how his culture affects his mental health." In Martinez, Ricardo Arguijo (Ed.). *Hispanic culture and health care.* St. Louis: The C. V. Mosby Co.

Wintrob, R. 1973. "The influence of others; witchcraft and rootwork as explanations of behavior disturbances." *Journal of Nervous and Mental Diseases, 156.*

Wolf, Rosalie S. 1978. "A social systems model of nursing home use." *Educational Trust,* Summer.

Zborowski, Mark. 1952. "Cultural components in response to pain." *Journal of Social Issues,* (4).

APPENDIX

Community profile*

This outline for a community profile is intended to help the individual worker or agency to develop a detailed picture of the community within which services are located. The profile should serve to highlight the basic population distribution of the community, and the relationship between its location and access to major transportation routes; these in turn may affect access to places of employment, health and welfare services, and recreational facilities.

Also important is a picture of existing health and welfare resources, as well as gaps in these resources. Resources are defined to include the formally organized helping institutions such as those developed by the public sector, trade unions, and churches, as well as those more informal resources such as identifiable helping networks, folk healers, and the like.

Of importance is the political structure, the representation of ethnic minority groups on the staffs of community institutions such as the schools and social agencies, and the attention to the special language, cultural dispositions, and needs of groups represented in the community.

Such a profile can be developed by use of census data, publica-

*Adapted from the "Community Profile" developed by Professor David Antebi, Graduate School of Social Work, Rutgers University.

tions developed by local organizations (e.g., League of Women Voters, County Planning Boards, Health and Welfare Councils), interviews with community leaders, and data available in the agency's files.

Identification

1. Name of community (e.g., "The North Ward," "Watts," etc.)
2. City (or township, borough, etc.)
3. County
4. State
5. Type of government

Local history

1. When settled
2. Changes in population
3. Major historical incidents leading to present-day development
4. Principal events in the life of the community, etc.
5. Traditions and values

Geography and transportation

1. Location—is it located near any of the following?
    a. Principal highways
    b. bus routes
    c. Truck routes
    d. Railroad routes
    e. Airports-air routes
    f. Rivers, oceans, lakes
2. Do any of the above facilitate/hamper residents' ability to get to work, major recreational centers, community services?

Population characteristics

1. Total size of population
2. Breakdown by
    a. Age
    b. Sex
    c. Minority groups
    d. Other ethnic groups
    e. Religious affiliation
3. Educational level
    a. Median educational level for total adult population
    b. Median educational level for women
    c. Median educational level for each of the major ethnic and minority groups

4. Have there been major shifts in the population composition over the past 5 to 10 years (e.g., in migration of minority groups, departure of sizable numbers of people in any one population group)?
    a. Are there any major urban renewal or other redevelopment efforts?

Employment and income characteristics

1. Employment status
    a. Major sources and type of employment for total adult population
    b. Major sources of employment for women
    c. Major sources of employment for each of the major ethnic and minority groups
2. Median income
3. Income characteristics below poverty level
4. Type of public welfare system (e.g., state, county jurisdictions; state involved in Medicaid program?)

Housing characteristics

1. Prevailing housing type (apartments, private homes, mix)
2. Percentage of population owning, renting own homes
3. Housing conditions (e.g., percentage characterized as "dilapidated" by the census)

Educational facilities and level

1. Types of schools available
2. Do the schools have bilingual programs?
3. Are minority and ethnic group members found in the members of staffs, school boards?
4. Are the schools aware of the particular problems and strengths of minority and ethnic group members?
5. Do the schools promote cultural awareness and sensitivity programs?

Health and welfare resources

1. What are some of the important resources available?
    a. Health and medical (hospitals, clinics, public health facilities, "folk healers")
    b. Recreational and leisure-time facilities
    c. Social agencies
2. Are staff members bilingual where appropriate?
3. Is there adequate representation of minority-ethnic group members on the staffs of hospitals and social agencies?
4. Do these facilities develop cultural awareness and sensitivity programs?
5. What are the prevailing formal and informal community networks?
    a. "Swapping networks"

b. Church-supported health and welfare groups
c. Ethnic-based lodges, fraternities, benevolent societies
d. Union-sponsored health and welfare facilities
e. Self-help groups of people with special problems (e.g., alcoholics, the physically handicapped)

Special problems and strengths

1. What are the major social problems (e.g., prevalent health problems; housing; school)?
2. Is there a particular concern with crime, delinquency, underemployment?
3. Are there particular intergroup tensions; efforts at intergroup coalition?

Evaluation

1. What do you consider are some of the major problems of this community?
2. Does this community have a positive identity, loyalty? Describe.
3. What are the major strengths and weaknesses of the health and welfare community?
4. What are the major gaps in services?

Index